DUALISATION OF PART-TIME WORK

Also available in the series

Welfare, populism and welfare chauvinism

By **Bent Greve**

Why, in a time of increasing inequality, has there been a recent surge of support for political parties who promote an anti-welfare message? Using a mixed methods approach and newly released data, this book aims to answer this question and to show possible ways forward for welfare states.

HB £75.00 **ISBN** 978-1-4473-5043-9
176 pages June 2019

Forthcoming titles

The moral economy of activation
Ideas, politics and policies

By **Magnus Hansen**

By rethinking the role of ideas and morality in policy changes, this book illustrates how the moral economy of activation leads to a permanent behaviourist testing of the unemployed in public debate as well as in local jobcentres.

HB £75.00 **ISBN** 978-1-4473-4996-9
208 pages September 2019

Local policies and the European Social Fund
Employment policies across Europe

By **Katharina Zimmermann**

Comparing data from 18 local case studies across 6 European countries, and deploying an innovative mixed-method approach, this book presents comparative evidence on everyday challenges in the context of the European Social Fund (ESF) and discusses how these findings are applicable to other funding schemes.

HB £75.00 **ISBN** 978-1-4473-4651-7
224 pages October 2019

For a full list of all titles in the series visit:

www.bristoluniversitypress.co.uk/
research-in-comparative-and-global-social-policy-1

DUALISATION OF PART-TIME WORK

The Development of Labour Market Insiders and Outsiders

Edited by
Heidi Nicolaisen, Hanne Cecilie Kavli
and Ragnhild Steen Jensen

First published in Great Britain in 2019 by

Policy Press
University of Bristol
1-9 Old Park Hill
Bristol
BS2 8BB
UK
t: +44 (0)117 954 5940
pp-info@bristol.ac.uk
www.policypress.co.uk

North America office:
Policy Press
c/o The University of Chicago Press
1427 East 60th Street
Chicago, IL 60637, USA
t: +1 773 702 7700
f: +1 773-702-9756
sales@press.uchicago.edu
www.press.uchicago.edu

British Library Cataloguing in Publication Data
A catalogue record for this book is available from the British Library

Library of Congress Cataloging-in-Publication Data
A catalog record for this book has been requested

978-1-4473-4860-3 hardback
978-1-4473-4861-0 ePdf
978-1-4473-4862-7 ePub
978-1-4473-4863-4 Mobi

Cover design by Andrew Corbett
Printed and bound in Great Britain by CPI Group (UK) Ltd,
Croydon, CR0 4YY
Policy Press uses environmentally responsible print partners

Contents

**Part One: Institutional and organisational regulations
of part-time work**

Part Two: The quality of working conditions and part-time work

List of tables and figures

Tables

Figures

List of contributors

Sonja Bekker, Dr, Associate Professor and Jean Monnet Chair, Tilburg Law School, The Netherlands. Email: s.bekker@tilburguniversity.edu

Heejung Chung, Dr, Associate Professor (Reader), University of Kent's School of Social Policy, Sociology and Social Research, UK. Email: H.Chung@kent.ac.uk

Jonas Felbo-Kolding, Dr, Post doc, Copenhagen Business School, Denmark. Email: jf.egb@cbs.dk

Dalila Ghailani, Senior Researcher, European Social Observatory, Brussels, Belgium.

Belinda Hewitt, Dr, Professor of Sociology, School of Social and Political Sciences, University of Melbourne, Australia. Email: belinda. hewitt@unimelb.edu.au

Kenneth Hudson, Dr, Associate Professor of Sociology and Social Work, University of South Alabama, USA. Email: ckhudson@ southalabama.edu

Anna Ilsøe, Dr, Associate Professor, Employment Relations Research Centre, University of Copenhagen, Denmark. Email: ai@faos.dk

Ragnhild Steen Jensen, Dr, Senior Researcher, Fafo Institute for Labour and Social Research, Oslo, Norway. Email: rsj@fafo.no

Arne L. Kalleberg, Dr, Professor of Sociology, University of North Carolina at Chapel Hill, USA. Email: arnekal@email.unc.edu

Hanne Cecilie Kavli, Senior Researcher, Fafo Institute for Labour and Social Research, Oslo, Norway. Email: hanne.kavli@fafo.no

Trine P. Larsen, Dr, Associate Professor, Employment Relations Research Centre, University of Copenhagen, Denmark. Email: tpl@faos.dk

Sophia Seung-yoon Lee, Dr, Associate Professor, Department of Social Welfare, Ewha Womans University, Seoul, South Korea. Email: sophia. sy.lee@ewha.ac.kr

Margarita León, Dr, Associate Professor Political Science and Senior Researcher, Institute of Government and Public Policies (IGOP), Universitat Autònoma Barcelona, Spain. Email: margarita.leon@uab.cat

Lara Maestripieri, Dr, Marie Skłodowska-Curie Fellow, Institute of Government and Public Policies (IGOP), Universitat Autònoma Barcelona, Spain. Email: lara.maestripieri@uab.cat

Jouko Nätti, Dr, Professor of Social Policy, University of Tampere, Finland. Email: jouko.natti@uta.fi

Kristine Nergaard, Senior Researcher, Fafo Institute for Labour and Social Research, Oslo, Norway. Email: kristine.nergaard@fafo.no

Heidi Nicolaisen, Dr, Senior Researcher at Fafo Institute for Labour and Social Research, Oslo, Norway, and the Research Unit at the Norwegian Work and Welfare Administration. Email: heidi. nicolaisen@fafo.no

Roy A. Nielsen, Senior Researcher, Fafo Institute for Labour and Social Research, Oslo, Norway. Email: roy.nielsen@fafo.no

Birgit Pfau-Effinger, Dr, Professor, University of Hamburg, Germany. Email: Birgit.Pfau-Effinger@wiso.uni-hamburg.de

Thordis Reimer, Researcher, University of Hamburg, Germany. Email: Thordis.Reimer@wiso.uni-hamburg.de

Min Young Song, PhD Candidate, Department of Social Welfare, Ewha Womans University, Seoul, South Korea. Email: smy911@ ewhain.net

Sissel C. Trygstad, Dr, Research Director, Fafo Institute for Labour and Social Research, Oslo, Norway. Email: sissel.trygstad@fafo.no

Mara A. Yerkes, Dr, Associate Professor, Interdisciplinary Social Science, Utrecht University, The Netherlands. Email: M.A.Yerkes@ uu.nl

Acknowledgements

This book is developed within the framework of the research project 'Part-time careers in Norway – the end of normalization?' (Grant number 237031), which was part of the Norwegian Research Council's programme Welfare, Working Life and Migration (VAM). The initial ambition was to explore the new realities and implications of part-time work in a few European countries. Gradually, it became clear that a more global perspective would provide richer insights into the many-faceted topic of part-time work. We warmly thank our contributing authors from Europe, the US, Australia and South Korea for excellent cooperation, stimulating discussions and for sharing their insights on how part-time work is regulated, practised and experienced around the world. We are grateful to the Norwegian Research Council for their generous funding that made it possible to broaden our perspectives and include a wider range of countries.

We also deeply appreciate all the competent support and assistance from the staff at Policy Press and the book series editors. Thanks are also due to the publishers' three anonymous reviewers for their useful comments.

Several scholars have encouraged the making of this book and contributed to its manifestation by generously sharing with us their knowledge, thoughts and insights; they are Heejung Chung, Anne Lise Ellingsæter, Lilja Mósesdóttir, Jon Rogstad and Sissel C. Trygstad.

We also owe many thanks to Fafo Institute for Labour and Social Research for supplying us with a generous and supportive working environment and to our colleagues for their many encouragements along the way. And last, but not least, thank you to our families who make sure we also have fun after office hours.

The Editors
April 2019

Series preface

Heejung Chung (University of Kent, UK)
Alexandra Kaasch (University of Bielefeld, Germany)
Stefan Kühner (Lingnan University, Hong Kong)

In a world that is rapidly changing, increasingly connected and uncertain, there is a need to develop a shared applied policy analysis of welfare regimes around the globe. *Research in Comparative and Global Social Policy* is a series of books that addresses broad questions around how nation states and transnational policy actors manage globally shared challenges. In so doing, the book series includes a wide array of contributions, which discuss comparative social policy history, development and reform within a broad international context. Initially conceived during a meeting of the UK Social Policy Association Executive Committee in 2016, the book series invites innovative research by leading experts on all world regions and global social policy actors and aims to fulfil the following objectives: it encourages cross-disciplinary approaches that develop theoretical frameworks reaching across individual world regions and global actors; it seeks to provide evidence-based good practice examples that cross the bridge between academic research and practice; not least, it aims to provide a platform in which a wide range of innovative methodological approaches – may they be national case studies, larger-N comparative studies, or global social policy studies – can be introduced to aid the evaluation, design, and implementation of future social policies.

Given the above aims, we are delighted that one of the first books in the series describes the current patterns and profiles of part-time work, with particular focus on how contemporary opportunity structures for labour market insiders and outsiders are shaped by actors and institutions at the global, national, sector/industry and workplace levels. The editors of the book – Heidi Nicolaisen, Hanne Cecilie Kavli and Ragnhild Steen Jensen – bring together expert scholars on part-time work strategies in Nordic, Central and Southern European countries, Australia, the United States, and South Korea, to collectively discuss cross-disciplinary perspectives on big policy issues. These include: atypical employment and labour market precariousness; gendered labour market outcomes and flexible work; industrial policy and the de-standardisation of organised labour; EU governance and the privatisation of public services. All of these policy issues are increasingly pertinent and need to be better understood by academic and non-academic stakeholders in the global knowledge economy. Current trends in global economic productivity, the fourth industrial revolution, family formation and transnational migration suggest that part-time work – at least – is here to stay. The book makes a crucial and timely contribution in providing a nuanced account on how it is currently regulated, practised and experienced in different labour market sectors in different cultural and political economy contexts. Through this, the book makes an important theoretical contribution for labour market scholars worldwide.

Introduction

*Heidi Nicolaisen, Hanne Cecilie Kavli
and Ragnhild Steen Jensen*

Introduction

This book reopens the debate on the position of part-time workers. Part-time employment is a topic of perpetual importance. It affects workers' pay and quality of life, as well as employers' costs and flexibility. It also affects society as a whole through its impact on the available workforce. For decades, working less than full-time has been associated with female workers and with precarious or marginal employment (Blossfeld and Hakim, 1997; O'Reilly and Fagan, 1998). Moreover, it is identified as a key indicator of being a labour market outsider (Vosko, 2010; Emmenegger et al, 2012). This presents a dilemma to both individual workers and politicians as part-time work is also a way for families in general, and women in particular, to reconcile family obligations with paid work.

Traditionally, there have been two main types of explanation for why people work part-time: One is related to demand factors and emphasises the influence from employers, as well as market conditions and occupational structures. The other focuses on supply-related factors, such as the employee's work–life balance and education, and the division of labour between men and women in the family (see, eg, Blossfeld and Hakim, 1997; O'Reilly and Fagan, 1998). Regulation of the labour market and social protection has the potential to modify the influence of demand and supply factors, and either maintain, reduce or enlarge the inequality between part-time and full-time workers, as well as between different groups of part-time workers. The dualisation perspective places emphasis on the role of politics, and we will draw on this perspective to strengthen understandings of how regulations can influence part-time work. A key question is whether the politics that regulate labour markets and social protection increase or decrease the divide between labour market insiders and outsiders. The contributions in this book demonstrate that changes in working-time patterns are rooted in various policy domains, often in more than one at a time, and the process of change may, or may not, pull in the same direction. We also examine differences not only between full-time and part-time workers, but also between different categories of part-time workers.

Political actors at the national and supranational levels have engaged, albeit to varying degrees and with different agendas, to address part-time work. By linking part-time work to current debates on precarious work and dualisation, this book provides an up-to-date account of what kind of labour market phenomenon part-time work represents to different categories of workers. The quality of part-time work is determined by numerous characteristics: if it is long or short; if it voluntary or involuntary; if the work schedule harmonises with standard hours or not; and if the predictability of work and leisure is high or low. For employees, the combination of short and involuntary part-time work tends to be bad in both economic and temporal terms. The quality of part-time work also relates to the stability of the employment relationship and a wider set of working conditions.

The book makes four contributions to the literature and to public debates on part-time work. First, it offers new perspectives and analyses on the regulation of part-time work at the supranational, national and workplace levels. Second, by focusing on similarities and differences among part-time workers, it develops a typology of part-time work that goes beyond the traditional insider–outsider divide and provides a more diverse vocabulary for later descriptions and discussions of part-time work. Third, it provides an up-to-date account of part-time work and its consequences in a range of countries and regime types. Fourth, it initiates a debate on part-time work among men.

In the following sections, we first define and clarify key theories and concepts used throughout this volume. Then, we move on and outline current knowledge and arguments pertaining to the three thematic sections of the book; the politics and regulations of part-time work at different levels; the quality of part-time work; and the influence of work–life balance policies. Based on the contributions in this volume, we then develop a new typology of part-time work. Finally, we present statistical information about part-time work across time and countries before we describe the chapter contributions.

Part-time work: theories and concepts

Theories and concepts about labour market insiders and outsiders are central to the study of part-time work. Whereas 'insiders' are positioned in a well-regulated part of the labour market, 'outsiders' face less stable and often harsher conditions. The concepts that have been developed to understand and investigate this insider–outsider divide both complement and overlap each other.

Many of the concepts take, more or less explicitly, the standard employment relationship as their reference point for a labour market 'insider'. The standard employment relationship, as defined by Bosch (2006), describes the traditional full-time core worker who enjoys job stability, and where social standards and protections are closely linked with permanent, full-time work. Others have added access to promotion, training, job content and work intensity (see, eg, Lyonette et al, 2010) as central aspects of job quality. A key hypothesis is that this ideal, or template, of the standard employment relationship is now breaking up in favour of a diversity of non-standard, atypical employment relationships, of which part-time work is one of several. Welfare states were initially designed to take care of the needs of male, full-time production workers. This departure from the standard employment relationship is therefore coupled with increased risks of poverty and loss of social protection, in particular, if welfare rights are closely linked to (full-time) employment (Palier, 2010). As pointed out by Rubery et al (2018: 510), policy responses to the growth in non-standard employment are taking different directions. On the one hand, there are examples of de-commodification by extending protection to workers in non-standard positions. One example is the European Union (EU) Part-Time Work Directive (97/81/EC), which makes it unlawful to provide part-timers with employment conditions, for example, pension, sickness health insurance and parental leave rights, that are inferior to those of full-timers (on a pro-rata basis). On the other, the 'activation agenda', targeting the unemployed, is increasingly 'normalising non-standard forms of employment as a route out of unemployment' (Rubery et al, 2018: 510). When the unemployed, through their dependence on public benefits, are obliged to accept 'any job', regardless of the job's conditions or quality, this opens the field for more precarious and fragmented forms of employment.

The discussion of labour market insiders and outsiders has a long tradition, and many concepts have been developed, for example, labour market segmentation (Rubery et al, 2002), dual labour markets (Doeringer and Piore, 1971) and 'the flexible firm' (Atkinson, 1984), which explain how primary and secondary labour markets are made. This happens because employers provide better employment conditions to core staff than to peripheral workers who can more easily be replaced. More recently, the concept of dualisation has been applied in studies of the ongoing changes in working lives and welfare states. We have been particularly inspired by the contribution of Emmenegger et al (2012) in their edited volume *The age of dualization*. Whereas the aforementioned concepts focus on how demand and supply factors contribute to the divide in the labour market, Emmenegger and colleagues emphasise the role of politics. Their argument, in short, is that policies matter and that dualisation 'implies that policies increasingly differentiate rights, entitlements and services provided to different categories of recipients' (Emmenegger et al, 2012: 10). Conceptually, they also differentiate between process (dualisation), output (institutional dualism) and outcome (divide). Dualisation can take three forms: a deepening of existing divides, making the differences between insiders and outsider more profound; a widening of the divides, moving previous insiders into outsider positions; and new institutional dualisms. These three forms of institutional dualism can occur both within politics that regulate social protection and within politics that regulate the labour market (Emmenegger et al, 2012: 11).

The dualisation perspective's emphasis on policy differs from the liberalisation perspective. In the latter, the causes and consequences of outsideness are explained by structural driving forces such as globalisation, deindustrialisation and firms' need to reduce labour costs (Häusermann and Schwander, 2012; Prosser, 2016). 'Dualisation' is also distinguished from other concepts by its orientation towards the *processes* that create inequality rather than being restricted to the more traditional focus on the outcomes for individuals. The outcome – the labour market divide – is traditionally described in terms of polarisation, segmentation and marginalisation. Moreover, Vosko (2010: 2) describes 'precarious work' as work characterised by 'uncertainty, low income, and limited social benefits and statutory entitlements'. As this definition recognises, precarious work is determined by the nature of the employment relationship, but it is also shaped by other factors, in particular, the extent and role of social protection.

The politics and regulation of part-time work

Twenty-five years ago, part-time work topped the agendas of policymakers at the supranational level. The Part-Time Work Convention implemented by the International Labour Organization (ILO) in 1994 recognised the importance of productive and freely chosen employment for all workers, as well as the economic importance of part-time work. Moreover, the Preamble of the convention pointed to the need for employment policies to take into account the role of part-time work in creating additional employment opportunities, as well as the need to ensure protection for part-time workers in the areas of access to employment, working conditions and social security.[1] The term 'comparable full-time worker' was defined and established as the reference category for the conditions of part-time workers. In article 1, 'comparable full-time worker' is defined as a full-time worker who: (1) has the same type of employment relationship; (2) is engaged in the same or a similar type of work or occupation; and (3) is employed in the same establishment, enterprise or branch of activity as the part-time worker concerned. Full-time workers affected by a temporary reduction in their normal hours are not considered to be part-time workers.

The ILO convention had a direct impact on the legislative process in the EU and the Part-time Work Directive[2] that came into effect three years later. The 1997 directive was based on similar principles and made it unlawful for member states to treat part-time workers as inferior to full-time workers. Now, more than two decades later, it is time to ask if, and how, supranational regulations influence part-time work. The capacity of supranational bodies to influence part-time work in different countries depends upon their authority, how regulations are advocated and implemented, and how individual countries respond. National institutions, for example, labour law and the system for collective bargaining, often adapt to supranational regulations and other types of change in ways that are compatible with the system's unique and original identity (see, eg, Soskice and Hall, 2001; Traxler, 2003). Hence, it is likely that the national level has a significant impact, and relative stability within countries is observed over time (Traxler, 2003). The EU Part-Time Work Directive has had very different effects on labour laws in different member states. In some countries, the directive produced little change. This was the case in countries like Norway and Sweden, where part-time workers had had equal employment conditions to those of full-timers for decades (Andersen, 2003). In other countries where part-time work had been less regulated, such as Ireland, the implementation of the directive had a more substantial impact on national labour law (Nicolaisen, 2011).

The ability of actors to avoid, undermine or counteract regulations at any level will rely on the nature of the regulations, or the regulatory effectiveness of formal protections, their design, application and enforcement. If regulations are 'soft', voluntary and have a suggestive character, it is easier to escape implementation than if they are 'hard' and legally binding (Tomlinson, 2006; Sisson, 2013). However, strong regulations do not guarantee implementation (Kanbur and Ronconi,

2018). Without vigorous enforcement mechanisms (eg a labour inspectorate and labour court) and advocacy in the workplace (eg from trade union representatives or employers), working-time regulations may have limited practical application (Haipeter, 2006). Hence, a multi-level approach is required to understand the transformative capacity of politics and regulations. Moreover, it is not sufficient to examine regulations alone. Implementation and enforcement mechanisms need to be explored to get the full picture of the capacity of regulations to modify inequality. Several contributors to this book analyse how politics and regulations at different levels influence the conditions of part-time workers, the relative importance of different regulations and how they interact (see Chapters 2, 4, 6, 10 and 12). Key regulatory levels are the supranational, the national and the workplace.

The quality of part-time work

Employers tend to provide 'good' and 'bad' part-time positions systematically to different categories of workers. In the primary labour market, they offer good part-time work to attract and retain core workers who, for some reason, cannot or will not enter into a full-time contract (see, eg, Tilly, 1996; Blossfeld and Hakim, 1997; Webber and Williams, 2008). These workers benefit from the 'standard employment relationship' (Bosch, 2006), in which work is well paid, integrated at the workplace and entitles workers to social protection. As for more disposable workers in the secondary labour market, employers offer part-time jobs with poorer conditions to give their businesses numerical and financial flexibility (Atkinson, 1984; Tilly, 1996). This type of part-time employment is characterised by working conditions and social protection of low quality and often a very low number of contracted hours (Blossfeld and Hakim, 1997; O'Reilly and Fagan, 1998).

While some factors, like gender and occupational class, are clearly important in any analysis of the quality of part-time work, defining a set of more detailed indicators quickly grows into a more complex task (Warren and Lyonette, 2018). A central aspect of a job is, of course, what it pays, but the quality of a job also includes dimensions like job security, autonomy, promotions, training, predictability and working time – both with regard to the hours and to the timing of these hours (Kalleberg, 2011; Carre et al, 2012; Gallie, 2013; Green et al, 2015). In their review of the literature about quality part-time work, Lyonette et al (2010) suggest a revised definition of the concept. Their starting point is very similar to the basic principles of the ILO Part-Time Work Convention (No. 175) and the EU directive: quality part-time jobs provide the same (pro-rata) terms and conditions, development, and progression opportunities as comparable full-time jobs. Moreover, quality part-time jobs enable the job-holder to maintain or enhance their skills, to achieve an acceptable work–life balance and to increase the number of working hours if desirable for the worker and feasible for the employer (Lyonette et al, 2010).

To understand how 'good' and 'bad' part-time work is regulated, practised, rationalised and experienced by workers and employers, more studies are needed. Several researchers have pointed out how it can be misleading to categorise the quality of part-time jobs (and full-time jobs) as either 'good' or 'bad' (see, eg, Sengupta et al, 2009; Kalleberg, 2011; Vidal, 2013; Warren and Lyonette, 2018). More often, they are better described in terms of degrees. In this book, we return to the core issue of how, but also to what degree, the working conditions of part-timers vary within different regulatory contexts.

While part-time work is a voluntary and good alternative for some, it is involuntary and, in this respect, bad for others. Combined with the concern that part-time workers are also more exposed to poor working conditions and less social protection than full-time workers, this duality has inspired a debate on the mobility of part-time workers (see, eg, Nätti, 1995; O'Reilly and Bothfeld, 2002; Böheim and Taylor, 2004; Gash, 2008; Nergaard, 2010; Kitterød et al, 2013). The question of part-time workers' mobility relates to a larger debate in labour market studies on the rigidity of 'primary' and 'secondary' labour markets. The gravity of being an 'outsider' will depend on its permanency. If part-time work is transitory and followed by full-time work and better working conditions, the consequences for the individual will be less pronounced than if part-time work is permanent or followed by unemployment. Hence, it is important to explore how the mobility patterns among part-time workers relate to precarious or marginalised work and its associated insecurities. Is part-time work a 'stepping stone' into full-time work and better working conditions, or is part-time work an 'end station' instead, locking workers into bad jobs?

Existing studies show that there are considerable country differences in transition patterns among part-time workers (for an overview, see Fagan et al, 2014). The Nordic countries, for example, have comparatively high levels of transfer from part-time to full-time work (Nergaard, 2010), while only a very small share (of women) in Britain and Germany were able to use part-time work as a stepping stone into full-time work (O'Reilly and Bothfeld, 2002). In general, women and workers with limited education are less likely to move from part-time to full-time positions than men and workers with higher education

(Fagan et al, 2014). There is less knowledge of the transfers between working-time statuses among migrants – a category of workers who are growing in number across Europe and who are particularly exposed to bad jobs with poor working conditions (see, eg, Emmenegger et al, 2012). This stands out as an important question as migrants tend to be over-represented in part-time positions and more often work part-time involuntarily than natives do (Rubin et al, 2008; OECD, 2010).

Work–life balance, gender and part-time work

Part-time work is often seen, both in politics and in the research literature, as a key strategy to achieve a better work–life balance (O'Reilly and Fagan, 1998; see also the EU Part-Time Work Directive). As a policy issue, 'work–life balance' seems to pertain almost exclusively to women, and to mothers in particular. It is less commonly suggested that men should achieve a better work–life balance through part-time work.

The perception of part-time work and its role in facilitating a better work–life balance for women varies across countries. In the Nordic countries, part-time work became a major strategy to combine paid work and care for women who entered the labour market in large numbers during the 1970s and 1980s. Many found work in the expanding public sector, where high-quality part-time work was provided. The long-standing provision of equal rights is seen as a result of the large-scale feminisation of the workforce at a comparably early stage (see, eg, Nicolaisen, 2011; Ellingsæter and Jensen, 2019). Hence, a large-scale feminisation of the workforce can have an independent effect on regulations, although this, of course, depends on the country-specific context (Ellingsæter and Leira, 2006). This argument prompts the question of how new work–life balance policies may influence the quality of part-time work, in particular, its gendered aspects.

Whether policy initiatives to increase female labour market participation are effective depends not only on the existence of a policy to reconcile work and family, but also on the quality of supporting institutions like parental leave and publicly provided childcare. How part-time work is viewed by employers and society in general also matters. Moreover, the gendered division of paid and unpaid work is deeply rooted in national cultures and traditions in ways that are partly, but not fully, captured by studies of formal regulations and institutions (Pfau-Effinger, 2012). Nation-specific gender cultures may influence individual, as well as collective, practices. An important question is therefore how country-specific cultures, institutions and practices influence the labour market participation of different categories of female workers. In this book, contributions from different countries examine women's and men's labour market participation against the backdrop of work–life balance policies and regulations (see, eg, Chapters 2, 3, 11 and 12). This will inform a discussion of the effects of work–life balance policies on women's labour market participation and work quality.

A typology of part-time work

Part-time work varies along two important dimensions: its quality and its voluntariness. The quality of part-time work in terms of *working conditions* and *social protection* varies between countries with different institutional structures, but also within countries, between sectors and occupations. More specifically, the quality of part-time work may differ from full-time work in terms of average hourly earnings, job security, health risks, opportunities for training or promotion, scheduling patterns, and the predictability of work and leisure. In addition, even if part-time workers have working conditions equal to those of full-timers, less time in employment may result in reduced access to unemployment benefits should they become unemployed, and to old-age or health-related pensions or other contribution-based benefits. Of course, full-time jobs also vary in quality and may provide low job security, low wages, limited fringe benefits, limited influence over one's own work activities and little opportunity for the flexibility needed to manage non-work issues (see, eg, Kalleberg, 2011: 7–10). That said, part-time work merits its own discussion as many part-time jobs are still of a poorer quality than full-time jobs (Fagan et al, 2014). In practice, it is difficult to draw a sharp line between good and bad part-time work,[3] or between labour market insiders and outsiders more generally. Some workers are in between 'good' and 'bad' – they enjoy some, but not all, of the benefits associated with a standard employment relationship. Oorschot and Chung (2015) argue that the vulnerability of workers situated in this intermediary labour market is not necessarily related to their employment contract, but related to their pay, income and skill levels, as well as to social security benefits stemming from employment.

A second dimension central to the evaluation of part-time work is its voluntariness. Alongside temporary work, *involuntary part-time* work is a core indicator of being a labour market outsider (Kalleberg, 2000; Vosko, 2010; Emmenegger et al, 2012). The distinction between voluntary and involuntary part-time work has been at the heart of debates on part-time work in general (and female part-time work in particular) for years. While some workers clearly state that they would like to work more hours, others accept part-time jobs even if they are of poor quality. Why? Hakim (2000) argues in her 'preference theory' that some women choose part-time jobs – sometimes of poor quality – because they are family-oriented rather than work-oriented. According to Hakim, women in modern, prosperous societies are increasingly able to follow their preferences, and to manoeuvre within or around the structural constraints and opportunities that surround them. This perspective has spurred extensive debate on the relative importance of individual preferences and structural constraints (see, eg, Crompton and Harris, 1998; Hakim, 2006; Halrynjo and Lyng, 2009). How much room is there for individual choice regarding working time? For our purposes, it is sufficient to conclude that part-time work can, indeed, be both voluntary and involuntary but that the lines between the two are sometimes hazy and even changeable (Tomlinson, 2006).

Inspired and informed by the contributions to this volume and the general debates on part-time workers as labour market insiders or outsiders, we outline a typology of part-time workers. This typology has not been the point of departure for the contributing authors, but gradually developed as a result of the insights and perspectives that they provided. We base the typology on the two dimensions discussed earlier: (1) the quality of working conditions and social protection associated with the job; and (2) if working less than full-time is voluntary or not.

Part-time work can be attractive for people who give priority to some other non-labour market activity, for example, mothers, students and pensioners (Blossfeld and Hakim, 1997). Workers who have voluntarily taken part-time positions can have access to working conditions and social protection of varying quality. These variations are not easy to capture if we restrict our perspective to either 'good' or 'bad'. We will argue that there is also a middle category with a mix of good and bad. Consequently, we differentiate between good, mixed or bad working conditions and social protection. Along the dimension of voluntary part-time work, we suggest a division between workers who are (1) equalised, (2) semi-secured and (3) transitionals. Among workers who find themselves involuntarily in a part-time position, we suggest a division between workers who are (4) underemployed, (5) precarious and (6) marginalised (see Table 1.1). We should hasten to add that all involuntary part-timers are, of course, underemployed. The argument here is that there is a difference between the three groups in their access to good working conditions and social protection.

Table 1.1: A typology of part-time work and part-time workers

	Working conditions and social protection		
	Good	Mixed	Bad
Voluntary	1. Equalised	2. Semi-secured	3. Transitionals
Involuntary	4. Underemployed	5. Precarious	6. Marginalised

Equalised part-time workers work part-time on a voluntary basis and enjoy similar working conditions and social rights to those of comparable full-timers. The exception is entitlements earned, like pension benefits and unemployment benefits. Employers can be willing to create so-called retention part-time jobs to motivate and retain valued employees (Tilly, 1996; Webber and Williams, 2008). Typical examples are highly educated women who prefer part-time work when they become mothers, or senior workers with valuable competence who are approaching retirement. The employees that fill these jobs are likely to be 'permanent' rather than temporary workers. Although part-time work can have negative career consequences and long-term consequences for pension benefits, these workers tend to have a financial situation that allows them to earn a reduced income and a competence to offer the employer that enables them to influence the length and the organisation of their working time. They will also typically be able to re-enter a full-time position at relatively short notice. In the Norwegian health-care sector, employers tend to offer equalised part-time jobs to occupational groups who are in demand (trained nurses), but actively avoid providing these to low-skilled and more readily available workers (auxiliary nurses, nurse assistants) (see Chapter 4). In the US, however, retention part-time jobs are fewer than normally assumed and men are more likely than women to have these types of part-time jobs (see Chapter 8).

Semi-secured part-time workers work part-time on a voluntary basis but have poorer working conditions, less influence on working time organisation and less social rights than full-time workers. A possible example of a semi-secured part-timer would be a secondary earner who chooses part-time work to achieve a good work–life balance but is not able to secure or to negotiate the good working conditions that are available for equalised part-time workers with a stronger bargaining position in relation to their employer. In terms of social protection, the position of semi-secured part-time workers will vary between countries and welfare regimes, depending on how closely knit social protection is to the standard employment relationship and to the family structure. Blossfeld and Hakim (1997) pointed out that many part-time workers, especially women, enjoy better economic conditions and social protection than their position on the labour market indicates because they are protected financially through their families. Emmenegger et al (2012: 306), however, argue that, over time, women have become less protected through their families and derived benefits than they were in the industrial age, especially in corporatist conservative welfare systems, because policymakers do not adjust policies to compensate new groups who become exposed to precarious conditions. In other words, 'semi-secured women' may have become more exposed over time, as is illustrated in the contribution from South Korea (see Chapter 12). Women have partly taken up part-time work as a response to policies designed to combat unemployment, economic downturns and declining fertility rates, but they risk ending up in a semi-secure position compared to full-timers because their type of employment provides inferior wages and social security.

Transitionals work part-time voluntarily but have 'bad' working conditions compared to full-time workers. Typical examples of transitionals are students who take up a part-time job to supplement student loans, or young people who work for a limited period after they have finished their obligatory schooling to consider what path to follow in life. These jobs will often be characterised by short and unpredictable hours of work, work outside 'normal' hours, and limited entitlement earnings with regard to social rights. Also, as illustrated in the case of the Danish service industries (see Chapter 6), young workers in these industries may have lower hourly wages compared to older workers. Many of these young workers are students and when they take on bad jobs in a transitional phase, they are not what we normally associate with precarious or marginalised workers. That said, there is still the issue of how employers' access to transitionals may influence the working conditions of employees who are less mobile. There is also the question of the transitionals' actual ability to move on, either to further education or to other types of jobs. Private services like retail, industrial cleaning or hotels and restaurants will typically contain many transitionals who cater to employers' need for flexibility. For workers who are, in fact, *not* heading elsewhere, employers' access to transitionals may 'tip the balance' in their disfavour in terms of negotiating better working conditions.

The *underemployed part-timers* have the same working conditions and social protection as comparable full-time workers but would like to work more hours. One example is a worker who is situated in the 'primary' labour market with good working conditions and social protection, has the role of the household main breadwinner, and is forced to accept a part-time position during a period of economic recession. Reduced working time in this category can take several forms. In other cases, workers may be forced to accept part-time employment through various forms of work sharing or work rotation schemes during temporary layoffs. These are ways for employers to increase flexibility and reduce costs without having to fire core staff during times of economic recession (Crimmann et al, 2010; Olberg, 2015). Another category of workers who are underemployed according to the definition used here are those who cannot manage a full-time position because of their health, the particular job requirements or their family situation. These workers are not classified as underemployed in statistical terms because they are unable to accept full-time work even if it was offered. Of course, this particular form of involuntary part-time work can be present within our typology among the underemployed, the precarious and the marginalised part-time workers. Among workers in this category, we might find single parents in particular, but also employees in the health–care sector who struggle to combine (full-time) shift work with care responsibilities (see Chapter 4). The share of female underemployed part-timers will also vary substantially between countries, based on the work–family policies that may – or may not – be in place.

There may also be a more precarious category of involuntary part-time workers where the status is more mixed in terms of working conditions and social protection, and whose options to achieve a full-time position are more uncertain. *Precarious part-time workers* are typically in an intermediary position. They want to work more hours and lack access to some of the benefits enjoyed by full-time workers, but they are not (yet) permanently positioned in poor conditions. They are, however, 'at risk'. A factor that may influence the size and magnitude of this part-time group is the presence and intensity of activation and workfare policies. The obligation to take any available job offer as a way out of unemployment may normalise non–standard forms of employment (Rubery et al, 2018). An example of this is the German 'Minijobs' that are discussed in Chapter 10. Perhaps the most central question related to the future prospects of precarious part-timers is their mobility from 'precarious part-time work' into a preferably 'good' full-time position. The question of whether involuntary part-time work is likely to be followed by an opportunity to move on to a better position in the labour market, or if part-time work is, in fact, more of a trap, is debated and will most certainly vary across countries and regime types (see, eg, O'Reilly and Bothfeld, 2002; Gash, 2008; Kitterød et al, 2013).

The final category – *marginalised part-time workers* – work part-time involuntarily and their social protection and working conditions are poor compared to most full-time workers. Moreover, their prospects for seeing improvements are low. They are more likely to move between marginalised jobs, or between marginalised jobs and unemployment, than to experience upwards mobility in working conditions, social protection and working time. This distinguishes the marginalised from the transitionals, who accept poor working conditions and limited social protection because they are heading elsewhere – presumably into jobs with better working conditions and more extensive social protection. An example of a part-time position with a high risk of marginalisation is the so-called 'zero hours' contract, where employers take workers on without guaranteeing any specific amount of work (see, eg, Broughton et al, 2016). Workers on such contracts have very low predictability in working-time organisation, number of hours of actual work and income level. This has become a topic of interest in, for example, the UK and Ireland, where concerns have been raised both about the use of 'exclusivity clauses' prohibiting workers from working for other employers and about a lack of transparency in the contracts.[4] Among the marginalised part-timers, we will typically find workers with low education in general and migrants with low education in particular. Employers have few incentives to offer them better contracts with longer hours because they are considered easy to replace. Migrants are in a particularly challenging situation as the judicial terms regulating both the right to work and the conditions to permanently reside in various host countries will further influence their ability to move out of precarious or marginalised positions.

The delineation between precarious and marginalised part-timers can be hazy, as can the borders between several of the other types of part-time work that we have outlined here. Workers will move between different types of part-time work of varying quality, as well as between part- and full-time work, or in and out of employment. Furthermore, while gender, age, education, occupational class, migration status and health will be important dimensions to consider in empirical investigations of the different forms of part-time work, the position of part-time workers will inevitably be closely related to factors such as economic fluctuations, national-level regulations and workplace practices. Last but not least, the empirical measurement of job quality and social rights – and their relative importance – deserves dedicated attention.

Across countries, the relevance of the six part-time categories will vary both in terms of their size and of the characteristics of their 'members'. Some countries provide better protection to those who are positioned at the margins of the labour market (Esping-Andersen, 1990, 2009; Lewis, 1992; Soskice and Hall, 2001). In regimes where central aspects of social protection are left to employers, and where the responsibilities of employers are gradually being deregulated, workers will be more exposed. For example, on average, marginalised part-time workers in the Scandinavian countries will be fewer and better off in terms of social protection than marginalised workers in countries of a liberal bent. Although countries are exposed to similar types of change, such as fiercer international competition, increased migration and a growing service sector, their responses will often be influenced by the original and unique identity of the country's national institutions. Examples of these are labour law and collective bargaining systems, the strength and priorities of trade unions, and the coverage and quality of care institutions (Traxler, 2003; Pfau-Effinger, 2012). The characteristics of labour market institutions, as well as gender cultures and family models, influence both the transformative capacity of policy, the insider–outsider divide in the labour market and the consequences of policy for people.

Part-time work across time and countries

The development of part-time work has been both suppressed and encouraged by political as well as cultural contexts. As the chapters in this book show, this has resulted in heterogeneous patterns of part-time employment across countries in terms of its scope, its voluntariness and its quality. Furthermore, these heterogenous patterns of part-time employment are still present in much the same way as before, although it has become more widespread in some OECD countries and less so in others (see Figures 1.1a and 1.1b).[5]

The Nordic countries are marked by high female labour market participation, but also by relatively high female part-time employment rates. This pattern is often explained with reference to the specific political and institutional development in social-democratic welfare state regimes. From the 1970s, and as women entered the labour market in increasing numbers, legislation and services were introduced to increase the employment of women and to reduce their economic dependence on a husband. Also, part-time work became a well-regulated employment category, showing few of the signs of marginal employment that would develop in other regimes (Ellingsæter, 2017). This does not preclude variations within the region. The part-time levels are currently well above the OECD average in Denmark (22%)

and Norway (19%), but significantly lower in Sweden and Finland (both 14%).

Other countries in Northern Europe have quite different levels of both female employment and part-time work. The Netherlands still holds the 'record', with a part-time share of 60% among women and 19% among men. The part-time share is also well above the OECD average among both women and men in Switzerland, the UK and Ireland. Countries that belong to liberal or corporate regimes have been far less committed than the Nordic countries to provide and design welfare benefits in a way that supports dual-earner families. In liberal regimes, such as the UK, but also Australia and the US, supporting the reconciliation of work and family, and facilitating dual-earner or dual-carer families, are not seen as state responsibilities. In corporate regimes like Austria, France and Germany, the state has been more strongly committed to preserving the traditional male breadwinner model, with family benefits designed to support motherhood and protect women through the husband and the family (Esping-Andersen, 1990, 2009).

In Southern Europe, both female participation in paid employment and the share of part-time work are lower than in Northern Europe. This is the result of a political and cultural context that favours the male breadwinner model, but also of a 'lagged position' in the transition from an agricultural to an industrial economy. This combination slowed down the development of labour market structures, family systems and welfare policy that could otherwise have shifted female employment patterns in new directions and increased the level of (female) part-time employment (Blossfeld and Hakim, 1997; O'Reilly and Fagan, 1998). Nevertheless, there are also variations within Southern European countries in terms of the development and levels of part-time work. While Portugal and Greece have part-time levels of 9% and 11%, respectively, the corresponding numbers in Spain and Italy are 14% and 19%.

In the former socialist countries of Central and Eastern Europe, employment was – and still is – typically full-time for both women and men. For example, in Russia and Hungary, the share of part-time workers is 3% among men and 5% among women. Apart from a period of economic crisis in the 1990s, South Korea has experienced rapid industrialisation and economic growth since the Second World War (Kalleberg and Hewison, 2013). In contrast to Japan – a country with a similar cultural context, economic development and levels of female employment – South Korea has part-time employment rates well below the OECD average (see Table 1.2).

Table 1.2: Key employment indicators 2016

	Total PT as % of total employed	Female PT	Male PT	Total labour force participation rate	Female LFPR	Male LFPR
Netherlands	38	60	19	64	59	70
Switzerland	27	45	11	69	63	74
Australia	26	38	15	65	59	71
UK	24	37	12	63	58	69
Japan	23	37	12	60	50	70
Ireland	23	35	12	60	53	68
Germany	22	37	9	61	56	66
Denmark	22	27	17	64	59	68
New Zealand	21	32	12	70	65	75
Austria	21	35	9	61	56	67
Canada	19	26	13	66	61	70
Norway	19	27	12	71	68	73
Italy	19	33	8	49	40	59
Belgium	18	30	7	53	48	59
Iceland	18	25	12	84	80	87
OECD average	17	26	9	60	52	69
France	14	22	7	56	52	61
Spain	14	22	7	59	54	65
Finland	14	18	11	66	63	68
Sweden	14	18	10	72	70	74
Luxembourg	14	24	5	59	54	64
Cyprus	11	14	8	62	57	67
Greece	11	16	7	52	45	60
South Korea	11	16	7	63	52	74
Turkey	9	18	6	52	32	72
Portugal	9	11	7	58	54	64
Estonia	9	12	6	71	66	76
Slovenia	8	11	5	57	52	61
Latvia	7	10	5	60	55	67
Lithuania	7	9	4	60	56	66
Poland	6	9	3	56	48	65
Slovak Republic	6	8	4	60	53	68
Czech Republic	5	8	3	60	52	68
Croatia	5	6	4	51	45	58
Russian Federation	4	6	3	70	64	76
Hungary	4	5	3	61	54	69
Romania	4	5	3	54	44	64

Notes: Part-time (OECD 'common definition') = less than 30 weekly hours of work in main job. PT = part-time; LFPR = labour force participation rate.

Source: OECD Labour Force Statistics

During the 1980s and 1990s, there was a strong growth in part-time employment in most OECD countries. This overall growth continued, or at least did not reverse, in the years preceding the financial crisis in 2007 and in the first years following the economic downturn (OECD, 2010). In Figures 1.1a and 1.1b, we extend the period of investigation and compare the part-time shares among women and men between 2000 and 2016.

In 2016, the average rate of part-time work for women in OECD countries was 26%. The levels ranged from 60% in the Netherlands and 45% in Switzerland, to around one third in Austria, Italy and Ireland, and 6% or less in the Russian Federation, Hungary and Romania. There is no clear-cut relation between the national level of part-time employment and the rise or fall of part-time rates over the last 15 years (see Figure 1.1a). Among the countries with the most notable increases, we find Austria, Italy and Japan, with relatively high levels of part-time employment, but also countries with lower levels like Greece and South Korea. The most notable decreases in female part-time work have been seen in Iceland, Poland, Norway and Belgium.

For men, the part-time levels in 2016 are far lower, with an OECD average of 9%. The Netherlands has the highest level of male part-time work (19%) but Denmark and Australia have also reached levels of 17% and 15%, respectively. The Russian Federation, Hungary and Romania are at the other end of the scale, with male part-time levels of 3%. Between 2000 and 2016, the overall share of men in part-time work increased in almost all OECD countries, but most notably in Denmark, Austria and the Netherlands. Denmark and the Netherlands already had comparatively high levels of men in part-time work, while Austria, Spain and Greece started at a far lower level.

Involuntary part-time work

Different demographic groups vary in their risk of working part-time involuntarily. Men who work part-time are more likely than women to do so involuntarily, older workers less so than younger workers and migrants more so than natives (OECD, 2010: 214). On average, in OECD countries, 16.3% of the part-time workers are involuntary and the share of involuntary part-time workers increased substantially between 2007 and 2016 (see Figure 1.2). There is, however, considerable variation between the countries contributing to this average. In the Southern European countries of Greece, Spain and Italy, who were hit hard by the economic crisis, more than half of the part-time workers would like to work longer hours and the

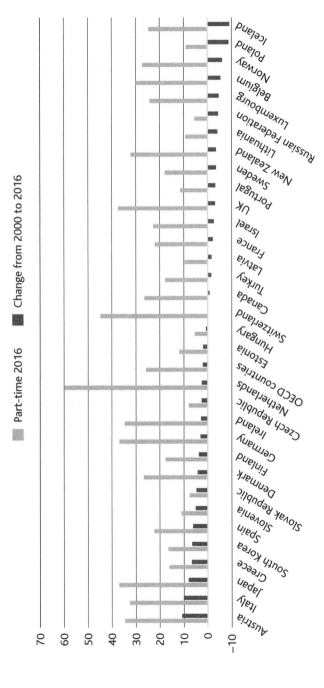

Figure 1.1a: Female part-time workers as a percentage of total employed in 2016, and change in share of female part-time workers between 2000 and 2016, by country, organised by percent change

Note: Part-time = less than 30 weekly hours of work in main job.

Source: OECD stat 2016

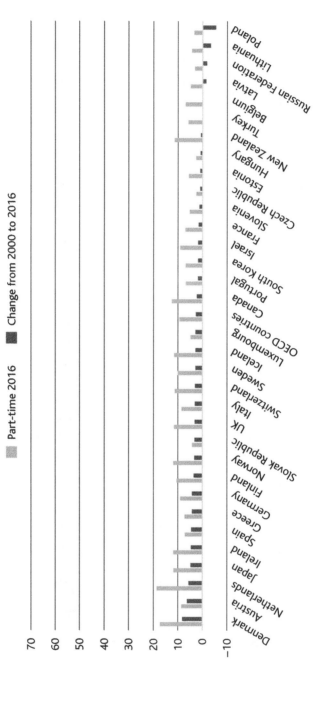

Figure 1.1b: Male part-time workers as a percentage of total employed in 2016, and change in share of male part-time workers between 2000 and 2016, by country, organised by percent change

Part-time 2016   Change from 2000 to 2016

Note: Part-time = less than 30 weekly hours of work in main job.
Source: OECD stat 2016

share of involuntary part-time work increased substantially between 2007 and 2016. At the other end of the scale, we find countries like Germany, the Netherlands, the UK, the US and Norway, all with reported levels of involuntary part-time work well below 15% of all part-time employees and either no increase in involuntary part-time work since 2007 or only a slight increase. In some countries, there has been a decline in the share of involuntary part-time work – most notably, in Germany, Sweden and Belgium.

It should be noted that statistical data have their obvious limitations in measuring involuntary part-time work. The distinction between voluntary and involuntary part-time work in Figure 1.2 is based on labour force surveys, where workers state their reasons for working part-time. In most countries, only those who answer that they have not been able to find a full-time job are categorised as involuntary part-time workers. However, the decision to work part-time may also be driven by external constraints, such as care responsibilities, a lack of affordable or good quality childcare facilities, or an inability to work longer hours due to health problems and/or the particular working conditions of the job at hand. The level of involuntary part-time work reported in Figure 1.2 will therefore most likely underestimate the actual level of involuntary part-time work, particularly among women (see also Chapter 4).

The structure of the book

This book will demonstrate that part-time workers are dissimilar in terms of their motivations to work part-time, their working conditions, their access to social protection and their prospects of transitioning from a position as a labour market outsider to a position as a labour market insider. The contributions look at the regulations and the quality of part-time work in a wide range of countries and contexts, as well as from a variety of analytical perspectives and methodological approaches. The book is organised thematically into three parts. The contributions in Part One focus on the *institutional and organisational regulations of part-time work*, and shed light on the influence of politics, institutions and organisations. The authors discuss the effectiveness of regulations at different levels (supranational, national and workplace), as well as the consequences for part-time workers. How relevant are supranational attempts to regulate part-time work at the national level? How has the de-standardisation of labour contracts in Italy and Spain influenced women's opportunity to use part-time work as a way to ease work–family conflicts? Do national ambitions to reduce involuntary

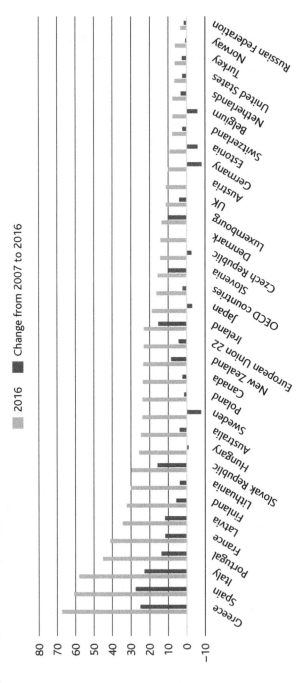

Figure 1.2: Involuntary part-time work as a percentage of total part-time employees in 2016, and change from 2007 to 2016, by country, organised by level of involuntary part-time work in 2016

■ 2016 ■ Change from 2007 to 2016

Source: OECD stat 2016

part-time work through 'hard regulations' in Norway trickle all the way down and create new workplace practices?

In Chapter 2, Sonja Bekker and Dalila Ghailani give an overview of EU norms and instruments and set the issue of part-time work in a wider context of gender equality. Their examination of recommendations from the European Commission to six member states shows that part-time work is not seen as a challenge or stand-alone issue in any of the cases. They argue that the EU Part-Time Work Directive is primarily an employment policy tool. The aim of the directive is to improve the working conditions of part-time workers, but it simultaneously legitimises the growth of this form of employment. This is problematic given that women face a much higher risk of having to deal with the structural and long-term disadvantages of part-time work, such as career penalties and lower pension entitlements.

In Chapter 3, Lara Maestripieri and Margarita León discuss the effects of employment de-standardisation trends on gender equality and living conditions in Italy and Spain. These Southern European countries have the highest share of involuntary part-time work in Europe and the element of involuntariness has increased during the economic crisis. The growth of non-standard contracts, including part-time, is seen as a consequence of labour market rigidity (eg strong restrictions on dismissals for permanent workers), and the authors argue that part-time employment appears to be a strategy to facilitate labour market flexibility, rather than work–family balance. Using an intersectional analytical approach, they show that the distribution of non-standard and involuntary part-time work is unequal among different groups of women, impacting the young (Italy) and the low educated (Spain) in particular.

In Chapter 4, Hanne Cecilie Kavli, Heidi Nicolaisen and Sissel C. Trygstad use the Norwegian health-care sector to discuss the possibilities, but also the limitations, of national legislation to combat involuntary part-time work. The workplace 'translation' of the amendments to the labour law had unintended consequences. While the amendments helped the most qualified part-timers to secure more hours, workers with less education became more exposed as employers adapted opportunistically to maintain their flexibility in staffing and scheduling. While the policy ambition was to reduce the gap between labour market 'insiders' and 'outsiders', this case shows that the most exposed workers still struggle to escape 'bad' part-time contracts.

Part Two, on the *quality of working conditions and part-time work*, addresses the consequences of part-time employment for the wider set of working conditions. When does part-time employment 'spill over' to other aspects of the employment relationship, and add to the disadvantages of part-time jobs? Under what circumstances is it a good way to facilitate a better work–life balance? In what parts of the labour market are part-time workers particularly exposed to poor working conditions and who among them are able to move on to better positions?

In Chapter 5, Heejung Chung examines part-time working women's access to schedule control, flexible start and finish times, and time off work to tend to personal issues. Based on data from 30 European countries, she shows that part-time work and other types of flexible working-time arrangements tend to complement rather than substitute for each other. In contrast to expectations, part-time working women were not worse off than full-timers in their access to family-friendly, flexible working arrangements. However, she also suggests that the real dualisation patterns may be found in the outcomes of flexible working, rather than in the access to such.

One such outcome is pay, a topic addressed in Chapter 6. Within the context of the private, low-wage sector in Denmark, Trine P. Larsen, Anna Ilsøe and Jonas Felbo-Kolding explore how institutional frameworks for working-time and wage regulation affect the prevalence of marginal part-time work and increased polarisation. While marginal part-time contracts in some instances facilitate a win–win situation for the employer and employees (mainly students), providing flexibility to both parties, the same types of contracts make it difficult to secure a living wage and therefore contribute to the marginalisation of young people (who are not students) and migrants, who may be more permanently positioned in these sectors and jobs.

Many migrants enter the labour market through part-time, low-paid, low-skilled jobs in the secondary sector (Rubin et al, 2008; Vosko, 2010; Standing, 2011; Emmenegger et al, 2012). In Chapter 7, Hanne Cecilie Kavli and Roy A. Nielsen use longitudinal register data from Norway to describe mobility patterns from part-time work among immigrants and non-immigrants. They find both upwards and downwards mobility from part-time work, but more so among immigrants than among non-immigrants. While the majority of 'movers' among both men and women, as well as immigrants and non-immigrants, increase their working time, immigrants are also more at risk of labour market exits. Employees in short part-time positions still face higher risks of labour market exits, and immigrants more so than non-immigrants.

The Norwegian institutional configuration is quite protective of part-time workers. If we move on to part-time work in one of the liberal regimes, the picture is different. In Chapter 8, Kenneth Hudson and Arne L. Kalleberg discuss part-time work in the US, a country where part-time work is both less common and less protected. They find that the level of part-time work has varied in response to fluctuations in the labour market since the 1980s and hence adjust the claims in the popular media that America is becoming a 'part-time nation'. An indicator based on part-time workers' pay level, access to health insurance, pension benefits and schedule flexibility is used to measure if part-time jobs are 'good' or 'bad'. They show that part-time workers are more likely to have bad jobs, and they are more apt to live in families that are poor. Furthermore although some part-time jobs offer health and retirement benefits, most do not. Black people, Hispanic non-citizens and persons of mixed-race descent are more likely to work part-time, and part-timers are more likely to have jobs in the secondary labour market.

Returning to the Nordic welfare and labour regimes in Chapter 9, Jouko Nätti and Kristine Nergaard study the characteristics of part-time workers and their mobility between different working-time categories over the last two decades in the Nordic countries. They show that there are pockets of precariousness among Nordic part-time workers that might moderate the overall impression of the low risks and high quality that have been associated with part-time work in this region. Furthermore, part-time work is characterised by high stability, especially in Norway. Hence, the results do not give support for the increased polarisation of part-time work.

Part-time work is often framed as a way to facilitate employment among women. In Part Three, on *work–life balance, gender and part-time work*, the focus is on the link between work–family balance policies, part-time work and gender equality. The key question is if and how national work–family reconciliation policies affect women's, and particularly mothers', labour market participation and conditions of work.

In Chapter 10, Birgit Pfau-Effinger and Thordis Reimer analyse how demand- and supply-side factors interact with welfare state institutions and politics in the production of marginal employment for women in part-time jobs in Germany. The so-called 'Minijobs' have created favourable opportunities for firms to employ workers in marginal jobs. Minijobs were originally introduced in the 1960s to provide opportunities for housewives to earn some additional income for the household. The Red–Green Coalition government reintroduced the 'Minijob' legislation in 2000 to increase labour market flexibility and employment. Compared to regular part-time and full-time employment, Minijobs are marked by substantially lower wages and higher social security and poverty risks. The authors find that Minijobs contribute to the persistence of traditional structures of gender inequality in Germany and also increase inequality in the labour market.

In Chapter 11, Mara A. Yerkes and Belinda Hewitt compare the Netherlands, a country with a high protection of part-time workers, with Australia, where protection is minimal. Their contribution illustrates that while mothers in both countries use part-time work as a strategy to combine work and care, the conditions under which these strategies are used differ significantly. Their findings suggest that inequality exists between part-time workers and full-time workers in both countries, as well as among part-timers, even in the Netherlands, where part-time work is well protected.

Women's participation in the labour market has also increased rapidly outside of Europe and modified former gender-traditional patterns of labour market participation. In Chapter 12, Min Young Song and Sophia Seung-yoon Lee examine the effect of government attempts to increase women's labour market participation in South Korea. They argue that a series of policies intended to help families to increase their income, on the one hand, and work–life balance for married women, on the other, have led to a rise in part-time employment opportunities for women. However, most part-time jobs have been created on the basis of temporary contracts where the hourly wage levels are lower than for full-time workers, and hence place women on the outskirts of the labour market.

In Chapter 13, Hanne Cecilie Kavli and Heidi Nicolaisen summarise the volume's main findings. They return to the question of the dualisation of part-time work and discuss the capability of policy and regulations to influence the divide between good and bad part-time jobs, as well as labour market insiders and outsiders. The future prospects of part-time work and part-time workers depend on numerous factors. Some are well within the reach of political action – others are not. In our opinion, a good way forward is to apply a more nuanced perspective of what part-time work entails for different categories of workers and within different institutional and cultural contexts. The typology presented in this introductory chapter can provide a framework for further analyses of part-time work and part-time workers within different institutional contexts.

Notes
[1]   From the Preamble, Part-Time Work Convention 1994 (No. 175).

[2] Part-Time Work Directive, 97/81/EC.

[3] The concepts of 'good/mixed/bad' part-time work can be seen as somewhat normative, representing an employee perspective. However, their content corresponds with the 'high/low' protection of workers through regulations and is well established in the literature about differences between different categories of workers in the labour market (see, eg, Kalleberg, 2011).

[4] See: www.eurofound.europa.eu/observatories/eurwork/articles/working-conditions/government-consults-on-regulating-zero-hours-contracts

[5] International comparisons of working time are seldom straightforward. The OECD defines part-time work as working less than 30 hours per week, but many countries have their own legal thresholds defining part-time work. In labour surveys, it is left up to the workers to describe their position as either part- or full-time.

References

Andersen, S.K. (ed) (2003) *EU og det nordiske spil om lov og aftale: de nordiske lande og de europaeiske aftaler/direktiver om deltid og tidsbegraenset ansaettelse*, Stockholm: Arbetslivsinstitutet.

Atkinson, J. (1984) 'Manpower strategies for flexible organisations', *Personnel management*, 16: 28–31.

Blossfeld, H.-P. and Hakim, C. (1997) *Between equalization and marginalization: women working part-time in Europe*, Oxford: Oxford University Press.

Böheim, R. and Taylor, M.P. (2004) 'Actual and preferred working hours', *British Journal of Industrial Relations*, 42: 149–66.

Bosch, G. (2006) 'Working time and the standard employment relationship', in J.-Y. Boulin, M. Lallement, F. Messenger and F. Michon (eds) *Decent working time: new trends and new issues*. Geneva: ILO, pp 41–64.

Broughton, A., Green, M., Rickard, C., Swift, S., Eichhorst, W., Tobsch, V., Magda, I., Lewandowski, P., Keister, R., Jonaviciene, D., Ramos Martín, N.E., Valsamis, D. and Tros, F. (2016) 'Precarious employment in Europe. Part 1: patterns, trends and policy strategy', study for the EMPL Committee.

Carre, F., Findlay, P., Tilly, C. and Warhurst, C. (2012) 'Job quality; scenarios, analysis and interventions', in C. Warhurst, F. Carre, P. Findlay and C. Tilly (eds) *Are bad jobs inevitable?*, London: Palgrave, pp 1–22.

Crimmann, A., Wießner, F. and Bellmann, L. (2010) *The German work-sharing scheme: an instrument for the crisis*, Geneva: International Labour Office.

Crompton, R. and Harris, F. (1998) 'Gender relations and employment: the impact of occupation', *Work, Employment and Society*, 12: 297–315.

Doeringer, P. and Piore, M.J. (1971) *Internal labor markets and manpower adjustment*, New York, NY: DC Heath and Company.

Ellingsæter, A.L. (2017) *Vår tids moderne tider: det norske arbeidstidsregimet*, Oslo: Universitetsforlaget.

Ellingsæter, A.L. and Jensen, R.S. (2019) 'Politicising women's part-time work in Norway: a longitudinal study of ideas', *Work, Employment and Society*. Available at https://doi.org/10.1177/0950017018821277

Ellingsæter, A.L. and Leira, A. (2006) *Politicising parenthood in Scandinavia: gender relations in welfare states*, Bristol: The Policy Press.

Emmenegger, P., Häusermann, S., Palier, B. and Seeleib-Kaiser, M. (2012) 'How we grow unequal', in P. Emmenegger, S. Häusermann, B. Palier and M. Seeleib-Kaiser (eds) *The age of dualization: the changing face of inequality in deindustrializing societies*, Oxford and New York: Oxford University Press.

Esping-Andersen, G. (1990) *The three worlds of welfare capitalism*, Cambridge: Polity.

Esping-Andersen, G. (2009) *Incomplete revolution: adapting welfare states to women's new roles*, Cambridge: Polity.

Fagan, C., Norman, H., Smith, M. and González Menéndez, M.C. (2014) 'In search of good quality part-time employment', Conditions of Work and Employment Series No. 43, International Labour Office Geneva.

Gallie, D. (2013) 'Economic crisis, the quality of work, and social integration', in D. Gallie (ed) *Economic crisis, quality of work, and social integration: the European experience*, Oxford: Oxford University Press, pp 1–29.

Gash, V. (2008) 'Preference or constraint? Part-time workers' transitions in Denmark, France and the United Kingdom', *Work, employment and society*, 22: 655–74.

Green, F., Felstead, A. and Gallie, D. (2015) 'The inequality of job quality', in A. Felstead, D. Gallie and F. Green (eds) *Unequal Britain at work*, Oxford: Oxford University Press, pp 1–21.

Haipeter, T. (2006) 'Can norms survive market pressures? The practical effectiveness of new forms of working time regulation in a changing German economy', in J.-Y. Boulin (ed) *Decent working time: New trends, new issues*, Geneva: International Labour Organization.

Hakim, C. (2000) *Work–lifestyle choices in the 21st century: preference theory*, Oxford: OUP.

Hakim, C. (2006) 'Women, careers, and work–life preferences', *British Journal of Guidance & Counselling*, 34: 279–94.

Halrynjo, S. and Lyng, S.T. (2009) 'Preferences, constraints or schemas of devotion? Exploring Norwegian mothers' withdrawals from high-commitment careers', *British Journal of Sociology*, 60: 321–43.

Häusermann, S. and Schwander, H. (2012) 'Varieties of dualization? Labor market segmentation and insider–outsider divides across regimes', in P. Emmenegger, S. Häusermann, B. Palier and M. Seeleib-Kaiser (eds) *The age of dualization: the changing face of inequality in deindustrializing societies*, Oxford and New York: Oxford University Press, pp 27–51.

Kalleberg, A.L. (2000) 'Nonstandard employment relations: part-time, temporary and contract work', *Annual Review of Sociology*, 26: 341–65.

Kalleberg, A.L. (2011) *Good jobs, bad jobs*, New York: Russell Sage Foundations.

Kalleberg, A.L. and Hewison, K. (2013) 'Precarious work and the challenge for Asia', *American Behavioral Scientist*, 57: 271–88.

Kanbur, R. and Ronconi, L. (2018) 'Enforcement matters: the effective regulation of labor', *International Labour Review*, September. Available at https://doi.org/10.1111/ilr.12112

Kitterød, R.H., Rønsen, M. and Seierstad, A. (2013) 'Mobilizing female labour market reserves: what promotes women's transitions between part-time and full-time work?', *Acta Sociologica*, 56: 155–71.

Lewis, J. (1992) 'Gender and the development of welfare regimes', *Journal of European Social Policy*, 2: 159–73.

Lyonette, C., Baldauf, B. and Behle, H. (2010) *Quality part-time work: a review of the evidence*, London: Government Equalities Office.

Nätti, J. (1995) 'Part-time work in the Nordic countries: a trap for women?', *Labour*, 9: 343–57.

Nergaard, K. (2010) 'Mobility in and out of part-time work', in T.E. Berglund (ed) *Labour market mobility in Nordic welfare states*, Copenhagen: TemaNord.

Nicolaisen, H. (2011) 'Increasingly equalized? A study of part-time work in 'old' and 'new' part-time work regimes', *Nordic Journal of Working Life Studies*, 1: 95.

OECD (Organisation for Economic Co-operation and Development) (2010) *OECD Employment Outlook 2010. Moving beyond the job crisis*, Paris: OECD. Available at: https://doi.org/10.1787/19991266

Olberg, D. (2015) 'Regulating the temporary layoff institution – coalitions and drift', in F. Engelstad and A. Hagelund (ed) *Cooperation and conflict the Nordic way*, Berlin: De Gruyter Open.

Oorschot, W.V. and Chung, H. (2015) 'Feelings of dual-insecurity among European workers: a multi-level analysis', *European Journal of Industrial Relations*, 21: 23–37.

O'Reilly, J. and Bothfeld, S. (2002) 'What happens after working part time? Integration, maintenance or exclusionary transitions in Britain and Western Germany', *Cambridge Journal of Economics*, 26: 409–39.

O'Reilly, J. and Fagan, C. (1998) *Part-time prospects: an international comparison of part-time work in Europe, North America and the Pacific Rim*, London and New York: Routledge.

Palier, B. (2010) *A long goodbye to Bismarck? The politics of welfare reforms in Continental Europe*, Amsterdam: Amsterdam University Press.

Pfau-Effinger, B. (2012) 'Women's employment in the institutional and cultural context', *International Journal of Sociology and Social Policy*, 32: 530–43.

Prosser, T. (2016) 'Dualization or liberalization? Investigating precarious work in eight European countries', *Work, Employment and Society*, 30: 949–65.

Rubery, J., Earnshaw, J., Marchington, M., Cooke, F.L. and Vincent, S. (2002) 'Changing organizational forms and the employment relationship', *Journal of Management Studies*, 39: 645–72.

Rubery, J., Grimshaw, D., Keizer, A. and Johnson, M. (2018) 'Challenges and contradictions in the 'normalising' of precarious work', *Work, Employment and Society*, 32: 509–27.

Rubin, J., Rendall, M.S., Rabinovich, L., Tsang, F., Van Oranje-Nassau, C. and Janta, B. (2008) *Migrant women in the European labour force: Current situation and future prospects*, Cambridge: RAND Europe.

Sengupta, S., Edwards, P.K. and Tsaj, C.-J. (2009) 'The good, the bad, and the ordinary: work identities in "good" and "bad" jobs in the United Kingdom', *Work and Occupations*, 36(1): 26–55.

Sisson, K. (2013) 'Private sector employment relations in Western Europe: collective bargaining under pressure?', in I.A.P.V. Arrowsmith (ed) *The transformation of employment relations in Europe*, New York, NY, and London: Routledge.

Soskice, D.W. and Hall, P.A. (2001) *Varieties of capitalism: the institutional foundations of comparative advantage*, Oxford: Oxford University Press.

Standing, G. (2011) *The precariat: the dangerous new class*, London and New York: Bloomsbury Academic.

Tilly, C. (1996) *Half a job: bad and good part-time jobs in a changing labor market*, Philadelphia: Temple University Press.

Tomlinson, J. (2006) 'Part-time occupational mobility in the service industries: regulation, work commitment and occupational closure', *The Sociological Review*, 54: 66–86.

Traxler, F. (2003) 'Bargaining, state regulation and the trajectories of industrial relations', *European Journal of Industrial Relations*, 9: 141–61.

Vidal, M. (2013) 'Low-autonomy work and bad jobs in post-Fordist capitalism', *Human Relations*, 66(4): 587–612.

Vosko, L.F. (2010) *Managing the margins: Gender, citizenship, and the international regulation of precarious employment*, Oxford and New York: Oxford University Press.

Warren, T. and Lyonette, C. (2018) 'Good, bad and very bad part-time jobs for women? Re-examining the importance of occupational class for job quality since the "Great Recession" in Britain', *Work, Employment and Society*, 32(4): 747–67.

Webber, G. and Williams, C. (2008) 'Mothers in "good" and "bad" part-time jobs: different problems, same results', *Gender & Society*, 22: 752–77.

PART ONE
Institutional and organisational regulations of part-time work

PART ONE

2

European Union regulations and governance of part-time work

Sonja Bekker and Dalila Ghailani

Introduction

This chapter focuses on the European Union (EU) dimension of part-time work. It gives a broad overview of EU norms and instruments, and sets the issue of part-time work in the wider context of gender equality. Connecting part-time work with gender equality facilitates the analysis in two ways. First, it enables linking the EU's employment policies to fundamental rights, such as equal labour market opportunities for men and women. Via this fundamental rights approach, the EU's view on part-time work may be tied to concerns of labour market dualisation. Second, it helps to analyse the degree of conflict between the aims of the different EU instruments. For instance, do the Part-Time Work Directive and the European Employment Strategy (EES) both aim for equal employment opportunities, or do other goals prevail? By answering such questions, the chapter not only reveals the different ways in which the EU deals with part-time employment, but also uncovers whether or not there is coherence between the different EU-level instruments.

Combinations of EU legislation and coordination to tackle inequality

This chapter places the issue of part-time employment in the wider context of the EU's pursuit of gender equality and improving employment policies. The EU uses a wide range of different instruments to influence national laws and employment policies. Jointly, these instruments form a complex mix of governance patterns (Armstrong, 2011). It means that seemingly distinct coordination tools may have an impact on each other. This understanding of the EU having a range of instruments that are interlinked is the basis of this chapter. It facilitates a broad analysis of the EU's position on part-time work, connecting it to fundamental rights such as gender equality and equal opportunities, while also taking account of the EU's employment policy aims, for instance, to increase employment rates. All these aims are furthered using both 'hard' and 'soft' law tools (Fagan and Rubery, 2018). EU hard law consists of primary law, such as treaties, and secondary law, such as directives, as well as the rulings of the European Court of Justice (CJEU), which are binding on member states. By contrast, soft law consists of different policy documents, recommendations and declarations that rely on the power of persuasion, the spreading of good practice and softer instruments (Kantola, 2010). Potentially, these different instruments evaluate part-time work differently, emphasising its positive aspects (eg improving labour market flexibility for employers and employees) or looking at its negative consequences (eg lower earning capacity or career penalties). The different instruments could thus complement each other when pursuing common goals (Trubek and Trubek, 2007; Smismans, 2011), for instance, if gender equality is not only set in treaty norms, but also pursued using the EES. Yet, rivalry could also occur, which might result in a competition for dominance (Trubek and Trubek, 2007), for instance, if part-time employment is seen as a means to get people into the labour market without really minding the negative consequences. From a labour market inequality perspective, paying attention to the negative consequences of part-time employment is essential, especially if these negative consequences are not distributed equally among the different labour market groups. Indeed, groups incurring a particularly high risk of being in atypical employment may be seen as 'outsiders' to the labour market (Emmenegger et al, 2012). Part-time work is highly gendered: women are employed part-time much more often than men. Although part-time work gives women an option to combine work and care, it also comes with disadvantages, such as career penalties and lower pensions upon retirement (Ghailani, 2014; Lyonette, 2015). The question is how the different hard and soft law instruments of the EU deal with part-time work. This chapter explores whether 'part-time' has different meanings and implications when it comes to the different EU instruments that guide policies for employment and equal opportunities in member states.

The next sections first outline how gender equality is dealt with in the EU legal framework: the treaties, directives and case law. Whereas the treaties do not address part-time employment, it does set norms regarding the equal opportunities for men and women, including on labour market participation. Such norms are relevant in assessing the

Part-Time Work Directive and related case law. Then, the chapter looks at soft law instruments dealing with both gender equality and part-time work, including the overall views and purposes of the EES. Next, the chapter focuses on the specific recommendations that the EU has made on part-time employment to six of its member states in 2017 and 2018. The conclusion discusses whether there is coherence in the goals of the different instruments, or if there is a degree of rivalry.

Gender equality in the EU legal framework

Gender equality is a fundamental human right and a moral imperative linked to principles of justice and equity, with political, economic, social and cultural aspects (Ghailani, 2014). It is considered to be a key factor for well-being and happiness (by the Organisation for Economic Co-operation and Development [OECD]), and is guaranteed internationally (by the International Labour Organization [ILO] and the United Nations [UN]) and at European (by the Council of Europe) and national levels by a substantial body of legislation (Ghailani, 2014). The EU has been a front-runner in gender equality on a number of occasions. It included gender pay equality as a principle in the 1957 Treaty of Rome, and afterwards introduced legal directives on equal pay and sex discrimination, applicable to all member states, in the mid-1970s (Rubery, 2015; Fagan and Rubery, 2018). Although the original focus on equal pay and on avoiding distortions of competition between member states has gradually been replaced by concerns for equality as a fundamental right, its economic roots still constitute an integral part of the gender-equality principle (Bain and Masselot, 2012). The EU's approach to gender reflects three conceptualisations of equality (Plomien, 2018): equal treatment, granting legal equality rights; equal opportunities, providing for different statuses via positive action; and equal outcome, requiring attention to all aspects and processes involved in (re)producing inequality and bringing about their transformation through mainstreaming. Plomien (2018) underlines that gender equality can be achieved through these combined approaches by overcoming the equality–difference dilemma and facilitating the transformation of unequal gender relations. These approaches partly come back in the use of the different hard and soft law instruments that the EU has, providing input to analyse which perspective the EU's instruments take when dealing with part-time work and inequality.

Gender equality and part-time work in hard law: treaties, directives, case law

Under the EU legal framework, treaties and directives must be complied with. Originally, Article 119 of the Treaty Establishing the European Economic Community (EEC) (1957) (now 157 TFEU) was the only provision setting out the principle of equal pay for men and women for equal work or work of equivalent value. Its purpose was strictly economic: to eliminate distortions of competition between companies established within the EEC. Its fundamental character has been completed with the addition of Article 13 EEC (Article 19 TFEU), making it possible to adopt a directive on gender equality outside the workplace. The Treaty of Amsterdam promoted gender equality as one of the central tasks of the EU (Article 2 EC), and introduced the concept of 'gender mainstreaming', requiring the European legislator to take account of the principle of gender equality when drafting and implementing all legislation (Article 3 EC). Article 141(4) EEC (Article 157(4) TFEU) allows positive action measures granting specific advantages for the under-represented sex in working life. These provisions were confirmed in the Treaty of Lisbon (2009). In addition, the EU Charter of Fundamental Rights (2000) recognises the right to gender equality in all areas, allows for the possibility of positive action (Article 23), sets out rights relating to the reconciliation of family and working life, and bans any discrimination on the grounds of sex (Article 21). Since the entry into force of the Treaty of Lisbon, the Charter has become a binding list of fundamental rights (Article 6(1) TEU) (Burri and Prechal, 2014; Ghailani, 2014). In case law, the CJEU has undeniably contributed to the progress made in gender equality. It has handed down essential rulings based on scanty legal provisions, interpreting these generously and extending the substantial protection offered by EEC law to many areas, including pregnancy, positive action and occupational pensions. It has strengthened the application of the law by developing the principle of the direct effect of directives, the concept of indirect discrimination and the concept of the reversal of the burden of proof, all principles codified in the form of directives (Carracciolo di Torella and Masselot, 2010).

The strengthening of the gender dimension of social policy, including on part-time work, was laid down in secondary law in the form of directives. Between 1975 and 2010, 15 directives were adopted in order to ensure the equal treatment of men and women at work, prohibiting discrimination in social security schemes, setting out minimum requirements on parental leave, providing protection to pregnant workers and recent mothers, and setting out rules on access to employment, working conditions and remuneration, as well as legal rights for the self-employed. According to the European Commission (Commission or EC), these measures aim to create uniform rules by removing obstacles to women's participation in the labour market, and by combating stereotypes. However, the idea of an unselfish Commission guided exclusively by a wish to improve gender equality must be taken with a pinch of salt. Stratigaki (2004) points out that these measures, defined as gender–equality policies, are, in fact, designed to create a more flexible labour force by incorporating flexible and temporary work carried out by women (see also Fagan and Rubery, 2018). From this perspective, European efforts to increase gender equality are merely a way of reformulating neoliberal internal market principles, thus making them more attractive to public opinion. The Part-Time Work Directive (97/81/EC) is a particularly good example, with its dual goal of removing discrimination against part-time workers while promoting flexible employment (Bell, 2011).

Despite their wide development, the EU has only recently begun to regulate flexible working arrangements. Initially, changes in working patterns were reached by private arrangements, lacking relevant legislation both at the national and EU levels. As mothers are often engaged in these forms of employment, flexible working arrangements have raised gender-equality concerns (Caracciolo di Torella and Masselot, 2010). In June 1994, both the ILO's Part-Time Work Convention No. 175-2 and Recommendation No. 182 on Part-Time Work were adopted, regulating part-time work under international law for the first time. According to Murray (1999), the adoption of the said convention has had a direct effect on the legislative process of the EU in this field. In December of the same year, the Essen European Council stressed that the promotion of employment may be achieved 'in particular by a more flexible organization of work in a way which fulfils both the wishes of employees and the requirements of competition' (Guobaitė-Kirslienė, 2010: 319). Thus, in contrast to the EU equality regulation implemented in the 1970s and 1980s, the Part-Time Work Directive is not primarily formulated in terms of the equal treatment of men and women (Council of the European Union, 1997). However, gender equality is explicitly mentioned, arguing that good-quality part-time work contributes to equal opportunities for men and women, and increases the number of job opportunities. Still, the directive was especially designed as a tool of employment policy, codifying the use of atypical work and contributing to the aim of increasing employment rates. On the one hand, it aims to remove discrimination against part-time workers and to improve the quality of part-time work. On the other hand, it facilitates the development of part-time work on a voluntary basis and contributes to the flexible organisation of working time, meeting both the needs of employers and workers (Annex, Clause 1). Some scholars underline this balancing act of the directive (Barnard, 2006; Bell, 2011), improving the employment conditions of part-time workers while legitimising the expansion of this form of work. Increasing the number of part-time jobs assisted the EU in meeting its objectives for raising employment rates under the EES (1997). Moreover, while the directive guarantees equal access to the European labour market for workers with care-giving tasks, it does so without guaranteeing them a minimum level of social welfare. As highlighted by Bleijenberg et al (2004), the EU recognises workers' needs to combine a job with domestic responsibilities but leaves the financial and practical consequences of this combination to the individual. Clause 5 crystallises the flexibility agenda: it requires member states, and social partners, to review obstacles to part-time work and 'where appropriate' to eliminate them. In addition, employers are placed under a duty 'to give consideration' to requests to transfer between full-time and part-time work (and vice versa). Employers should also 'facilitate access to part-time work at all levels of the enterprise' (Clause 5).

Several authors (Jeffery, 1998; Bleijenbergh et al, 2004; Bell, 2011) have questioned the effectiveness of the directive, although for some countries, a number of positive effects may be noticed as well (see Chapter 1; see also Fagan and Rubery, 2018). Caracciolo di Torella and Masselot (2010) conclude that while the directive might have increased labour market flexibility, it has failed to advance the reconciliation of work and family life. It forbids discrimination on the grounds of unfavourable treatment but may introduce hazardous justifications. It encourages part-time work but does not allow employees to really have control over their choices. It seeks to improve the quality of part-time work but relevant research shows that flexible working arrangements are frequently confined to low-skilled and low-paid jobs, whose inherent precariousness has a negative impact on reconciliation (Fudge and Owens, 2006). These jobs remain heavily gendered and reinforce either women's poverty or financial dependency on their partners (James, 2009). Table 1.1 in Chapter 1 illustrates how gendered part-time employment is, although the gap between male and female part-time employment widely varies per country. In OECD countries, 26% of women work part-time, while this percentage is much lower for men (9%). In the Netherlands, 60% of women work part-time.

Although Dutch men also often work part-time (19%), this percentage is much lower than for women. In Poland, part-time employment is much less widespread, being 6% of total employment in 2016 on average.

Not all part-time work is involuntary (see, eg, Figure 1.2 in Chapter 1). In some countries, part-time workers seem satisfied with the number of working hours they have. Here, the scores per country show wide variety. Moreover, in some countries, involuntary part-time work is rising (Italy, the Netherlands and Ireland), while in other countries, it is decreasing (Germany). Building on the findings that especially women tend to work part-time more often, Figure 2.1 gives more details on the reasons why women work reduced hours. Figure 2.1 gives the reasons for working part-time, focusing on the six case countries that will be explored in more depth in the remainder of the chapter.

Figure 2.1: Main reason for part-time employment, women aged 20–64, 2017 (%)

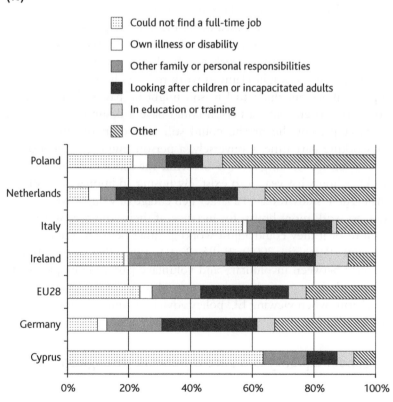

Source: Eurostat

Again, there is a wide variety across countries. In Italy (57%) and Cyprus (63%), the majority of part-time working women say that they could not find a full-time job, likely referring to underemployment. In the Netherlands and Germany, less than 10% of part-time working women state this reason. German and Dutch women often mention care for children or incapacitated adults as a reason for working reduced hours. It is unclear whether we should interpret their answers as being voluntarily or involuntarily in part-time employment. In Ireland, women also give care responsibilities as a main reason for working part-time. Conversely, in Poland, care responsibilities are much less often mentioned. Here, other reasons prevail. Based on this information, it is difficult to judge whether these workers would be in good, mixed or bad working conditions and social protection.

The difference across countries suggests that the economic and institutional settings of countries pose different obstacles to women in their choices to work either part-time or full-time (see also Bekker et al, 2017). This is why authors call for paying better attention to a latent desire to work more hours. This tends not to show up in statistics that measure (in)voluntary part-time work (see Chapter 1). Bollé (2001) recommends measuring involuntary part-time work in several complementary ways as the distinction between involuntary and voluntary part-time work is not always straightforward. For instance, a person might claim to work reduced hours due to family responsibilities but the actual reason might be past inability to find work. Moreover, while a person could have a desire to work more hours at present, he or she could still give their original reason for working part-time. Conversely, a person might give economic reasons for not working more hours while the actual desire to increase working hours has ceased to exist. By posing additional questions, a small Dutch study revealed a larger percentage of women who would want to work more hours, for instance, if their employer would ask them to or if they could adjust working times better to their private situation (Portegijs, 2009). Bollé (2001) argues that distinguishing properly between involuntary and voluntary part-time employment helps in designing suitable economic and social policies. This could be relevant when viewing EU policy advice to countries, for instance, via the EES (see later).

EU gender equality and part-time work through soft law

Together with the standard legislative and binding legal instruments, soft law instruments have gradually gained more importance in the field of gender-equality and labour market policies (Plomien, 2018). In 1997, the EU launched the EES, a key example of soft law. Other examples are strategic programming tools such as the European Pact for Gender Equality 2011–2020 and the Commission's Equality Strategy. At the beginning, gender equality was strongly present in the EES but it is no longer visible as a distinct goal in the EU's current growth strategy. In the EES, it formed one of its four pillars, which included: improving employability; developing entrepreneurship and job creation; encouraging the adaptability of businesses and their employees; and strengthening equal opportunities for women and men. The equal opportunities pillar was based on four principles: adopting gender mainstreaming; tackling gender gaps in unemployment, job segregation, pay and employment; reconciling work and family; and facilitating reintegration into the labour market (Plantega et al, 2008). In 2000, the EU adopted a strategy for Europe to become a leading knowledge economy (the so-called Lisbon Strategy), complementing the EES objectives. It adopted a specific women's employment rate target of 60% by 2010 (alongside a 70% target for both sexes combined). Targets for childcare coverage were added at the 2002 EU Barcelona summit, complementing the employment rate targets. Being voluntaristic, the effectiveness of these processes in promoting gender equality has been questioned. Rubery (2015) puts forward two arguments to show that they kept gender equality on the agenda in member states with limited traditions of addressing gender equality. First, all member states had to engage with the issue of gender equality in their employment action plans. Second, these principles of gender equality and gender mainstreaming were included in the criteria for accessing European structural funds. However, she recognised that the early 2000s may be considered a high watermark for EU gender-equality policy, with a gradual erosion of some of these commitments. The equality issue has progressively become less visible as there has not been a separate equality guideline since the mid-2000s (see also Fagan and Rubery, 2018). The Europe 2020 Strategy for smart, sustainable and inclusive growth, agreed in 2010, reinstated social policies into the EU agenda but no longer stipulated any quantified goals on gender equality. As part of Europe 2020 and the EES, the Commission makes joint evaluations of all member states in their Joint Employment Report (JER) and evaluations of individual countries in the so-called country reports. Occasionally, these country reports address how the Commission sees the link between part-time work and gender equality, and places these issues in the wider context of employment and social policies (see later).

The objective of the EES to increase the rate of employment to 75% can hardly be achieved, according to Pimminger (2015: 5), without increasing female labour participation. This argument is also put forward in the Commission's Equality Strategy. Recently, however, the European Pillar of Social Rights (ESPR) has brought some changes, with an explicit re-articulation of social objectives for fair labour markets and welfare systems, and commitments to gender equality (Plomien, 2018). It is to be implemented through a combination of hard and soft law (EC, 2017). The clear status of gender equality in the EPSR's principles and rights can be seen as an improvement on the invisibility of gender in the Europe 2020 Strategy. In the preliminary outline, gender equality was contained in the fifth domain dedicated to 'gender equality and work–life balance' (EC, 2016a). The final proposal made substantive improvements by bringing gender equality up to the second domain and moving 'work–life balance' to Chapter II on fair working conditions. This resulted in giving gender equality a more general and important place, and included work–life balance among the issues dealing with the working environment (Plomien, 2018).

European Pact for Gender Equality 2011–2020

A connection between the position of women on the labour market and gender equality is also part of the European Pact for Gender Equality, originally adopted in 2006. The Pact emphasises the importance of using women's untapped potential in the labour market. In the context of Europe 2020, it emphasises the need to remove obstacles to women's participation in the labour market in order to meet the objective of a 75% employment rate by promoting women's empowerment in economic and political life and taking steps to close gender gaps, combat gender stereotypes and promote better work–life balance for both women and men, and so on. This set of instruments is intended to integrate the gender perspective into all policies carried out at European and national levels by including this aspect in the impact assessments carried out before new policies are developed. The weak point of the Pact is the lack of precise, quantified targets (Ghailani, 2014).

In 2010, the Commission adopted a 'Strategy for equality between women and men 2010–2015' (EC, 2010), providing a global framework for defending gender equality. It combined specific measures with developing an equality perspective into all EU policies. It included a series of actions based on the five priorities identified in the Women's

Charter (2010) (Ghailani, 2014). The strategy emphasised the contribution made by equality to economic growth and sustainable development, and defended the creation of a gender-equality dimension in the Europe 2020 Strategy. It led to a better knowledge of the various dimensions of gender inequalities, to a greater awareness within the population and policymakers of the necessity to address gender inequalities, and to the elaboration of models and indicators in favour of gender mainstreaming (Heine, 2015). However, Crepaldi et al (2015) highlighted two main defects of the strategy: first, a lack of sufficient resources for effective implementation because no budget has been earmarked for the strategy; and, second, the evident deficiency caused by the weak institutionalisation of gender mainstreaming in the EU decision-making process. Faced with the Commission's reluctance to adopt a new strategy in 2015, the competent ministers and secretaries of state from 21 member states wrote an open letter urging the EU commissioner responsible to adopt a new gender-equality strategy (Pimminger, 2015). The Commission finally issued a 'Strategic engagement for gender equality 2016–2019' (EC, 2015). It focuses on five priority areas, of which the first may be seen as having a direct link to part-time employment: increasing female labour market participation and equal economic independence; reducing the gender pay gap; promoting equality in decision-making; combating gender-based violence and human trafficking; and promoting gender equality and women's rights across the world. Hubert and Stratigaki (2016) note that whereas this text contains interesting benchmarks, it is not a Communication to the European Parliament and the Council; it has the lowest status as an internal document issued by Commission services without the agreement of the College of Commissioners and contains no binding provisions or requests for member state commitments. Even the Council criticised the Commission's approach as 'a large number of Member States stressed that a formal Strategy endorsed by the Commission was needed and expressed their disappointment in having received an informal working document instead' (Council of the European Union, 2015).

Digging deeper into soft coordination: the role of part-time work in policy recommendations

As mentioned earlier, the EU has an ambiguous view on part-time work, especially in the directive. It wants to increase labour market flexibility while also being mindful of the protection of part-time workers and setting norms for gender equality. In this section, we put the EU coordination of member state policies to the test. Do the evaluations of the EU on national labour market and social policies take notice of part-time work? Do these evaluations address the negative aspects of part-time work and its gendered character? Figures 1.1 and 1.2 (Chapter 1) and Figure 2.1 show that national labour market trends are quite dissimilar, which might reflect differences in national institutional settings, such as the availability of affordable childcare, which affects the choices of (wo)men to work either part-time or full-time. Via the EES, the Commission may draft recommendations suggesting improvements for national policies and institutions. However, the overall labour market evaluation in the JER 2017 only occasionally addresses part-time work, for instance, the gender employment gaps that are especially acute for parents. The Commission (EC, 2016b) notes that women are more likely than men to accept childcare responsibilities and more often involved in long-term care responsibilities. Moreover, women face financial disincentives when entering the labour market or wanting to work more, and are consequently more likely to reduce working hours or exit employment altogether. The Commission also addresses the gender pay gap, and concludes that a reason for the lower earnings of women is their higher involvement in part-time employment, which is less well remunerated than full-time jobs per hour of work. Lower earnings also have consequences for pension entitlements. Here, the Commission clearly sketches the negative aspects related to part-time work while noticing that women more often work part-time and are therefore more often exposed to the negative consequences of part-time work.

As said earlier, the latest guidelines of the EES have been better attached to the ESPR priorities, including gender equality. The guidelines give guidance to the member states on implementing reforms, and form a basis for country-specific recommendations (CSRs) to the member states. The introduction to the guidelines refers to the objectives of full employment and social progress, as set out in Article 3 TFEU. Analogous to the treaty, the guidelines do not mention part-time employment, but give attention to equality between men and women. For instance, in Guideline 6 on 'Enhancing labour supply: access to employment, skills and competences', the EU aims to remove barriers to participation and career progression in order to ensure gender equality and to increase the labour market participation of women. This also means equal pay for equal work, the reconciliation of work and family life, and access to suitable family leaves and flexible working arrangements for both women and men. In Guideline 8 on 'Promoting equal opportunities for all, fostering social inclusion and combating poverty', similar social security provisions are mentioned, also from the perspective of gender equality.

Thus, the norms on gender equality are present in the employment guidelines, yet part-time employment is not mentioned as a separate issue. Also, the more visible parts of employment coordination, such as the quantitative targets of the Europe 2020 Strategy, do not consider part-time work. For instance, the target to have an employment rate of 75% does not consider part-time employment. All persons who, during the reference week, did any work for pay or profit for at least one hour are regarded as employed. Thus, from the EES itself, few conclusions can be derived on the standpoint of the EU regarding part-time employment; rather, there are more general references to aims such as higher female participation in the labour market, gender equality and equal opportunities. The next section explores whether this is different when it comes to tailored policy advice to countries.

Employment policy coordination: CSRs

After the evaluation of each country, and having the employment goals in mind, the Commission drafts CSRs, which constitute policy advice tailored to the particular situation of a country. This section summarises the evaluation of six countries, selected based on their dissimilar incidence of (involuntary) part-time employment. The analysis is based on the CSRs for 2017 and 2018, supplemented by information from the 2017 country reports that provide background information on countries. All these documents are publicly available on the Commission's website.

Matching the differences in part-time work between the six countries, the EU's policy advice on employment differs considerably. However, in none of the countries is part-time employment seen as a challenge or a stand-alone issue. Rather, the evaluations address chances to move into the labour market and labour market institutions that support or hinder the employment and income of (mostly) women. Consequently, the Commission mentions childcare facilities and leave arrangements as policies that countries could develop; however, such observations hardly ever translate into a CSR. For the Netherlands, the country with the highest part-time employment rates but low scores on involuntary part-time work, the issue is not addressed at all. This is remarkable as Dutch women often state that care for children and/or incapacitated adults keeps them from getting a full-time job. Likewise, for Cyprus, the evaluation hardly addresses the high incidence of involuntary part-time work.

The country reports are much more interesting for viewing the Commission's view on part-time work, and thus also the outlook on how countries could (or should) reform their employment policies in order to improve the position of and support for part-time workers. Here, the Commission connects the issues of part-time employment and gender equality to wider labour market and social security issues. Depending on the country, these may include the taxation system, pension entitlements, care facilities and parental leave systems. For example, at times, the country report on Ireland addresses the gender employment gap and the main reason to work part-time, observing that Irish parents are frequently forced into inactivity and part-time work due to the lack of care services. Around 27.4% of inactive women aged 20–64 do not work because of care responsibilities for children or incapacitated adults (compared to 4.5% of Irish men aged 20–64). Especially single parents, most often women, suffer from the lack and high cost of childcare support. Interestingly, the Commission broadens the analysis to include the meagre care facilities for fathers as an obstacle to female labour participation. Although Ireland has recently introduced paid paternity leave, parental leave is still unpaid, thus encouraging the secondary earner (mostly women) to step out of the labour market to take care of children. These evaluations reveal the ability of the Commission to look beyond the statement of women that they work part-time due to care responsibilities for children, thus questioning whether this choice is 'voluntary' (cf Bollé, 2001). However, the Commission does not undertake this same exercise for all countries, as the case of the Netherlands illustrates. In spite of the high levels of part-time employment in the Netherlands, this issue is hardly addressed in the 2017 country report. The Commission observes an employment gap between Dutch men and women in terms of full-time equivalents, and knows that this gap is one of the highest in the EU. However, contrary to the conclusion for Ireland, the Commission explains the Dutch situation as voluntary choices regarding work–life balance. Although the Commission sees that institutions and policies may encourage such choices, it does not challenge Dutch policy choices.

In its analysis of the German labour market, the Commission again nuances statistics that look well at first sight, developing complex analyses on part-time work and gender equality. It is a clear demonstration of the (accumulating) negative aspects of part-time work that particularly women have to deal with. Whereas the country report acknowledges Germany's strong labour market performance, it underlines that this relates to an increase of part-time work, particularly among women. Moreover, the Commission finds that disincentives to work remain in place, especially for secondary earners. Due to the high share of part-time work, Germany ranks in the bottom third of member states in terms of its full-time equivalent employment rate of women, especially affecting women with a migrant background and women with care responsibilities. The Commission also points at quality full-time childcare, all-day schools and long-term care as ingredients for increasing woman's labour participation. In this respect, the Commission also addresses the high gender pay gap. Moreover, the taxation system regarding secondary earners (mostly women) hampers female full-time employment. The Commission furthermore relates the rise in in-work poverty to the high share of part-time employment. Lastly, part-time employment is linked to low pension coverage as there is a high risk of the insufficient accrual of public pension benefits. Such observations have been converted into CSRs prior to 2017, yet Germany has made little progress in addressing the negative side effects of part-time employment and in removing the causes of part-time work. Moreover, there is little progress in reducing disincentives to work for secondary earners.

The Commission also takes a broad approach when analysing Italy. The country report addresses female employment predominantly as an underutilisation of employment potential, based on the very low employment rate of Italian women. The Commission sees this as a large economic cost as women have relatively higher educational attainment rates than men. The tax system discourages secondary earners from participating in the labour force, and the inactivity trap (financial disincentives to move from inactivity and social assistance to employment) is larger than the EU average. This is combined with limited access to affordable childcare, related also to the widening employment gender gap in households with children and elderly persons. As in Ireland, the Commission notices that Italian paternity leave is among the shortest in Europe, affecting both women's employment and gender equality. Part-time employment is not mentioned, and it seems that in the case of Italy, the Commission finds that getting a job is, at present, more important than the length of the working week.

Furthermore, the evaluation of Cyprus pays little attention to the incidence of part-time employment, in spite of the high rates of involuntary part-time employment. The country report raises concerns about the growing inequality in Cyprus, and points to the worsened working conditions during the crisis as a main factor of increased inequality, including involuntary temporary and part-time employment, and downwards-adjusted wages. Female employment is addressed slightly, discussing the low public investment in long-term care, leaving the provision of such services to the private sector or informally to family members. In this respect, the Commission observes that some people with care responsibilities, mainly women, could be pushed into flexible working arrangements or out of the labour market. At the same time, a recent growth in the number of live-in carers has had a positive effect on female employment.

Within the six countries, there are two observations where part-time work is welcomed as improving labour market performance. One is concerning Germany, where the country report addresses *Flexi-Rente*, which facilitates the transition of older workers into retirement via combining early retirement and part-time work by reducing pension deductions in the event of extra income. The second is Poland, where part-time employment rates are low. Although part-time work is hardly raised in the 2017 country report, the Commission sees the limited use of part-time employment as limited labour market flexibility. It suggests that this may be problematic, in particular, for older workers or people with care obligations (often women). Clearly, part-time work is seen here as a means to improve labour market flexibility without potential negative consequences.

Although the country reports connect the issue of female employment to issues of care facilities, taxation systems and income, the 2017 and 2018 CSRs hardly prioritise these matters. The Netherlands and Cyprus did not receive CSRs at all, either on part-time employment or on the employment opportunities of women. In 2017 and 2018, both Poland and Italy received a CSR to increase labour market participation. For both countries, this also included CSRs on the employment of women or 'secondary earners'; however, in 2018, the CSR to Poland no longer specifically mentions women's employment. Germany was recommended to lower disincentives to work for secondary earners and to facilitate transitions to standard employment in 2017 (see Chapter 10), while the 2018 CSRs quite clearly address the issue of part-time work by recommending Germany to reduce disincentives to work more hours, including the high tax wedge. Ireland was recommended to improve the social infrastructure, including quality childcare, both in 2017 and 2018. It seems that whereas the country reports address the complex issue of part-time employment and its potential negative consequences, also in view of gender equality, this does not find a full translation into CSRs. Rather, the CSRs, if given at all, focus on getting women into employment, regardless of the number of working hours. Moreover, CSRs do not address whether part-time work should be voluntary and of high quality. Of the six countries explored, only the CSR for Ireland speaks of supportive facilities to enable (wo)men to combine work and care better.

Conclusion

This chapter takes a broad approach to the EU dimension of part-time work, setting it in the wider context of gender equality. It thus explores the EU governance mix of hard and soft law for addressing part-time work, answering the question of whether the different EU-level instruments are coherent or pursue conflicting goals. Whereas the treaty does not mention part-time work, it sets a clear norm on gender equality as a fundamental human right. From this perspective, part-time employment may be questioned, for women have a much higher risk of being in this type of atypical employment, and consequently deal more often with related structural and long-term disadvantages, such as career penalties and lower pension entitlements. However, part-time work also facilitates the combination of work and care, giving not only employees, but also employers, flexibility in the labour market. The Part-Time Work Directive illustrates this ambiguity nicely. It refers to gender equality but is set up as a tool for employment policy. It is seen as a balancing act of improving the working conditions of part-time workers while legitimising the growth of this form of employment.

The evaluation of the Commission as regards 'soft' employment policy coordination activities reveals a similar ambiguity. While the employment guidelines include concerns about gender equality, they do not mention part-time employment. At times, the 2017 country-specific evaluations of and recommendations for six countries show the capacity of the Commission to take a broad approach to the labour market position of women, connecting it to the institutional setting of a country, such as childcare facilities or taxation systems. Occasionally, it even connects the poor paternity leave rights of fathers to the labour market position of mothers. However, such a broad approach is not part of the analysis of all countries. In this respect, it is interesting to see how Ireland gets questions about the reason why women work part-time (care responsibilities), while similar statistics do not lead to questions of the Netherlands. Moreover, to some countries, such as Italy, increasing female labour participation seems more relevant than their working time per week. In Germany and Poland, more part-time work is seen as a way to get or keep some groups (older workers, women) in employment, without questions being asked about potential disadvantages.

Overall, one could conclude that clear EU norms on gender equality are not always taken into account when dealing with part-time work. On the one hand, this may be seen as a mismatch between legislative instruments and coordination instruments, where each tool has a different focus, with, at times, conflicting goals. On the other hand, part-time work is often a form of employment that is assessed in different ways in different national contexts, having both positive and negative characteristics. Depending on the country and its labour market situation, priorities might differ for legitimate reasons. However, viewing the gendered character of part-time employment, concerns on equal opportunities deserve a higher priority when assessing part-time employment in European labour markets.

References

Armstrong, K.A. (2011) 'The character of EU law and governance: from "community method" to new modes of governance', *Current Legal Problems*, 64(1): 179–214.

Bain, J. and Masselot, A. (2012) 'Gender equality law and identity building for Europe', *Canterbury Law Review*, 18: 97–117.

Barnard, C. (2006) *Commission employment law*, Oxford: Oxford University Press.

Bekker, S., Hipp, L., Leschke, J. and Molitor, F. (2017) 'Part-time fathers and mothers? Comparing part-time employment in Germany, Sweden, Ireland and the Netherlands', *Bulletin of Comparative Labour Relations*, 98: 27–50.

Bell, M. (2011) 'Achieving the objectives of the Part-Time Work Directive? Revisiting the part-time workers regulations', *Industrial Law Journal*, 40(3): 254–79.

Bleijenbergh, I., De Bruijn, J. and Bussemaker, J. (2004) 'European social citizenship and gender: the Part-time Work Directive', *European Journal of Industrial Relations*, 10(3): 309–28.

Bollé, P. (2001) 'Part-time work: solution or trap?', in M. Fetherolf Loufti (ed) *Women, gender and work*, Geneva: ILO, pp 215–38.

Burri, S. and Prechal, S. (2014) *EU gender equality law. Update 2013*, Brussels: European Commission.

Burrows, N. and Robinson, M. (2007) 'An assessment of the recast of Community equality laws', *European Law Journal*, 13(2): 186–203.

Caracciolo di Torella, E. and Masselot, A. (2010) *Reconciling work and family life in EU law and policy*, Basingstoke, Palgrave Macmillan.

Council of the European Union (1997) 'Council Directive 97/81/EC of 15 December 1997 concerning the Framework Agreement on part-time work concluded by UNICE, CEEP and the ETUC', OJ L 14, 20 January 1998, pp 9–14.

Council of the European Union (2015) 'Council decision (EU) 2015/1848 of 5 October 2015 on guidelines for the employment policies of the Member States for 2015', L 268/28.

Crepaldi, C., Loi, D., Pesce, F. and Samek, M. (2015) *Evaluation of the strengths and weaknesses of the Strategy for Equality between Women and Men 2010–2015*, Research Paper, Brussels: European Commission.

EC (European Commission) (2010) 'Strategy for equality between women and men 2010–2015', COM(2010) 491 final.

EC (2015) 'Strategic engagement for gender equality 2016–2019', SWD(2015) 278 final.

EC (2016a) 'First preliminary outline of a European Pillar of Social Rights – annex 1 accompanying to the communication from the Commission to the European Parliament, the Council, the European Economic and Social Committee and the Committee of the Regions – launching a consultation on a European Pillar of Social Rights', COM(2016) 127 final.

EC (2016b) 'Draft joint employment report 2017', COM(2016) 729 final.

EC (2017) 'Commission recommendation of 26.04.2017 on the European Pillar of Social Rights', COM(2017) 2600 final.

Emmenegger, P., Häusermann, S., Palier, B. and Seeleib-Kaiser, M. (eds) (2012) *The age of dualization: The changing face of inequality in deindustrializing societies*, New York: Oxford University Press.

Fagan, C. and Rubery, J. (2018) 'Advancing gender equality through European employment policy: the impact of the UK's EU membership and the risks of Brexit', *Social Policy & Society*, 17(2): 297–317.

Fudge, J. and Owens, R. (eds) (2006) *Precarious work, women, and the new economy: the challenge to legal norms*, Oxford: Hart Publishing.

Ghailani, D. (2014) 'Gender equality, from the Treaty of Rome to the quota debate: between myth and reality', in D. Natali (ed) *Social developments in the European Union 2013*, Brussels: ETUI and OSE, pp 161–84.

Guobaitė-Kirslienė, R. (2010) 'The features of legal regulation on part-time work', *Social Sciences Studies*, 4(8): 317–38.

Heine, S. (2015) 'The EU approach to gender: limitations and alternatives', *European Policy Brief*, 40(December): 1–10.

Hubert, A. and Stratigaki, M. (2016) 'Twenty years of EU gender mainstreaming: rebirth out of the ashes?', *Femina Politica*, 2: 21–36.

James, G. (2009) *The legal regulation of pregnancy and parenting in the labour market*, London: Routledge Cavendish.

Jeffery, M. (1998) 'Not really going to work? Of the Directive on Part-Time Work, 'atypical work' and attempts to regulate it', *Industrial Law Journal*, 27(3): 193–213.

Kantola, J. (2010) *Gender in the European Union*, Basingstoke: Palgrave Macmillan.

Lyonette, C. (2015) 'Part-time work, work–life balance and gender equality', *Journal of Social Welfare and Family Law*, 37(3): 321–33.

Murray, J. (1999) 'Social justice for women? The ILO's Convention on Part-Time Work, "atypical work" and attempts to regulate it', *International Journal of Comparative Labour Law and Industrial Relations*, 15: 3–19.

Pimminger, I. (2015) *A quiet farewell? Current developments in EU gender equality policy*, Berlin: Friedrich-Ebert-Stiftung.

Plantega, J., Remery, C. and Rubery, J. (2008) *Gender mainstreaming of employment policies: A comparative review of thirty European countries*, Brussels: European Commission, Directorate-General for Employment, Social Affairs and Equal Opportunities Unit G1.

Plomien, A. (2018) 'EU social and gender policy beyond Brexit: towards the European pillar of social rights', *Social Policy & Society*, 17(2): 281–96.

Portegijs, W. (2009) 'Vrouwen met een kleine deeltijdbaan', in S. Keuzenkamp (ed) *Deeltijd (g)een probleem; Mogelijkheden om de arbeidsduur van vrouwen met een kleine deeltijdbaan te vergroten*, The Hague: SCP, pp 63–92.

Rubery, J. (2015) 'Austerity and the future for gender equality in Europe', *ILR Review*, 68(4): 715–41.

Smismans, S. (2011) 'From harmonization to co-ordination? EU law in the Lisbon governance architecture', *Journal of European Public Policy*, 18(4): 504–24.

Stratigaki, M. (2004) 'The cooptation of gender concepts in EU policies: the case of "reconciliation of work and family"', *Social Politics: International Studies in Gender, State & Society*, 11(1): 30–56.

Trubek, D.M. and Trubek, L.G. (2007) 'New governance and legal regulation: complementarity, rivalry, and transformation', *Columbia Journal of European Law*, 13: 1–26.

3

So close, so far? Part-time employment and its effects on gender equality in Italy and Spain[1]

Lara Maestripieri and Margarita León

Introduction

In comparison with most other European countries, part-time employment does not make up a high percentage of employment in Spain and Italy. Part-time work by men is negligible in both countries and is also limited for women. A different picture is drawn, however, when other forms of non-standard employment are considered. When compared with countries such as France, the Netherlands, Sweden or the UK, both Italy and Spain show a high level of involuntary work, either in the form of fixed-term or permanent part-time contracts. In Spain, involuntary part-time work increased steadily during the economic crisis, in parallel with the sharp rise in unemployment, consolidating at about 16% of all employment once the crisis ended. It has now become a form of underemployment and is a way for employers to avoid dismissals.

In this chapter, the authors assess the extent to which the process of de-standardisation in labour contracts has turned part-time work into a form of precarious employment in these two countries rather than a way to ease work–family conflict. They aim to analyse insider–outsiders cleavages among women working part-time in Italy and Spain, assuming intersectionality as an analytical strategy (Collins, 2015). To do so, they use an inter-categorical approach to intersectionality, as put forward by McCall (2005). This approach implies a strategic use of intersectional categories in order to stress the multiple inequalities that arise when different dimensions of disadvantage collide (McCall, 2005; Winker and Degele, 2011; Walby et al, 2012). The idea is to look at the multiplicative effects that specific intersections might have on the general condition of disadvantage suffered by women in order to understand the dynamics that lie beneath the integration of women in non-standard working positions. The intersectional approach puts in question the intra-group similarity of women, highlighting the differences that occur among women with different educational levels, of different ages and having different childcare responsibilities.

In highly dualised labour markets, the chances for part-timers to escape from insider–outsider dynamics are limited. Yet, while the 'voluntariness' of part-time work is, in itself, a reflection of the type of part-time work available, there are multiple differences among various groups of workers that require more nuanced observations. The focus of this chapter is on the differences between women with regard to access to the labour market and their different working arrangements. The authors will show how particular combinations of educational level, age and household composition increase marginality within the labour market.

Italy and Spain belong to the 'corporate' welfare regime cluster that has certain 'Mediterranean traits' distinct enough, according to some authors, to fall under an altogether different typology. Despite the centrality of occupational welfare, and because of a certain degree of fragmentation in social provision, the Southern European welfare model has always performed rather poorly in the development of universal services and family policy. As is to be expected in a conservative welfare regime, the state relies on the 'caring family' but does not do so through specific policies that preserve the role of the traditional family and, specifically, the role of women within the family, as in Continental Europe. What Saraceno (1994) has termed 'unsupported familialism' refers to a limited capacity of these welfare states to foster employment and social policies that enhance women's chances to reconcile their work and family life (such as, for instance, part-time work). The lack of effective work–family balance mechanisms and care policies has a negative impact on fertility dynamics and the participation of women in the labour market.

In the last two to three decades, the two countries have gone through what Rueda (2015: 109) calls the protectionist processes of industrialisation, where labour market regulations to protect insiders have contributed to reduced labour productivity and high income inequality. In many countries, the deregulation and flexibilisation of employment has led to an across-the-board increase of atypical forms of employment, with the subsequent deepening of insider–outsider labour market dynamics (Emmenegger et al, 2012). The origins and reasons for this labour market dualisation are beyond the aim of this chapter. However, it is nonetheless essential to understand: (1) the extent to which flexibility conveys a very different meaning in countries of the South; and (2) the specific ways in which it affects women and young people. In Spain, the rapid increase in female employment has coincided with a very strong increase in occupational polarisation, which means that differences between women belonging to different occupational groups have widened over recent years. In Italy, labour market deregulation has always been proposed 'at the margins', meaning that those who were already employed when the new regulation was implemented have not been affected by the worsening of working conditions (for instance, more flexible dismissal procedures) (Firinu and Maestripieri, 2018). Differences due to gender and age have been widening. As in Spain, women and young people are more exposed to precariousness and underemployment; differently from Spain, however, women and young people are only partially protected by a higher educational level (Villa, 2010).

In both countries, part-time employment is right at the heart of this process of differentiation between categories of workers with unequal access to social and employment rights, such as unemployment benefits and old-age pensions. In a recent case, for instance, the European Court of Justice declared that the Spanish legislation on part-time employment was not compliant with the European Union (EU) directive on equal treatment for men and women in matters of social security.[2]

The implication for gender equality is that more women than men are affected by atypical employment and, together with the young and workers of foreign origin, women suffer the consequences of an increasingly precarious labour market. As will be shown later in this chapter, the incidence of involuntary part-time work is much higher among women than men. Following gender, the probability of having involuntary part-time work or a fixed-term contract is highly determined by age, skill level and type of occupation. For this reason, it is important to use an intersectional approach that takes this socio-economic and socio-demographic differentiation into account.

From a sociological perspective, the term 'non-standard employment contract' is used to refer to any contract that deviates from the full-time permanent dependent contract that is taken to be the standard (Bosch, 2006). In this analysis, non-standard forms of work thus include fixed-term contracts, part-time contracts and non-dependent self-employment. Several combinations of non-standard work can be given with multiple layers of de-standardisation (ie part-time contracts that are also temporary contracts). Each has a different distribution by gender and by age: self-employment is more diffuse among adult men; part-time work is more common among adult women; and part-time and fixed-term contracts are equally shared among young workers of both sexes.

This section provides an overview of part-time employment and other forms of non-standard work in the two countries on which the authors focus. To help situate Italy and Spain within a wider European comparative framework, the authors also look at the situation in France, Sweden, the Netherlands and the UK. In the latter three countries, women's non-standard employment is mainly composed of part-time work voluntarily chosen by the person (see Table 3A.1). Other forms of non-standard employment, such as temporary, self-employment or involuntary work, are less common, comparatively speaking. In Italy, Spain and, to some degree, France, non-standard employment moves away from the ideal of 'good work' as it is mostly involuntary fixed-term and part-time employment.

In Spain, the hegemonic form of non-standard employment is a fixed-term job (see Table 3A.1). Almost 90% of non-standard contracts held by men and about 60% of the contracts held by women are fixed-term contracts, it is the only country with more women on a fixed term than a part-time contract. The temporary nature of contracts in Spain is evident when the contracts held by younger generations are analysed: more than 70% of the total number of employed workers under 24 years of age are temporary workers, compared with about 55% each in France, Italy, the Netherlands and Sweden.[3] The difference with other countries is salient as well for older workers: 38.5% in Spain versus about 20% in the other countries for 25–34 year olds, and 23% versus about 10% for 35–49 year olds. As already argued, this high level of temporary work has serious consequences for labour market polarisation. Spain is one of the countries where having a fixed-term contract has the highest associated penalty regarding larger gaps in earnings per hour (Conde Ruiz and Marra de Artíñano, 2016). Additionally, 58% of non-standard employment in Spain is involuntary.

In Italy, on the contrary, self-employment is the most diffuse non-standard form of employment: in 2016, almost one worker in five was self-employed, whereas in countries such as Spain, the Netherlands and the UK, only 15% are self-employed, and in France and Sweden, the percentages are even lower (about 10%). Nevertheless, this type of contract is strongly gendered in all the countries considered as it is the most popular form of non-standard work for men: self-employment represents 64% of total non-standard work in Italy and the UK, and about 40% in the other countries. Non-standard employment among women is mostly represented by part-time work strongly characterised by involuntariness, as in Spain.

The level of part-time work in the two countries is low in comparative terms, especially in Spain (see Table 3A.2). With the exception of the Netherlands and the UK, migrants are more likely to be employed on a part-time basis, but the difference compared with the native population is especially strong in Italy. Young adults under 25 years of age are usually more exposed to part-time employment, but only in Italy and Spain is there a clear linear correlation between age and part-time work. In all the other countries, part-time work grows among workers older than 50 who are making their exit from the labour market, but this does not occur in Spain and Italy. Education is linearly correlated with part-time work in all the countries: low-educated workers are the most exposed to this contract, but in Spain and Italy, high-skilled workers have particularly low levels of part-time work. Finally, what really distinguishes Spain and Italy is that there is a relatively lower proportion of men employed part-time, the majority being under 34 years old.

In comparison with other countries in Europe, however, Spain, Italy and, to a certain extent, France distinguish themselves by having a higher level of female involuntary non-standard work, meaning those part-time workers who would prefer to work full-time (see Figure 3.1). As a matter of fact, Southern European countries have

Figure 3.1: Share of part-time work that is involuntary, by gender, 15–64 year olds

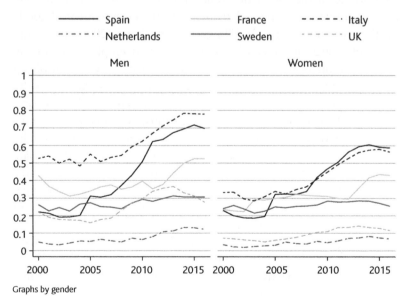

Graphs by gender

Source: Authors' own elaboration on the European Labour Force Survey (2000–16)

witnessed the substantial growth of involuntariness during the years of the economic crisis, affecting both women and men. Among those working part-time in Italy and Spain in 2016, more than 65% were doing so involuntarily, that is, the majority of part-timers would rather work full-time. The level of involuntary part-time workers is thus much higher in Italy and Spain than in the other countries included in our comparison and the difference has grown in the last 10 years (45.2% in France, 34.6% in Sweden, 16.8% in the UK and 13.1% in the Netherlands).

Involuntary part-time workers can be considered to be sub-employed as their condition is of partial unemployment since their working potential is not entirely satisfied by the labour market (Bodnár, 2018). According to the Spanish Labour Force Survey (EPA), the chances of involuntary part-timers moving to a permanent position are small (about 17%); thus, part-time work does not seem to represent a stepping stone to more standard forms of employment. Rather, part-time work represents one of the main dimensions through which we detect 'bad jobs' (Nicolaisen et al, Chapter 1, this volume) and by which dualisation has been implemented in Southern European labour markets (Rueda, 2015).

Origins of part-time work in Italy and Spain

The timing of the influx of women into the labour market in Italy and Spain might have been detrimental to the development of good-quality part-time work. As Ellingsaeter and Leira (2006) argue, the entry of a large number of women into paid employment in the Nordic countries in the 1970s and 1980s, many of whom took up part-time employment, coincided with favourable conditions for the introduction of labour regulations that ensured equal rights for part-timers. A few decades later, however, similar favourable conditions were non-existent further south. Italy and Spain have historically had very low rates of female employment. Prior to 1990, the female activity rate was below or just above 30%, about 20 percentage points lower than in other European countries. Both countries have since started to slowly catch up, although the growth rate has been more spectacular in Spain than in Italy.

Spain departed sharply from these low levels in the mid-1990s, with the rate of female employment increasing to 41.2% and 55.3% in 2000 and 2007, respectively (Eurostat online database[4]: 15–64). While both female and male unemployment increased rapidly during the most recent economic crisis, activity rates have not decreased, which indicates a stable pattern of participation in the labour market that does not fluctuate with the economic cycle or family circumstances, which was the case in the past.

Part-time work was not introduced to foster female employment. In fact, in 1980, part-time employment in Spain was heavily restricted to specific groups of workers (the unemployed and young workers under 25 years old). Only in 1984, with the first statutory reform, was the option of part-time work opened up to the entire workforce. Even then, no social or political actor advocated an expansion of part-time work as a way to develop good working opportunities for women (Ibáñez, 2011). In Italy, the first law on part-time employment was not enacted until the mid-1980s. Prior to this law (L. 863/1984), there were sporadic and unsystematic reductions of working schedules that were applied in the context of a legal vacuum to meet the rising need for flexibility. Even in cases where trade unions opposed the new law, it established arrangements concerning part-time work through national collective agreements (Santucci, 2017).

In both countries, national legislation on part-time work has subsequently been amended to comply with the European directive (97/81/CE). However, none of the labour market reforms implemented in either Italy or Spain have succeeded in presenting forms of reduced working time that are attractive to employees. Rather, labour market reforms over the last three decades have helped in many different ways to increase dualisation by maintaining high levels of protection for a core group of insiders while allowing for the expansion of poorly protected employment at the margins. In other words, while the road to increasing internal flexibility, that is, 'good' part-time work as a way to ease the tensions between work and care (or life more generally), has never been travelled, external flexibility at the contract level, whether in fixed-term employment, agency work or involuntary part-time work, has been on a continuous upward trend since the mid-1990s. This form of flexibility, proposed as a way forward in the context of high unemployment and sluggish economic growth, reinforces, rather than alleviates, tensions between family life and work (Muffels and Wilthagen, 2011) and ends up being a key dualisation mechanism in itself. Within the framework of the most recent Italian reform, the Jobs Act (Decree 34/2014), part-time contracts were further liberalised (Dlgs 81/2015). Employers can now add to the number of hours established in a part-time contract by up to 25% in the form of overtime. At the same time, however, the new regulation offers full-time workers the chance to apply for a working-time reduction for personal reasons (own illness or the illness of a family member, having a disabled relative in the household or having children under 13 years old in the household). Furthermore, the law now gives workers the possibility to use their parental leave to temporarily work part-time, that is, to work up to 50% fewer hours within the limits of the parental leave (10 months shared between the two parents until the child's 12th birthday). It is quite revealing that these new measures regarding part-time work were included within the decree that regulates employment contracts (Dlgs 81/2015) and not in the decree that deals specifically with work–family conciliation measures (Dlgs 80/2015) (Santucci, 2017).

Intersectional analysis

The following analysis uses microdata collected for the European Labour Force Survey (2005–16). It identifies trends in time and differences in the composition of non-standard employment in the two countries.[5] Comparing the two countries is somewhat interesting since despite their apparent similarity, they exhibit different patterns in terms of integrating women into the labour market.

Given reduced numbers, the authors decided to include only women and exclude men from the analysis since the detailed observation of trends pertaining to all the intersectional categories would have been statistically difficult. The migrant working population usually has different patterns of labour market integration, which require a specifically oriented analysis. To reduce the complexity of the analysis presented in this chapter, it was decided to focus on the native population only. Furthermore, the analysis focuses on women of childbearing age (25–49 years). Above and below this age group, part-time employment is a residual phenomenon in Southern Europe.

Microdata also allow the creation of a series of typologies that explore the characteristics of women's labour force participation by taking into account: first, their ability to access the labour market on the basis of their paid work time; and, second, the type of their non-standard working arrangements. Table 3A.5 distinguishes among standard, non-standard and involuntary non-standard work: the first category includes all workers who work full-time with a permanent contract; the second category includes all non-standard workers that have voluntarily chosen a non-standard job (including self-employment and fixed-term and part-time contracts); and the third category includes all part-timers and fixed-term workers that are employed in a non-standard job because it was not possible to find an equivalent standard job. Levels of involuntariness among self-employment might be underestimated: in the European Labour Force Survey, there is no question asking a self-employed person if they would have rather worked as a dependent worker.

Tables 3.1a and 3.1b focus on different types of part-time employment, with the idea of analysing how different groups of women are distributed within certain categories at risk of marginalisation (Nicolaisen et al, Chapter 1, this volume), namely: marginal part-time work (Hakim, 1997), including all those part-timers that work less than 10 hours/week; involuntary part-time work, that is, part-time contracts accepted because it was impossible to find an equivalent full-time job; and bogus part-time work, that is, persons who officially declare themselves as working part-time but are, in fact, working more than 30 hours/week on average. This latter category is derived from the concept of bogus self-employment, as introduced by Pedersini and Coletto (2010). This is a practice that, as Bodnár (2018) points out, has been liberalised in Southern Europe in recent years thanks to recent reforms in the labour market but that might cover practices of potential contractual abuses.

Marginal and bogus part-time work are treated independently according to why the person has accepted a reduced hours schedule (for care reasons or involuntarily), on the assumption that their actual condition in the labour market is a potential risk in itself for the welfare of that person. In the first case – marginal part-time work – there is a potential risk of becoming working poor (Hallerod et al, 2015); in the second case – bogus part-time work – there is a potential risk of covering exploitative undeclared work (Firinu, 2015).

The last category that we take in account in our analysis is part-time work for care reasons; in this case, a reduced working schedule is chosen voluntarily to cope with care responsibilities. Despite its voluntary nature, we consider that part-time work in this case might constitute a potential source of gender inequality as almost no man opts for part-time work because of family responsibilities. It is also important to highlight that even when part-time work is voluntarily chosen by the person, as in this case, a reduced working schedule is a potential source of economic dependency: working part-time provides a lower individual income, lower hourly pay and reduced career opportunities in the future as employers perceive it as less career-oriented (Maestripieri, 2015). Moreover, less paid hours might result in lower social protection given a reduction in social security contributions. Nevertheless, we do not include this type of part-time work in the group of part-timers at risk of marginalisation; in itself, voluntary part-time work chosen for care obligations cannot be considered as a condition risking labour market marginalisation (Nicolaisen et al, Chapter 1, this volume).

Three periods of time are considered in the analysis: before the economic crisis (2005–08), during the acute crisis period (2009–12) and the post-crisis years (2013–16). During the last decade, part-time work in Southern Europe has grown, especially its involuntary component. This is in line with the dualisation hypothesis: rates of non-standard work in general and involuntary part-time work in particular are congruent with a marginalisation strategy that provides employers with a source of cheap labour, mostly offered to women and young people (Kalleberg, 2008). It can hardly be interpreted as a reconciliation strategy offered by employers to retain workers with a preference for reduced working hours (Kalleberg, 2008).

For the empirical analysis, the authors developed a classification that simultaneously takes into account the workers' educational level (low = ISCED[6] 1–2; medium = ISCED 3–4; high = ISCED 5–8), their age (25–34 year olds and 35–49 year olds) and gender. The resulting classification comprises 12 groups. All the gender gaps in the following section are calculated by subtracting the percentages of women from the percentages of men. The scope is to test the assumption that the marginal position of women in the labour market is evidenced by part-time employment, measured in terms of how many children under the age of 14 are present in the household. Age or education (as sources of dualisation in labour market) are important explanatory factors; we hypothesise that they drive labour market outcomes more than family obligations.

Access to the labour market and standard work

Before going in-depth into the analysis of the quality of women's employment, it is interesting to highlight how Italy and Spain differ in terms of women's participation in the labour market, focusing first on the population that is currently not in employment (see Tables 3A.3a and 3A.3b). First, education counts (see Table 3A.3a): over 50% of young and adult women with a low-skill profile are inactive in the two countries. Still, Italian women with a lower educational level are more likely to be inactive when compared to Spanish women with the same age. Conversely, there is a relative advantage of young women holding high-skilled positions in Spain compared with Italy (their inactivity is 26.9% for Spain and 37.8% for Italy). Among adult women, however, the situation is reverted (22.4% and 16.8% in Spain and Italy, respectively). Education differentials explain the Spanish women's higher labour market participation compared to Italy: in Spain, half of the women have a tertiary education (53.5% among the young; 45.8% among adults), while in Italy, only one out of every five adult women have a tertiary education (33.1% among the young).

Family obligations impact on labour market participation as well, but the impact of children on women's employment is mediated by their age and education. The analysis of the distribution of gender gaps by the number of children under 14 years old in the household (see Table 3A.3b) makes it clear that the difference in terms of inactivity is not only a matter of family responsibilities: childcare responsibilities only magnify a situation of disadvantage among women compared to men that becomes more evident when women have a low educational background. Men and women are equally participating in the labour market only in Spain and only if they are young and childless: just one child is enough to increase women's inactivity in both countries, but the magnitude of the gender gap is determined by age and education, and it is more pronounced in Italy.

As well as being less employed than men, women also work fewer hours (see Tables 3A.4a and 3A.4b). Gaps may be interpreted as a persisting division of roles between partners: when there are children involved, households tend to follow a more traditional division of labour – men increase hours of paid work while women reduce their working hours. The higher the number of children in the household, the less paid work women take up; the correlation between the number of children and women working less is more evident among the lower educated and stronger in Italy. This interpretation is nevertheless not entirely satisfactory as even high-skilled childless young women work about three hours per week less than men. A concurrent interpretation regards the role of involuntary part-time work in determining women's involvement. Figures 3.2 and 3.3 show how involuntary non-standard employment has grown in all groups during the crisis but that the growth has been stronger for women and young people.

Figures 3.2 and 3.3 confirm the lower quality of the jobs undertaken by women and young people. There is no evident difference between Spain and Italy; however, Spain has a higher rate of involuntary non-standard employment given the wider diffusion of temporary jobs. Men are more likely to have more standard employment and were better able to maintain their standard contracts even during the crisis. Women, on the contrary, are more likely to have non-standard employment; the last few years also show a clear trend towards involuntary work at the detriment of voluntary non-standard jobs.

Figure 3.2: Levels of standard and non-standard employment before, during and after the economic crises, by gender, 25–49 year olds, Spain and Italy

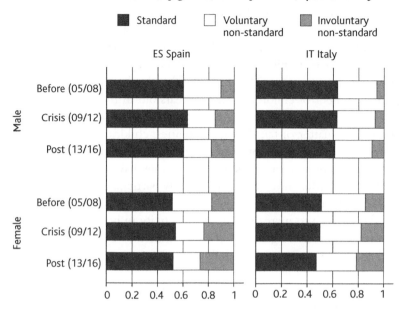

Source: Authors' own elaboration from the European Labour Force Survey (2005–16)

Figure 3.3: Levels of standard and non-standard employment before, during and after the economic crises, by age, Spain and Italy

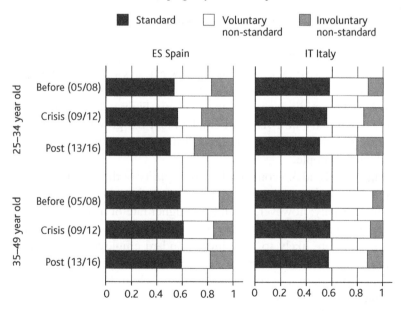

Source: Authors' own elaboration from the European Labour Force Survey (2005–16)

What characterises workers in involuntary non-standard jobs?

There is extensive literature which demonstrates that non-standard jobs are associated with worse social and economic conditions (Maestripieri, 2015). The data presented in Table 3A.5 confirm that when a person is involuntarily employed in a non-standard job, segmentation and occupational segregation is high. First of all, voluntary non-standard work is mostly carried out by self-employed workers. Unfortunately, the European Labour Force Survey data do not provide information on the voluntariness of self-employment, which is one of the most important types of non-standard jobs, especially for adult men. Thus, it cannot be established whether freelancers who are now active in the labour market have been pushed into independent jobs or whether they were attracted to self-employment by better working opportunities (Pedersini and Coletto, 2010). As a consequence, rates of voluntary non-standard employment might be overestimated among adult men.

Second, of the total number of workers in fixed-term employment, involuntary job-takers represent 81.6% in Italy and 88.2% in Spain. Similarly, 63.8% of part-timers in Spain and 52% in Italy are involuntary part-timers. Indicators of segmentation show the greater exposure of involuntary non-standard workers to underemployment (42.2% in Spain and 14.1% in Italy of non-standard workers would like to work more hours) and the reduced investment of employers in their human capital, as demonstrated by the low access to in-work training (more pronounced in Italy). Involuntary job-takers are mostly skilled and unskilled service workers in women's segregated sectors, such as traditional services (ie retail, accommodation and restaurants), care and education. Quite remarkably, there is a minor but not negligible percentage of 18% of involuntary non-standard workers who are employed in advanced business services. Among professionals and managers, involuntary non-standard workers represent 18.3% and 13.4% in Spain and Italy, respectively. This evidence questions traditional theories of labour market segmentation (Yoon and Chung, 2016).

Focusing only on involuntary part-timers (see Table 3A.6), our empirical evidence shows how this phenomenon has an intersectional dimension. First, even if it is true that involuntariness in part-time work is higher among men, it still remains a residual phenomenon affecting one in every 10 young workers and one in every 20 adult workers, especially when they are low educated. Second, involuntary part-time work among women is not homogeneously distributed across groups: Italian women are more exposed than Spanish women, and young women are more exposed than adult women. Among the adult population, there is a linear correlation between education and involuntary part-time work: adult women with higher education are the least exposed to the phenomenon in all the intersectional categories.

The impact of children on part-time types

The percentage of part-time employment in total employment rises when there is at least one child in the family, with different percentages in Italy and Spain. In both countries, the lowest percentage of part-time employment in total employment is found among tertiary-educated adult women with no children (see Table 3.1a). Among the lower-educated young and adult women, the percentages of part-timers grow, especially when women have childcare responsibilities (40.5% in Spain; 46.2% in Italy) (see Table 3.1b). However, higher-educated women with children are more likely to voluntarily choose part-time work, while lower-educated women are in the majority involuntarily employed on a part-time basis even when there is at least one child in the family (about 46% for young adults and about 38% for adults).

Childcare responsibilities influence the reasons behind the choice of part-time work among women but only partially the quality of part-time employment that women undertake. In fact, Tables 3.1a and 3.1b show how the percentage of women working part-time for care reasons varies significantly in the intersectional categories. However, the types of part-time work that the authors considered to be at possible risk of marginalisation (involuntary, marginal and bogus part-time work) still represented over 70% of the total number of workers in part-time employment in the case of childless women and over 50% in cases where there is a child in the household. Women with a tertiary education are less likely to work with a part-time contract at risk of marginalisation (eg involuntary part-time, bogus part-time or marginal part-time); when they have children, their risk is lower compared to less-educated women, especially when they are older than 35 years. Nevertheless, they are still more likely to be bogus part-time employed than their childless counterparts, that is, working more than 30 hours per week while officially being employed on a part-time basis. In total, over 50% of part-timers can still be considered at risk even among those who possess the highest human capital.

Table 3.1a: Types of part-time employment among childless women aged 25–49 years old, by intersectional categories (age, education), Spain and Italy (%)

	Part time	Care	Marginal	Involuntary	Bogus	Total marginal	% total
Spain							
Young adult (25–34)							
Low educated	3.5	0.8	12.9	67.9	14.9	95.7	21.6
Medium educated	13.4	0.7	15.5	57	13.3	85.8	23.4
High educated	11.4	0.5	16.8	58.7	12.6	88.1	22
Totals by age	10.8	0.5	16	59.6	13.1	88.7	22.2
Adult (35–49)							
Low educated	13.4	6.2	25.3	48	7.2	80.5	33.3
Medium educated	15.5	3.5	14.3	54.1	12.5	80.9	18.5
High educated	12.9	4.9	14.4	52.6	15.2	82.2	11.6
Totals by age	13.7	5.3	19.8	50.6	10.6	81.1	19.5
Italy							
Young adult (25–34)							
Low educated	7.1	2.5	9	63.6	17.7	90.3	36.2
Medium educated	11.3	1.5	7.6	59.1	20.4	87.1	31.3
High educated	12.3	0.9	15.3	51.4	20.1	86.8	22.7
Totals by age	11.2	1.4	10.5	56.9	20	87.4	28
Adult (35–49)							
Low educated	10	9.1	14.2	51.3	15.4	80.9	37.7
Medium educated	12.4	13.6	8.3	43.8	21.9	74	25
High educated	15.2	7.1	15.1	42.7	19.9	77.7	16.3
Totals by age	11.9	10.8	11.7	46.6	19	77.4	26.4

Note: Part-time at risk of marginalisation is the sum of marginal part-time (less than 10 hours per week), involuntary part-time (part-timers who would like to work full-time but did not find a full-time job) and bogus part-time (official part-time contract when workers usually work more than 30 hours per week)

Source: Authors' own elaboration on the European Labour Force Survey (averages 2013–16)

Further inferences can be made about childless women on the basis of the survey data. In the case of childless women, the role of part-time work for care reasons is almost negligible. Only a minority of childless women (not more than 15% in any category) voluntarily choose to work on a part-time basis. Apart from this involuntariness, they are also affected by marginal part-time work (on average, 15% in the two countries) and bogus part-time work (15% in Spain; 20% in Italy). Bogus part-time work is especially high among higher-educated adult women, perhaps because of an abusive use of this type of contract by employers. The level of education does not seem to protect against marginal part-time work, which is nonetheless

Table 3.1b: Types of part-time employment among women with children aged 25–49 years old, by intersectional categories (age, education), Spain and Italy (%)

	Part time	Care	Marginal	Involuntary	Bogus	Total marginal	% total
Spain							
Young adult (25–34)							
Low educated	6.7	23.2	14.1	46.1	9.8	70	39.9
Medium educated	9	34.6	12.4	32.7	11.3	56.4	33.3
High educated	8.9	36.3	10.2	27.9	16.7	54.8	23.6
Totals by age	8.1	30.7	12.3	36.3	12.6	61.2	30.9
Adult (35–49)							
Low educated	9.1	21.7	21.9	38.6	8.7	69.2	40.5
Medium educated	10.4	35.1	11.5	30.2	12.8	54.5	30.4
High educated	10.8	37.4	8.2	24.2	19.5	51.9	22
Totals by age	10.2	32.2	13	29.8	14.7	57.6	27.5
Italy							
Young adult (25–34)							
Low educated	3	23.5	13.9	46	13.6	73.5	46
Medium educated	4	30	6.6	34.7	24.6	65.9	41.8
High educated	5.2	31.7	8.8	30.3	24	63.1	28.9
Totals by age	4.1	29	8.6	36.1	22.2	66.9	38.8
Adult (35–49)							
Low educated	5	25.7	13.6	38.6	17.1	69.3	46.2
Medium educated	5.4	36.7	5.9	25	27	57.9	41.1
High educated	5.6	33.2	9.4	22.1	29.6	61.1	28.6
Totals by age	5.3	33.3	8.5	27.4	25.4	61.3	38.1

Note: Part-time at risk of marginalisation is the sum of marginal part-time (less than 10 hours per week), involuntary part-time (part-timers who would like to work full-time but did not find a full-time job) and bogus part-time (official part-time contract when workers usually work more than 30 hours per week).

Source: Authors' own elaboration on the European Labour Force Survey (averages 2013–16)

prevalently involuntary. Bogus part-time work is especially frequent in Italy, while marginal part-time work is more frequently found in Spain. However, involuntarily part-timers remain the most frequent category of part-timers in the two countries for all the intersectional types identified in the analysis if the woman has no children.

Conclusions

In many countries, part-time employment developed during the 1970s and 1980s in parallel with the incorporation of women into the labour market in large numbers. At a time when caring responsibilities were placed squarely upon the shoulders of women, part-time work was put forward as an attractive solution to women of childbearing age who wanted to work but could not do so on a full-time basis. Although this has created strong gender wage gaps, working conditions have been by and large good. The discussion of part-time employment in Italy and Spain, however, takes a very different direction. In these two countries, part-time work, together with other forms of non-standard employment, expanded much later as a response to severe constraints on the core of the labour market, such as strong restrictions on the dismissal of permanent workers. Non-standard contracts, such as fixed-term and part-time work, started to rise in this context of labour market rigidity and strong hindrances to job growth. Hence, it is virtually impossible to disassociate the evolution of part-time work from the logic of labour market dualisation. This is, indeed, very different from how part-time work developed in other European countries. Part-time employment as a long-term activation strategy in the Netherlands, for instance, allowed for a positive inclusion of non-standard work in the form of equal treatment in wages and access to social security rights. Dutch trade unions played a key role in the creation of this win–win scenario of working time and organisational flexibility (Visser and Hemerijck, 1997; Hemerijck, 2013). In the two Southern European countries, the security element of flexible working arrangements has always been conspicuously absent. The power of insiders in organised labour and the political weakness of Left cabinets have been major hindrances to the introduction of more secure forms of labour market activation (Beramendi, 2015). Employers' demand for greater external flexibility at the contract level has been accommodated only for non-core occupational groups and new entrants. In both countries, national legislation on part-time work has subsequently been amended to comply with the European directive (97/81/CE) but this has still not prevented part-time work from becoming an expression of deepening dualisation dynamics.

As this chapter has shown, a large majority (over 60%) of part-time workers in Italy and Spain have not voluntarily chosen to work part-time. If they were given the chance, they would work more hours. The proportion of part-time workers who consider their status involuntary has increased with the economic crisis as it offers a way for employers to reduce labour costs and secure flexibility. It could be argued that, overall, part-time work in these two countries did not become an option for workers who prefer to work shorter hours, but became a way to make employment more flexible in the context of increasing labour precariousness.

Using an intersectional perspective, the authors investigated the possible interlocking effects of disadvantage that occur when multiple factors intersect to define the living and working conditions of individuals. Through their common set of structural features but differentiated outcomes, the comparison between Italy and Spain is interesting on several counts. The analysis presented in this chapter has shown the relative advantage of women with high skill levels in both countries, although more so in Spain. Highly skilled women have lower employment gaps and are penalised less when they become mothers. In almost every category, gender gaps are stronger for women with low to medium education levels, including the number of hours worked. The presence of children in the household magnifies a situation of disadvantage that characterises all women, linked to educational level in Spain and age group in Italy, where the youngest adults and lowest educated are the most exposed to non-standard contracts. Only a minority of part-time contracts are chosen for reasons of care: over 80% of female part-timers with no children are affected by marginalised working conditions in part-time work, including extremely reduced working hours (less than 10 hours/week), involuntariness and an officially stated part-time contract when the worker usually works more than 30 hours per week. Recent years have shown an increasing level of involuntariness behind non-standard employment, while involuntary non-standard employment magnifies the exposure to segregation and segmentation that characterises these types of contracts.

Involuntary part-time work is growing among all categories of workers, especially among young women without children. Bogus part-time work is growing among medium and highly skilled women with young children but, at least, marginal part-time work (ie working less than 10 hours/week) remains stable and residual. While the younger generations are the most affected by this dynamic, a significant difference between the two countries is the extent to which education protects women against involuntary part-time work in Spain but not in Italy, where the disadvantage is driven by age.

Reflecting upon the typology presented in the introductory chapter, the evolution of part-time employment in Italy and Spain places these two countries in the 'marginalised part-time workers' type. The lagged position of the two Southern European countries in relation to their economic development, democratic consolidation and welfare state expansion made them miss the train of the *flexicurity* momentum in other European countries. The involuntary character of most part-time work signals a supply-side-driven development with the worst possible consequences for workers in the farthest part of the prevailing insider–outsider divide.

Notes

[1]   This chapter has received funding from the EU's Horizon 2020 research and Innovation Programme under the Marie Skłodowska-Curie Grant Agreement No 747433.

[2]   *Ms Espadas Recio v Servicio Público de Empleo Estatal (SPEE).* Ms Espadas Recio had been working part-time for a company for 12 years. When the unemployment insurance was calculated, the public service considered only the days of the week worked in respect of which contributions had been paid. The Court of Justice ruled that this was discriminatory against women because the vast majority of 'vertical' part-timers are women (Court of Justice of the EU Press Release No XX/17, 9 November 2017, available at: https://curia.europa.eu/jcms/upload/docs/application/pdf/2017-11/cp170116en.pdf).

[3]   Given the low barriers to dismissal among permanent workers in the UK, the rate of temporary work in this country is particularly low in comparison.

[4]   See: https://ec.europa.eu/eurostat/data/database

[5]   The analysis starts in 2005 as the data collected for the Italian Labour Force Survey prior to that date followed a different data-collection strategy that make comparisons between the waves before and after 2004 potentially difficult.

[6]   ISCED is the International Standard Classification of Education and it is used to compare educational levels across countries. For more information see: https://ec.europa.eu/eurostat/statistics-explained/index.php/International_Standard_Classification_of_Education_(ISCED)

References

Beramendi, P. (2015) 'Constrained partisanship and economic outcomes' in P. Beramendi, S. Häusermann, H. Kitschelt and H. Kriesi (eds) *The politics of advanced capitalism*, Cambridge: Cambridge University Press, pp 333–56.

Bodnár, K. (2018) 'Recent developments in part-time employment'. Available at: https://goo.gl/SL5pcH

Bosch, G. (2006) 'Working time and the standard employment relationship', in J.-Y. Boulin, M. Lallement, J.C. Messenger and F. Michon (eds) *Decent working time: New trends, new issues*, Geneva: International Labour Office, pp 41–64.

Collins, P.H. (2015) 'Intersectionality's definitional dilemmas', *Annual Review of Sociology*, 41(1): 1–20.

Conde Ruiz, J.I. and Marra de Artíñano, I. (2016) 'Gender gaps in the Spanish labour market', *Estudios sobre la Economía Española 2016/32*. Available at: http://documentos.fedea.net/pubs/eee/eee2016-32.pdf

Ellingsaeter, A.L. and Leira, A. (2006) (eds) *Politicising parenthood in Scandinavia: Gender relations in welfare states*, Bristol: The Policy Press.

Emmenegger, P., Hausermann, S., Palier, B. and Seeleib-Kaiser, M. (2012) *The age of dualization: The changing face of inequality in deindustrializing societies*, Oxford, Oxford University Press.

Firinu, A. (2015) 'La flessibilità irregolare: un fenomeno grigio della regolazione del lavoro', *Sociologia del Lavoro*, 138: 37–54.

Firinu, A. and Maestripieri, L. (2018) 'Lavoro marginale', in A. Zucca and C. Croce (eds) *Lavoro marginale e nuove vulnerabilità*, Milano: Giangiacomo Feltrinelli Editore.

Hakim, C. (1997) 'Sociological perspective on part-time work', in H.P. Blossfeld and C. Hakim (eds) *Between equalization and marginalization: Women working part-time in Europe and the United States of America*, Oxford: Oxford University Press, pp 22–70.

Hallerod, B., Ekbrand, H. and Bengtsson, M. (2015) 'In-work poverty and labour market trajectories: poverty risks among the working population in 22 European countries', *Journal of European Social Policy*, 25(5): 473–88.

Hemerijck, A. (2013) *Changing welfare states*, Oxford: Oxford University Press.

Ibáñez, Z. (2011) 'Part-time employment in Spain: a victim of the "temporality culture" and a lagging implementation', in A.M. Guillén and M. León (eds) *The Spanish welfare state in European context*, London: Ashgate, pp 165–86.

Kalleberg, A.L. (2008) 'Nonstandard employment relations and labour market inequality', in D.B. Grusky (ed) *Social stratification: Class, race and gender in sociological perspective*, Boulder, CO: Westview Press, pp 562–75.

Maestripieri, L. (2015) 'Gendering social vulnerability. The role of labour market de-standardisation and local welfare', in D. Kutsar and M. Kuronen (eds) *Local welfare policy making in European cities*, Berlin: Springer, pp 51–67.

McCall, L. (2005) 'The complexity of intersectionality', *Signs: Journal of Women in Culture and Society*, 30(3): 1771–800.

Muffels, R. and Wilthagen, T. (2011) 'Defining flexicurity indicators for the public sector in Europe', 1 March. Available at SSRN: https://ssrn.com/abstract=1968845 or https://dx.doi.org/10.2139/ssrn.1968845

Pedersini, R. and Coletto, D. (2010) *Self-employed workers: Industrial relations and working conditions*, Dublin: Eurofond. Available at: https://goo.gl/rU9Dhn

Rueda, D. (2015) 'The origins of dualism', in P. Beramendi, S. Häusermann, H. Kitschelt and H. Kriesi (eds) *The politics of advanced capitalism*, Cambridge: Cambridge University Press.

Santucci, R. (2017) 'Il contratto di lavoro part-time tra Jobs Act (decreto legislativo n. 81/2015) e diritto giurisprudenziale'. Available at: https://goo.gl/ffiiRa

Saraceno, C. (1994) 'The ambivalent familism of the Italian welfare state', *Social Politics*, 1(1): 60–82.

Villa, P. (2010) 'La crescita dell'occupazione femminile: la polarizzazione tra stabilità e precarietà', *Lavoro e diritto*, XXIV(3): 343–58.

Visser, J. and Hemerijck, A. (1997) *A Dutch miracle: Job growth, welfare reform and corporatism in the Netherlands*, Amsterdam: Amsterdam University Press.

Walby, S., Armstrong, J. and Strid, S. (2012) 'Intersectionality: multiple inequalities in social theory', *Sociology*, 46(2): 224–40.

Winker, G. and Degele, N. (2011) 'Intersectionality as multi-level analysis: dealing with social inequality', *European Journal of Women's Studies*, 18(1): 51–66.

Yoon, Y. and Chung, H. (2016) 'New forms of dualization? Labour market segmentation patterns in the UK from the late 90s until the post-crisis in the late 2000s', *Social Indicators Research*, 128(2): 609–31.

Appendix

Table 3A.1: Labour market indicators in the six countries – population aged 15–64, percentages, 2016

	Spain	France	Italy	The Netherlands	Sweden	UK
Inactivity rate (women)	31	32.5	44.8	24.9	19.8	28.1
Inactivity rate (men)	20.5	24.6	25.2	15.6	16.1	18
Unemployment (women)	21.5	9.9	12.9	6.5	6.7	4.8
Unemployment (men)	18.2	10.4	11.1	5.7	7.6	5.1
Rate of non-standard work in employment (women), of which:[a]	48.5	44.6	51.4	84.3	46.2	47.2
Fixed-term	63.7	43	34.7	27.0	41	14.4
Part-time	50.9	67.1	63.7	91.1	77.1	84.2
Self-employment	24.5	17.1	30.7	13.6	11.4	21.3
Involuntary non-standard employment	58	41.5	48.3	13	34.3	12.6
Rate of non-standard work in employment (men), of which:[a]	43.2	31.4	40	47.1	31	29.4
Fixed-term	88.8	79	69.5	55.1	67	36.9
Part-time	17.4	24.5	20.5	55.3	42	37
Self-employment	44.6	44.3	64	38.1	38	62
Involuntary non-standard employment	48.1	30.4	30.4	16.4	30.3	14.6

Note: [a] Given the possible overlapping between different form of non-standard contracts, the sum of fixed term, part-time and self-employment is not equal to 100.

Source: Authors' own elaboration from the European Labour Force Survey

Table 3A.2: Indicators on part-time employment in the six countries – population aged 15–64, percentages, 2016

	Spain	France	Italy	The Netherlands	Sweden	UK
Part-time employment (women)	24.7	29.9	32.7	76.8	35.6	39.8
Part-time employment (men)	7.5	7.7	8.2	26	13	10.9
Part-time employment (native)	14.8	18	17.4	50.1	23.7	25
Part-time employment (migrant)	19.4	24.8	28.2	42.7	27.1	20.5
Part-time employment (15–24)	40.3	24.5	29.6	80.2	49.1	35.7
Part-time employment (25–34)	18.3	15.4	22	40.6	21.9	18.4
Part-time employment (35–49)	13.9	17.4	18.9	43.7	19.6	22.7
Part-time employment (50–64)	11.6	20.6	14.6	47.5	21.3	26.9
Part-time employment (low education)	17.1	25.4	19.4	58.5	34.4	27
Part-time employment (medium education)	16.6	18.8	19.2	51.7	23.4	27.4
Part-time employment (high education)	13.2	15.1	15.7	42.8	21.2	20.8
Overall total part-time employment	15.3	18.4	18.5	49.8	23.9	24.5
Rate of involuntary part-timers in total part-time employment	68.4	45.2	65.6	13.1	34.6	16.8

Source: Authors' own elaboration from the European Labour Force Survey

Table 3A.3a: Percent inactive by intersectional categories (age, gender and education), Spain and Italy[a]

	Spain				Italy		
Young adult (25–34)	Men	Women	Gaps	Young adult (25–34)	Men	Women	Gaps
Low educated	40.1	50.7	–10.6	Low educated	41.7	66	–24.3
Medium educated	30.6 (ns)	35.7	–5.1	Medium educated	29.5	45.5	–16
High educated	24.3	26.9	–2.6	High educated	35.6	37.8	–2.2
Totals by age	31.8	34.7	–2.9	Totals by age	33.9	46.7	–12.8
Adult (35–49)	Men	Women	Gaps	Adult (35–49)	Men	Women	Gaps
Low educated	35.1	51.8	–16.7	Low educated	25.4	59.4	–34
Medium educated	20	35.5	–15.5	Medium educated	11.2	33.3	–22.1
High educated	12	22.4	–10.4	High educated	6.3	16.8	–10.5
Totals by age	22.8	34.7	–11.9	Totals by age	16.2	38.8	–22.6

Note: Gender gaps = men ÷ women. [a] Proportions with (ns) means that the proportion of the category is not significantly different from the rest of the population, measured at .95 probability with a two-sample test of proportion. The overall significance test anova has confirmed that the difference in means by country and intersectional categories are statistically significant.

Source: Authors' own elaboration on the European Labour Force Survey (averages 2013–16)

Table 3A.3b: Percent inactive by intersectional categories (age, education and number of children under 14 years old), Spain and Italy

	Spain					Italy				
Young adult (25–34)	0	1	2	3+	Total	0	1	2	3+	Total
Low educated	-0.6	-16.7	-25.8	-16.1	-10.6	-12.3	-29	-41.9	-45	-24.3
Medium educated	-0.9	-16.5	-22.3	-25.6	-5.1	-11.2	-27	-39.5	-59.2	-16
High educated	-0.6	-12.3	-17.3	-42.4	-2.6	-2.2	-15.6	-16.5	-30.8	-2.2
Totals by age	2.3	-11.7	-20.6	-20.5	-2.9	-7.3	-22	-34.4	-46.1	-12.8
Adult (35–49)	0	1	2	3+	Total	0	1	2	3+	Total
Low educated	-5	-24.8	-33.2	-33.7	-16.7	-24.4	-41	-45.6	-54.7	-34
Medium educated-	-7.3	-20.9	-24.2	-23.9	-15.5	-14.6	-25.1	-30.9	-38.5	-22.1
High educated	-4.1	-14.2	-15.9	-16.4	-10.4	-5.3	-13.7	-15.4	-19.2	-10.5
Totals by age	-4.1	-17.9	-19.9	19.7	-11.9	-16.4	-26.9	-28.9	-35.2	-22.6

Source: Authors' own elaboration on the European Labour Force Survey (averages 2013–16)

Table 3A.4a: Worked hours (self-declared)[a] by intersectional categories (age, gender and education), Spain and Italy (averages)[b]

Young adult (25–34)	Spain			Young adult (25–34)	Italy		
	Men	Women	Gaps		Men	Women	Gaps
Low educated	39.9	34	5.9	Low educated	40.2	32.1	8
Medium educated	39.9	34.6	5.3	Medium educated	39.7	33.7	6
High educated	38.9	35.1	3.8	High educated	38.6	33.9	4.7
Totals by age	39.4	34.8	4.7	Totals by age	39.6	33.6	6
Adult (35–49)	**Men**	**Women**	**Gaps**	**Adult (35–49)**	**Men**	**Women**	**Gaps**
Low educated	42	32.5	9.5	Low educated	41.1	32.2	8.9
Medium educated	41.7	35.1	6.6	Medium educated	41.1	33.1	8
High educated	41.1	36.2	4.9	High educated	40	32.5	7.5
Totals by age	41.5	35.1	6.5	Totals by age	40.9	32.7	8.2

Notes: [a] Using self-declared usual working time allows us to track the real working involvement of the person in the labour market, which might be different from what is officially stated in the contract (see, eg, bogus part-time work). [b] The overall significance test anova has confirmed that the differences in means by country and intersectional categories are statistically significant. Means are all significant. Gender gaps = men ÷ women

Source: Authors' own elaboration on the European Labour Force Survey (averages 2013–16).

Table 3A.4b: Gender gap in hours worked (self-declared) (men hours ÷ women hours) by intersectional categories (age, education and number of children under 14 years old), Spain and Italy

Spain

Young adult (25–34)	0	1	2	3+	Total
Low educated	2.4	9	12.2	7.2	5.9
Medium educated	4	7.2	10	13.7	5.3
High educated	3.2	6.8	5.5	5.5	3.8
Totals by age	3.4	7.4	9.1	8.2	4.7
Adult (35–49)	0	1	2	3+	Total
Low educated	8	10.1	12.6	9.5	9.5
Medium educated	4.5	7.6	8.9	8.2	6.6
High educated	2.6	6.3	6.5	7.1	4.9
Totals by age	4.6	7.6	8.1	7.5	6.5

Italy

Young adult (25–34)	0	1	2	3+	Total
Low educated	6.2	9.3	10.6	11.2	8.1
Medium educated	5	7.5	9.3	10.8	6
High educated	3.7	7.6	10.5	8.7	4.7
Totals by age	4.8	7.9	9.6	11	6
Adult (35–49)	0	1	2	3+	Total
Low educated	7.7	9.7	10.9	12.7	8.9
Medium educated	5.9	8.7	10.5	11.3	8
High educated	5.2	8.2	9.8	12.6	7.5
Totals by age	6.3	8.9	10.4	12.2	8.2

Source: Authors' own elaboration on the European Labour Force Survey (averages 2013–16)

Table 3A.5: Characteristics of standard and non-standard employment by involuntariness, 25–49 years old, Spain and Italy (percentages)

	Spain			Italy		
	Standard	Voluntary non-standard	Involuntary non-standard	Standard	Voluntary non-standard	Involuntary non-standard
% of temporary contract	–	11.8	88.2	–	18.4	81.6
% of part-time	–	36.2	63.8	–	48	52
Want to work more hours	6.7	11.6	42.2	2.2	5.4	14.1
Access to training	11.1	7.6	10.8	7.4	7.3	4.6
Managers and professionals	25.9	28.4	18.3	15.9	27.5	13.4
Technicians and clerks	29.3	16.3	19.4	40.4	28.3	25.8
Skilled service workers	18.2	26.9	23.5	12.8	19.2	27.6
Skilled manual workers	20.3	24.4	18.4	25	21.2	13.1
Unskilled manual workers	6.3	4	20.4	5.9	3.8	20
Total	100	100	100	100	100	100
Agriculture and manufacturing	20.7	15.1	15.6	31.4	15.3	17.7
Construction	4.6	9.2	6.4	5.6	9.2	3.4
Traditional services	27.9	41.1	29.8	23.4	35	34.2
Advanced business services	21.1	21.8	18.6	15.8	29.7	18.9
Public administration	10.2	1.5	5.8	9.1	0.9	2.9
Care and education	15.5	11.3	23.7	14.7	9.9	23
Total	100	100	100	100	100	100
% of total employment	56.6	21.4	22	55.1	30.2	14.6
% of women	42.3	45.3	55.4	36.3	44.3	62.9
% of young adults (25–34)	29.1	28.4	45.3	25.2	26.7	39.6

Source: Authors' own elaboration on the European Labour Force Survey (averages 2013–16)

Table 3A.6: Percentages of workers that declared to be involuntary part-timers by intersectional categories (gender, age and education), Spain and Italy[a]

Young adult (25–34)	Spain		Italy	
	M	F	M	F
Low educated	86.4	71.8	89.8	75.2
Medium educated	68.3 (ns)	65.1	85.2	66.6
High educated	75.9	69.9	81.7	70.2
Rate of part-time employment in the age class	11	25	9.7	31.8
Adult (35–49)	M	F	M	F
Low educated	81	67.4	86.4	64.8
Medium educated	75.7	53.5	76.1	44
High educated	69.3	41.9	68.2	42.8
Rate of part-time employment in the age class	4.9	24.1	5.3	32.8

Notes: [a] Proportions with (ns) mean that the proportion of the category is not significantly different from the rest of the population, measured at .95 probability with a two-sample test of proportion. The overall significance test anova has confirmed that the differences in means by country and intersectional categories are statistically significant.

Source: Authors' own elaboration on the European Labour Force Survey (averages 2013–16)

4

Workplace responses to national regulations to reduce involuntary part-time work

Hanne Cecilie Kavli, Heidi Nicolaisen and Sissel C. Trygstad

Introduction

Part-time work can be both 'good' and 'bad'. 'Bad' part-time work is often associated with short hours, involuntariness, unpredictability in terms of temporary contracts and a continuous challenge to secure a living wage (see, eg, Vosko, 2010; Kalleberg, 2011; Ilsøe, 2016). Although there is substantial cross-country variation, on average, involuntary part-time workers face a higher poverty risk than full-time workers in the European Union (EU) (Eurofound, 2017: 9). Workers on such contracts do not enjoy the job security and good working conditions that characterise the 'standard employment relationship' (Bosch, 2006). In this chapter, the ambition is to examine how – and why – some workers end up with 'bad' part-time contracts despite policymakers' efforts to the contrary. Emmenegger and colleagues (2012: 10) have argued that modern societies are 'growing more unequal'. Through a process of dualisation, policies make different rights and services available to different groups (Emmenegger et al, 2012). The process of dualisation can take place in three different ways: by deepening existing divisions between 'insiders' and 'outsiders'; by excluding former 'insiders'; and by political failure or unwillingness to address the development of new divisions. It follows from this that there are at least two avenues that political authorities can take to counter the increasing divide between 'insiders' and 'outsiders': they can include new and vulnerable workers into existing protective systems or they can create new rights. In Norway, the government has tried to combat involuntary part-time work by creating new rights for exposed workers. In 2006 and 2013, the Working Environment Act (WEA) was changed to make it easier for part-time workers to demand an increase in their working time. By doing this, policymakers also intended to resolve labour shortages in the health–care sector. The issue here, however, is whether the amendments have been effective in terms of preventing dualisation among part-time workers.

To investigate this question, this chapter examine workplace processes through in-depth interviews with employers and workers. Dualisation theorists argue that we get a richer understanding of labour market inequality if we study policies and processes that create inequality rather than just the outcome for individuals (Emmenegger et al, 2012). We argue that it is important to investigate the workplace level as this is where we see policy being implemented. It is where policies and regulations translate into practice, and where employers and workers negotiate employment contracts and working-time conditions. In the health–care sector, part-time work is an institutionalised practice, produced by both demand and supply factors. Changing this practice is a difficult task. Insight from institutional theory suggests that change requires a form of 'collective action' where actors who hold the same interests invest material and cultural resources in the new institution (Selznick, 1997: 17; Pierson, 2004: 258). Moreover, Scott (2014) argues that institutions consist of 'cognitive, normative, and regulative' pillars, which represent structures and activities that are intended to bring stability and meaning to the social context. Legal amendments are related to the regulative pillar, while norms, values and roles can be placed in the normative pillar. According to Scott, change is unlikely unless the regulative and normative pillars mutually support each other. Therefore, an important question in this study is whether norms and practices at the workplace level correspond with national-level policies and regulations, and therefore whether the responses of actors at the workplace are in line with policymakers' intentions. A lack of coherence between these structures may produce unintended consequences (Merton, 1996).

We have chosen the public health–care sector in Norway as our case for four reasons. First, it has a high proportion of part-time employees. Women dominate the sector, with more than half working part-time and some in marginal and involuntary part-time positions. Second, the sector employs a high proportion of low-skilled workers, but also workers with higher education levels. Third, it is an important port of labour market entry for migrants, which is a group of workers who often struggle to find 'good' jobs. Fourth, the public health–care sector in Norway is marked by high trade union density and all workers are covered by a collective agreement. From a comparative perspective, Norwegian employees benefit from regulations that warrant high-quality working conditions and job security. Based on these characteristics, we would expect that the new regulations will be put into practice. If this is the case, less attractive groups of workers should also have a reasonable chance of exiting 'bad' part-time contracts because of the new regulations.

In the following section, we discuss how insight from theories about the dualisation of the labour market, industrial relations, working time and institutional change can enhance our understanding of 'good' and 'bad' part-time work, and how part-time work is shaped in the context of the Norwegian health-care sector. We will then describe the more specific characteristics of working time in the health-care sector, as well as our data and methods, before empirically examining how processes at the workplace level influence the risk of involuntary part-time work among different categories of workers. Finally, we discuss how workplace adaptations to national policy regulations influence the dualisation of part-time work.

'Good' and 'bad' part-time work

Atypical work is often characterised by short and involuntary part-time employment and contrasts with the 'standard employment relationship' of the full-time core worker. An increase in atypical work is often seen as a development towards a more dualised labour market. Dualisation refers to a polarised process of change that results in increasing differences in working conditions between groups of workers. While the position of insiders may remain more or less constant, the position of outsiders deteriorates. It is also underlined that labour market dualisation may originate from 'institutionalised dualism' (Emmenegger et al, 2012), which refers to statutory or voluntarist regulations – or a lack of such. In the dualisation literature, atypical work plays an important role and part-time work is a key indicator of being a labour market outsider.

During the 1970s and 1980s in Norway, part-time work was viewed as a way for women to enter the labour market. It has later been argued that women's part-time work rapidly became 'normalised'. The 'normalised part-time worker' typically works relatively long hours and enjoys working conditions of the same quality as full-time workers (Ellingsæter, 1989: 258). While the Nordic countries still have a high level of employment protection for part-time workers, limited levels of involuntary part-time work and high levels of employees with long part-time jobs, new research suggests that this might be changing in parts of the labour market. New forms of atypical employment contracts, marginalised work and involuntary part-time work have increased in sectors and occupations at the 'bottom' of the labour market (Nicolaisen and Trygstad, 2015; Refslund and Thörnquist, 2016; Larsen et al, Chapter 6, this volume).

The statistical criterion for being categorised as an involuntary part-timer is that the worker seeks to increase their working time and is unable to do so at relatively short notice (Statistics Norway and Eurostat). The literature on working time indicates, however, that 'bad' part-time work also includes the 'time welfare' (Ellingsæter, 2017) of workers, which is strongly associated with the scheduling of working time, including the predictability of the hours to be worked. In a comparative study including 23 European countries, Steiber (2009) explores the subjective experience of work–family conflict. She draws a conceptual distinction between 'time-based' and 'strain-based' pressures. While 'time-based' pressures prevent the worker from devoting the time they want to their family, 'strain-based' pressures are related to how tired they feel after work and whether this prevents them from spending quality time with their family. While 'time-based' work pressures relate to the numbers of hours worked, unpredictable hours and working during evenings, nights or weekends are also potential causes of work–family conflict. The majority prefers to have time off at afternoons, evenings and weekends when their spouses, children and friends have time off (Sullivan, 1996; Warren, 2003; Fagan et al, 2012). Shift work makes coordinating time off with friends and family more difficult. 'Strain-based' pressures are related to work demands and job insecurity (Steiber, 2009). Within the health-care sector, lower levels of staffing during evening and night shifts may increase the strain-based pressures on both full- and part-time workers. Job insecurity and underemployment might be more prevalent among part-time than among full-time workers. To separate 'good' from 'bad' part-time work, we should therefore consider the timing of working hours, in addition to their number, and the work strain experienced.

Policymakers' efforts to boost women's labour market participation

National authorities have made several efforts to enable mothers to engage in paid work. Generous parental leave enables parents to remain employed during the first year after a child is born. Affordable childcare is then provided – even for very young children (Ellingsaeter et al, 2017). However, day nurseries are not open during evening, nights and weekends, and do not completely cover the needs of shift workers.

For several decades, the WEA has entitled part-time workers to the same rights as employees in full-time positions. In 2006, a new amendment (WEA, Section 14-3) gave priority to employees in part-time jobs when a full-time position becomes available. For this preferential right to apply, the employee must have the necessary qualifications for the position, and their employment in the position must not involve significant inconvenience for the employer. In 2013, a second amendment to the WEA (Section 14-4a) granted part-time workers the right to increase their contracted/agreed hours to match their actual working time in the preceding 12 months, unless the employer can demonstrate that the need for additional work (extra hours) no longer exists.

The changes were introduced to reduce involuntary part-time work (Alsos and Bråten, 2011) and reflect a change in public discourse. Rather than seeing part-time employment as a promising way for women to reconcile work with family life, it was framed as a barrier to gender equality, equal pay and pensions (Mósesdóttir and Ellingsæter, 2017). The changes to the WEA can hence be seen as policymakers' attempts to prevent a more institutionalised form of dualism, where labour market outsiders – the involuntary part-timers – become even more marginalised compared to the insiders.[1]

Interests and power at the workplace level

It is at the workplace level that employees negotiate work schedules with their employer. The power relationship between them is asymmetrical, but institutions (eg labour law, collective agreements and trade unions) aspire to 'level the playing field'. Although employees are generally the weaker participant, some may have a stronger position than others if they possess a resource that is attractive to employers. Power resources can be material or immaterial. To be effective, however, other actors in the system must value them and see them as critical (Borum, 1995). The ability of employees to mobilise and utilise their resources is a key factor in converting control over resources into power (Pfeffer, 1981: 98). Expertise is a valuable power resource in the workplace. We define expertise more widely than just formal education and work experience. Norwegian-language skills, as well as knowledge about relevant laws and agreements, are also a part of the worker's expertise and hence a power resource. The employee's expertise will affect how critical their skills are to the employer, as well as whether they are easy to replace or not (Crouch, 1982; Scheuer, 1986). Hence, we assume that access to power resources affects the employee's ability to secure a good part-time position. In the health-care sector, some employees have a strong bargaining position based on their expertise. The nurses administer medications in both hospitals and nursing homes and have the authority to provide medication as needed to the patients. Nursing homes are therefore obliged to have a trained nurse on site around the clock. Combined with a growing shortage of trained nurses, this provides this occupational group with more power to negotiate their terms than auxiliary nurses and assistants.

From the employers' point of view, the changes to the WEA in 2006 and 2013 can be regarded as efforts to limit their managerial prerogative, and their power, because they have the potential to restrain employment strategies and schedule flexibility. This may result in employer behaviours that undermine the WEA regulations aimed at combating involuntary part-time work. The discrepancy between rules/institutions and the underlying action is widely discussed within the framework of institutional theory. A main theoretical point is that because of the agendas – and sometimes conflicting interests – among the actors who implement rules, institutions cannot be seen as self-reproducing. This perspective can be useful when we examine the implementation of new part-time work regulations among actors who are likely to have partly conflicting interests. Based on this insight from institutional theory, we cannot expect implementation to be straightforward. Although the statutory regulations in the WEA are stable, they are subject to change if actors behave in an opportunistic way or in ways that undermine institutions (Mahoney and Thelen, 2010).

Employers are the leading stakeholders at the workplace level. If the rules are at odds with their interests, they may adopt a strategy that decouples formal regulations and practical action. For example, they may communicate loyalty to regulations but act in an opportunistic way (Meyer and Rowan, 1977: 352; Trygstad, 2017). The ability of actors to avoid, undermine or counteract regulations depends on the nature of the regulations and their design, application and enforcement (Vosko, 2010). If regulations are 'soft', voluntary and have a suggestive character, it is easier to escape implementation than if they are 'hard' and legally binding (Tomlinson, 2006). However, hard regulations are not necessarily implemented in practice (Kanbur and Ronconi, 2016). Without enforcement mechanisms (eg a labour court and labour inspectorate) and advocacy in the workplace (from trade union representatives and/or employers), working-time regulations may have limited practical application (Haipeter, 2006: 337–8).

Data and methods

Qualitative data allow us to examine how – and why – different types of part-time contracts are made at the workplace level. We concentrate on women as they are over-represented in part-time work and in the health-care sector. Our sample is highly diverse and includes part-time workers with different occupational backgrounds (trained nurses, auxiliary nurses and health-care assistants), as well as separate samples of migrant women. During 2015 and 2016, 40 interviews were conducted in the health-care sector. The informants can be split into two main categories: women in part-time employment (33 interviews) and top- or mid-level managers (eight interviews). Employees responded to questions on preferred and actual working time, causes for any discrepancy between preferences and practice, and how this was dealt with in the dialogue with managers and trade union representatives. The interviews also addressed work organisation, family and care obligations, and working-time adaptation throughout their career. The interviews lasted between 30 minutes and two hours (most were about one hour). With managers, topics included formal aspects of how the workplace was organised, and employer perspectives on part-time work and the WEA amendments.

Our informants mainly worked at public hospitals, nursing homes or municipal home-care services and were recruited through: (1) trade unions; (2) various organisations and individuals with broad networks among migrant women; and (3) employers. We chose different paths to recruit employees in order to avoid a sample bias in terms of either overly 'employer-friendly' or 'critical' employees. Their main characteristics are presented in Table 4.1. We also interviewed five mid-level managers who have personnel responsibility and who are responsible for staffing shifts, as well as three general managers. All but one employer representative were educated nurses.

We supplemented the qualitative interviews with the following secondary data: a short analysis of register data from Statistics Norway to quantify working time among women by occupation; a brief content analysis of cases brought before the Dispute Resolution Board (DRB) and their outcomes; and findings from an ongoing study among trade union representatives commenting on the WEA amendments and their work to inform and assist employees who considered trying their cases (Trygstad et al, 2017).

Table 4.1: Descriptive data on employee informants (part-time workers)

	Trained nurse		Auxiliary nurse/assistant		
	Norwegian	Immigrant	Norwegian	Immigrant	Total
Working time:					
Less than 50%	1	0	1	3	5
50–80%	5	3	4	7	19
More than 80%	4	3	1	1	9
Involuntary part-time	0	0	1	9	10
More than one job	1	0	0	2	3
Number of children:					
1 or 2	8	4	5	5	22
3 or more	2	2	1	6	11
Single parent	2	0	1	2	5
Age:					
35 and under	0	0	1	4	5
36–50	6	3	3	7	19
51 and above	4	3	2	0	9
N	*10*	*6*	*6*	*11*	*33*

Working time across occupations in the health-care sector

Labour Force Survey (LFS) data show that part-time work is unevenly distributed between occupations (see Table 4.2). While 54% of trained nurses were employed full-time, the proportion dropped to 36% among auxiliary nurses and 34% among health-care assistants. We also distinguish between short (1–19 hours) and long (20–34 hours) part-time work. Short part-time work is far more common among health-care assistants than among the higher-educated auxiliary nurses and trained nurses. Among migrants, part-time work varies according to occupation along the same patterns as for non-migrants. Nevertheless, part-time work is less common among migrants than non-migrants (see Table 4A.1).

With regard to involuntary part-time work, Nergaard (2016: 50) finds that 21% of trained nurses and 28% of auxiliary nurses in part-time positions wish to work more. If we exclude the substantial proportion of those in this sector who combine work and education, then 31% of trained nurses and 40% of auxiliary nurses wish to increase their working time.

The majority in the sector work split shifts and hence rotate between daytime, evening and night work. Full-time for those on split shifts is normally 35.5 hours per week, which is shorter than for those who only work daytimes (37.5 hours per week). For those who work

Table 4.2: Working time among women (20–64 years), by occupation (%)

	Short part-time	Long part-time	Full-time	N
Trained nurse	9	36	54	6,119
Auxiliary nurse	20	44	36	4,864
Health care assistant	27	40	34	1,647
Total (all women in NACE 86–88)	13	31	56	20,266

Notes: Students are not included. European industry standard classification system (NACE).
Source: Norwegian Labour Force Survey (2014–17), Statistics Norway

split shifts, a six-week work schedule typically consists of 12 daytime shifts, 10 evening shifts and eight night shifts. In addition, they work weekends (defined as Sundays). According to the WEA, no employee can work more than every second Sunday, although the nurses' union only accepts working every third Sunday. As for the collective agreements for auxiliary nurses and health-care assistants, the regulation of weekend work is more frequent and in line with the WEA.

Impact from the workplace level on dualised part-time work

In this section, we analyse interviews with managers and workers to illuminate how policy measures are implemented at the workplace level, and we identify workers that are most exposed to 'bad' part-time work.

Policymakers' regulations and employers' responses

In the health-care sector, employers' preferred working-time arrangement is a combination of long part-time (70–90%) among the core staff, and short part-time (10–20%) among 'weekend staff'. While a certain number of employees on short part-time contracts ensures flexibility, employees on longer hours provide continuity and competence.

Managers generally emphasise the need to staff every shift in a way that ensures that the necessary competence is available at all times. Each shift requires a trained nurse to administer and provide medications. Managers also make other assessments related to the overall competence of the workers. These can include workers' years of experience, ability to cooperate with colleagues, patients and next of kin, and Norwegian-language skills. Staffing the rota in a way that balances all these considerations weighs heavily on several of the mid-level managers we interviewed:

"Because of the rota, we need some part-time positions. It also helps us in periods with high levels of sick leave. But, there must be a balance. If we have too many in short part-time positions, that will reduce our ability to offer the residents continuity. To be frank, I sometimes worry that the service quality is not good enough, in particular on public holidays and at weekends." (Manager, nursing home)

High levels of sickness absence and a recurring need for on–call workers have been a challenge in the health-care sector for many years. Part-time workers provide flexibility as they can fill gaps in the rota at short notice. In these situations, availability tends to trump suitability. However, the WEA amendment that allowed workers the right to a position according to their actual working time made the question of suitability more pressing:

"They enter through the back door, so to speak. If they are competent, that's ok. But I was inattentive once and ended up having to employ a worker who did not know her trade. She started out with very few hours per week, but now holds an 80% position. I should have been more careful, but at the time, the sickness–absence level had almost reached 30%, I needed people all the time and she always said yes." (Manager, nursing home)

The WEA amendments reduce employers' opportunities to keep workers on short part-time contracts as a strategy to fill gaps in the rota. As illustrated in the previous quote, some employers are concerned that this can lead to suboptimal hiring. To avoid this, they have adapted to the new rules in different ways that are not always in line with policymakers' intentions. One strategy is to prioritise students over other part-time employees when extra shifts need to be staffed. The use of students is preferable for several reasons: first, students of medicine or nursing will have many of the qualifications needed; second, senior students also have the authority to medicate patients; third, students seldom have the intention of securing a full-time position; and, fourth, students are often available during evenings and weekends. Hence, the manager is able to staff the rota with qualified staff and avoid situations where part-time workers do claim more contracted hours with reference to the WEA.

Employers also pursue other strategies to avoid losing control over the hiring process. In one municipality, several auxiliary nurses tried to secure longer hours with reference to the WEA. One manager describes how this made it important to pay close attention to how extra work was distributed:

> "If you are not alert and let them take on extra shifts throughout the year, they often become entitled to a position with more contracted hours. But in these cases [when they use the WEA amendment], we give them a shitty work schedule or send them to different institutions. They are entitled to longer hours, but not at one workplace."
> (Manager, nursing home)

The aforementioned 'shitty work schedule' usually means that the extra hours that the worker secures are mainly scheduled in the evenings and at weekends or, as in the previous example, at different workplaces. Employees often find it hard to move between different sites. It becomes more challenging to 'find your way around' in practical terms, to establish a good relationship with your colleagues and to get to know the patients and their particular needs. It is reasonable to expect that this employer practice deters workers considering using the WEA amendments to increase their working time.

In summary, from the employers' perspective, the changes to the WEA are often seen as a political effort to limit managerial prerogative and the potential for flexibility when it comes to employment and scheduling strategies. To counter this regulation of managerial power and flexibility, strategies are in use to minimise the effect of the policy measures. In particular, for auxiliary nurses and health-care assistants, who are less in demand than trained nurses, the possibility of getting extra shifts, and, in the end, more hours, has become more difficult due to restrictive employer behaviours.

Policy regulations and employees' responses

Unsocial hours are a key element in all debates on working time in the health-care sector. Although the principle is that all workers must do their share of work at evenings, nights and weekends, our interviews uncover that employees' capacity to influence their individual work schedules varies by occupational group:

> "My evening shifts start when my children come home from school and end at 10.30 pm. This is difficult for me because I have nobody else to care for the kids.... I have

requested to work only daytimes, but they [the employer] do not permit that. If I want to work full-time, I must do more evening shifts. So, I now have a 75% position and chase as many extra day shifts as possible. Each month I take on four to six extra shifts in order to earn enough." (Auxiliary nurse, nursing home)

The previous quote is from a single mother of two children aged eight and 13. To her, unsocial hours are a major obstacle to applying for more contracted hours because it would leave her children unattended during afternoons, evenings, nights and weekends. Although she experiences her part-time status as involuntary, she does not meet the statistical criteria for being an involuntary part-time worker.

Unsocial hours is pointed out as a main obstacle to full-time employment by trained nurses as well:

"When you work full-time in split shifts, your working-time schedule will never match the opening hours of the day nursery. We don't have any family to help us out. So, today, I work 50% nights and 25% daytime. It's a good solution for the family and it is financially beneficial due to the extra pay for night work." (Trained nurse, hospital)

At first glance, the situation of the auxiliary nurse and the trained nurse seem similar. They both work around 75% of full-time and identify work at unsocial hours as the main reason for their part-time status. However, if we take a closer look, their situations are different. Although they both work split shifts, only the trained nurse has been able to escape the evening shifts that they both see as a main obstacle due to care obligations. Moreover, the trained nurse prefers a larger share of night shifts and has managed to secure this. In contrast, the auxiliary nurse must 'do her share' of all types of shifts. Hardly any of the interviewed health-care assistants or auxiliary nurses had managed to reduce their number of unsocial hours without also reducing their overall working time.

The trained nurses have a better match between their preferences and their actual work contract – in terms of both the length and scheduling of working time. The employers confirm this difference and justify it by the stronger market position of the trained nurses. For this group, part-time work is mainly a voluntary strategy to achieve a better work–life balance.

'Extra shifts' were a popular topic among the involuntary part-time workers. Although access to extra shifts reduced following the changes to the WEA, there are still many understaffed shifts because of the high levels of sickness absence in the sector. To workers, the consequences of 'chasing' extra shifts are unpredictable income and a reduced quality of social life. A former refugee from Afghanistan and the mother of a pre-school boy describes a frustrating and long-lasting period of unpredictability and underemployment:

> "I am very tired from thinking about extra shifts all the time. I ask – 'How many days will I get next week?'. It has been like this for four-and-a-half years now and it's tiring. And not just for me, but for my family as well." (Auxiliary nurse, 18.7% position, nursing home)

Despite her many extra shifts, she had not approached her union representative or tried her case through the WEA amendment. She feared losing shifts that she depended on financially, and not being chosen when new positions become available. She had repeatedly asked her manager for longer hours but was encouraged to be patient and then 'something' would surely turn up.

In summary, unsocial hours are unavoidable for most workers in the health-care sector, which, for some, is a major obstacle to working longer hours or full-time. We do identify, however, a dualised practice when it comes to the distribution of unsocial hours among different occupational groups. This practice contributes to more short and involuntary part-time employment among health-care assistants and auxiliary nurses than among trained nurses. Low-educated workers have limited opportunities to negotiate a good match between preferred and actual working time, while simultaneously avoiding (too many) unsocial hours. In several cases, such mismatches lock the employee into involuntary part-time work. Their care obligations make it difficult for them to work the number of unsocial hours required to contract more hours. Although policymakers' adjustment of the labour law formally entitles employees to apply for an increase in contracted hours based on their extra work, workplace-level practices can make this difficult.

Increasing educational demands and immigration – workplace responses

The health-care sector has been an important port of entry into the labour market for workers with limited formal education. In 2012, approximately 38% of employees in the sector were unskilled. To increase the quality offered to users and to meet future demands, it is a political priority to reduce the level of unskilled workers.[2] However, while the long-term political ambition remains, labour shortages in the sector still provide unskilled and low-skilled workers with employment opportunities, although their power to negotiate their working conditions in general, and their hours of work in particular, is weak.

While the WEA amendments were introduced to reduce underemployment, there is a clear precedence for ruling in favour of the employer if it can be justified that the worker lacks formal education. A case brought before the DRB is illustrative. A health-care assistant was employed in an 8.8% position by a municipal home-care facility. Within a period of 12 months, she worked over 1,000 extra hours. For more than half of these hours, she was doing work that formally required education as either a nurse or an auxiliary nurse. The DRB concluded that these hours should *not* be included in her request for longer hours as her formal education did not reflect the employer's needs.

The health-care sector is also an important employment arena for migrants with limited or undocumented formal education. However, as the share of migrants increased, the need to formalise language requirements became more pressing. In a nursing home with a staff comprising more than 30 nationalities, the manager describes increasing communication problems. She argues that while most shifts can handle one worker with limited Norwegian-language skills, too many make it harder to staff shifts in a way that ensures adequate communication and therefore quality of care. Employees also sometimes find it difficult to communicate efficiently with colleagues, in particular, during hectic shifts. In Oslo, requirements for language skills are now regulated and strongly enforced. To secure a permanent position (with longer hours), workers must pass both oral and written Norwegian-language tests at the pre-academic level.[3] Most of the managers were clear on the need for all employees to master Norwegian: "We require that you have passed Norwegian-language tests at level three. You see, it is about communication. Either with old people, colleagues or with the patients' next of kin" (department manager, nursing home).

Employees who fail the language test face a formal barrier to securing regular employment contracts. To our knowledge, the requirements of documented Norwegian-language skills have not (yet) been tested against the WEA in cases where the worker is otherwise formally qualified. It is consequently not clear how the two relevant WEA paragraphs will rank against the recent municipal demands for documented language skills if a case is tried.[4] Even so, it seems clear that the policy ambition to ensure a high-quality service by 'raising the bar' in the sector also contributes to increased dualisation in the labour market.

Immigrants with formal education enter the labour market to a larger degree than immigrants with limited or no education (Connor, 2010). However, they are more often overqualified for their jobs (Villund, 2008; Aleksynska and Tritah, 2013), and discrimination in hiring processes is well documented (Midtbøen, 2015). Even though immigrants with high education seem to have lower returns for their education compared to natives, the positive link between formal education and paid employment is clear. In the case of trained nurses, our data suggest that formal education and Norwegian-language skills 'trump' ethnicity in terms of securing a 'good' part-time contract as long as the skill possessed is in demand. The following account from a Somalian nurse is illustrative of several of the interviews:

> "I have been offered a full-time position several times, but I prefer part-time. My mother lives in England with my sister – this way, I can visit them more often.... I do take on some extra shifts, but convert them to annual leave, rather than more money." (Trained nurse, nursing home)

In summary, while trained nurses are in high demand and can make use of the WEA amendments if needed, workers with limited education and/or undocumented Norwegian-language skills face multiple formal barriers that reduce their opportunities to make use of the WEA amendments, increase their working hours and move out of the 'bad' part-time category.

Discussion and conclusion

In this chapter, we explored how workplaces respond to policymakers' efforts to combat short and involuntary part-time employment through legal regulations. Our study suggests that the characteristics of the work organisation and the power relations in the sector are essential to understand how and why part-time work becomes dualised. Workers with low education and limited Norwegian-language skills are more exposed to bad part-time work. We also argue that 'bad' part-time work is not just defined as short and involuntary part-time employment. Low predictability due to the scheduling of working hours or the need to work at different locations also impact on the everyday lives of marginal part-time workers. Although some workers manage to increase their working time with reference to the new rules, the rules have not had the capacity to really modify where 'good' and 'bad' part-time contracts are distributed and to whom.

National intentions, workplace realities

The workplace-level examination uncovered mechanisms that undermine policymakers' efforts to combat involuntary part-time work for occupational groups with limited power resources. We therefore observe a mismatch between the policymakers' intentions and how the regulations are translated into practice at the workplace level. Our data provide examples of auxiliary nurses who have secured longer hours with reference to the WEA amendments. Most of these cases were tried with the assistance of trade union representatives. However, there are also auxiliary nurses and health-care assistants who are trapped in short and involuntary part-time employment. This is explained, in part, by employers' desire to maintain flexibility. Workers on short part-time contracts in the health-care sector have always worked extra shifts and thus provided flexibility. The 2013 WEA amendment entitles them to increase their contracted hours accordingly, but employers avoid implementing the WEA regulations towards less attractive workers by refusing them extra shifts. Moreover, the workplace perspective reveals that the distribution of unsocial hours interacts with part-time work in dualised ways. For the occupational groups with low formal skills, an increase in contracted hours would entail increasing the amount of work at nights and evenings. For single parents, the inflexibility in the distribution of unsocial hours locks them into part-time work and prevents them from utilising the WEA entitlements. According to the statistical definition, their part-time work is voluntary, and in the part-time typology (see Chapter 1), they would have to be categorised as 'semi-secured' or 'equalised' workers with working conditions and social conditions quite equal to those of full-timers. Our study shows, however, that they cannot be seen as labour market insiders. They struggle financially and would prefer to work more if they could. The workplace perspective illuminates that the divide between voluntary and involuntary part-time work is not clear-cut. Consequently, while part-time work is a way for some to facilitate work–family balance, the most exposed part-time workers face both time- and strain-based pressures that lead them into part-time work, and consequently financial pressures. In the Norwegian health-care sector, the flexibility strategy of employers is geared towards schedule control and is based on a principle of equity rather than the principle of equality (see Chapter 5). If pursuing the equality principle, employers would provide flexibility to meet the needs of workers with the most family demands. However, employers are not able to choose freely among the strategies. The increasing educational demands in the sector also limit the potential to reduce involuntary part-time work.

Explaining the gap between rules and practice

This study illustrates the potential and promise, but also the limits, of political measures in providing more workers with good jobs. Regulations have provided most Norwegian part-time workers with good working conditions and rights equal to full-time employees, but there are still 'pockets of precariousness' that seems hard to remove. Can institutional theory help us understand the implementation deficit? This chapter has shown that, despite its ambitions, labour law does not protect all workers equally. Dualisation theories point to the fact that certain institutional arrangements can even cause the unequal division of labour market vulnerability. In some cases, the WEA amendments made the most vulnerable workers more exposed by reducing their access to extra shifts. Institutional theory scholars highlight the role of actors in how institutions change. The traditional focus on workers and employers as the key actors in the transformation of labour market institutions does not fully capture why the new rules were not implemented. Workers cannot be analysed as one homogeneous group as they differ in their access to power resources. This affects their capacity to enforce the rules. By focusing on the workplace level, we have captured how the skewed implementation is, in fact, produced in the relationship between employees and occupational groups with different power resources.

By applying a workplace perspective, we have found that employers interpret the labour law changes as attempts to limit the prerogative and power of management. While workers with sufficient power resources have been able to use the WEA amendments to their advantage, employers' opportunistic adaptation to the new policy has affected workers with limited power resources in a negative way. The result is a more dualised employer approach towards different occupational groups. Despite policymakers' efforts, the divide between 'good' and 'bad' part-time work in the health-care sector persists, and involuntary part-time work is still most manifest among the most marginalised workers.

Acknowledgement

The project is funded by the Research Council of Norway's programme on welfare, working life and migration (VAM), grant number 237031.

Notes

[1] Since 1982 and 2005, however, the WEA has allowed people to work part-time if they have young children or other care obligations (Sections 46A, 49), or poor health conditions and so on (Sections 10.2, fourth section, and 10-6, 10th section).

[2] White Paper 13 (2011–12) 'Education for welfare', p 29 (in Norwegian).

[3] A level that qualifies for enrolment in higher education (university or university college).

[4] So far, 351 cases have been brought before the DRB (RB 29/12-2017).

References

Aleksynska, M. and Tritah, A. (2013) 'Occupation–education mismatch of immigrant workers in Europe: context and policies', *Economics of Education Review*, 36: 229–44.

Alsos, K. and Bråten, M. (2011) 'Tvisteløsningsnemndas praksis i saker om fortrinnsrett for deltidsansatte', Fafo-rapport 2011:31, Oslo.

Borum, F. (1995) *Organization, power and change*, København: Handelshøjskolens forlag.

Bosch, G. (2006) 'Working time and the standard employment relationship', in J.-Y. Boulin, M. Lallement, J.C. Messenger and F. Michon (eds) *Decent working time. New trends, new issues*, Geneva: International Labour Organization.

Connor, P. (2010) 'Explaining the refugee gap: economic outcomes of refugees versus other immigrants', *Journal of Refugee Studies*, 23: 377–97.

Crouch, C. (1982) *Trade unions: the logic of collective action*, Glasgow: Fontana.

Ellingsæter, A.L. (1989) *Normalisering av deltidsarbeidet: en analyse av endring i kvinners yrkesaktivitet og arbeidstid i 80-årene*, Oslo/Kongsvinger: Statistisk sentralbyrå.

Ellingsæter, A.L. (2017) *Vår tids moderne tider: det norske arbeidstidsregimet*, Oslo: Universitetsforlaget.

Ellingsæter, A.L., Kitterød, R.H. and Lyngstad, J. (2017) 'Universalising childcare, changing mothers' attitudes: policy feedback in Norway', *Journal of Social Policy*, 46: 149–73.

Emmenegger, P., Häusermann, S., Palier, B. and Seeleib-Kaiser, M. (2012) 'How we grow unequal', in P. Emmenegger, S. Häusermann, B. Palier and M. Seeleib-Kaiser (eds) *The age of dualization: the changing face of inequality in deindustrializing societies*, Oxford: Oxford University Press.

Eurofound (2017) *In-work poverty in the EU*, Luxembourg: Publications Office of the European Union.

Fagan, C., Lyonette, C., Smith, M. and Saldaña-Tejeda, A. (2012) *The influence of working time arrangements on work–life integration or 'balance': a review of the international evidence*, Geneva: ILO.

Haipeter, T. (2006) 'Can norms survive market pressures? The practical effectiveness of new forms of working time regulation in a changing German economy', in J.-Y. Boulin (ed) *Decent working time: new trends, new issues*, Geneva: International Labour Organization.

Ilsøe, A. (2016) 'From living wage to living hours – the Nordic version of the working poor', *Labour & Industry: A Journal of the Social and Economic Relations of Work*, 26: 40–57.

Kalleberg, A.L. (2011) *Good jobs, bad jobs*, New York, NY: Russell Sage Foundation.

Kanbur, R. and Ronconi, L. (2016) 'Enforcement matters: the effective regulation of labor', *International Labour Review*, 1579(3): 331–56.

Mahoney, J. and Thelen, K. (eds) (2010) *Explaining institutional change*, Cambridge: Cambridge University Press.

Merton, R.K. (1996) *On social structure and science*, Chicago, IL: University of Chicago Press.

Meyer, J.W. and Rowan, B. (1977) 'Institutionalized organizations: formal structure as myth and ceremony', *American Journal of Sociology*, 83: 340–63.

Midtbøen, A.H. (2015) 'Etnisk diskriminering i arbeidsmarkedet', *Tidsskrift for samfunnsforskning*, 56(1): 4-30.

Mósesdóttir, L. and Ellingsæter, A.L. (2017) 'Ideational struggles over women's part-time work in Norway: destabilizing the gender contract', *Economic and Industrial Democracy*. Available at https://doi.org/10.1177/0143831X16681483.

Nergaard, K. (2016) 'Utbredelsen av deltid og ulike arbeidstidsordninger', in I.K. Ingstad (ed) *Turnus som fremmer heltidskultur*. Oslo: Gyldendal Norsk Forlag, pp 39–55.

Nicolaisen, H. and Trygstad, S.C. (2015) 'Preventing dualization the hard way – regulating the Norwegian labour market', in F. Engelstad and A. Hagelund (eds) *Cooperation and conflict the Nordic way: Work, welfare, and institutional change in Scandinavia*, Berlin and Boston, MA: Sciendo Migration and De Gruyter.

Pfeffer, J. (1981) *Power in organizations*, Marshfield, MA: Pitman Publishing Inc.

Pierson, P. (2004) *Politics in time: History, institutions and social analysis*, Princeton: Princeton University Press.

Refslund, B. and Thörnquist, A. (2016) 'Intra-European labour migration and low-wage competition – comparing the Danish and Swedish experiences across three sectors', *Industrial Relations Journal*, 47: 62–78.

Scheuer, S. (1986) *Fagforeninger mellem kollektiv og profession*, København: Nyt fra Samfunsvidenskaberne.

Scott, W.R. (2014) *Institutions and organizations: ideas, interests, and identities*, London: Sage Publications.

Selznick, P. (1997) *Lederskap*, Oslo: Tano Aschehoug.

Steiber, N. (2009) 'Reported levels of time-based and strain-based conflict between work and family roles in Europe: a multilevel approach', *Social Indicators Research*, 93: 469–88.

Sullivan, O. (1996) 'Time co-ordination, the domestic division of labour and affective relations: time use and the enjoyment of activities within couples', *Sociology*, 30: 79–100.

Tomlinson, J. (2006) 'Part-time occupational mobility in the service industries: regulation, work commitment and occupational closure', *The Sociological Review*, 54: 66–86.

Trygstad, S.C. (2017) 'Opposing forces: on whistleblowing in Norwegian working life', in F. Engelstad, H. Larsen, J. Rogstad and K. Steen-Johnsen (eds) *Institutional change in the public sphere: views on the Nordic model*, Warsaw: De Gruyter Open.

Trygstad, S.C., Ødegård, A.M., Skivenes, M. and Svarstad, E. (2017) *Fafo-rapport 2017: 04*, Oslo: Fafo. Available at: www.fafo.no/index. php/en/publications/fafo-reports/item/ytringsfrihet-og-varsling-i-norske-kommuner-og-fylkeskommuner-3

Villund, O. (2008) 'Riktig yrke etter utdanning?', Rapporter 2008/37, Oslo: Statistisk sentralbyrå.

Vosko, L.F. (2010) *Managing the margins: Gender, citizenship, and the international regulation of precarious employment*, New York, NY: Oxford University Press.

Warren, T. (2003) 'Class and gender-based working time? Time poverty and the division of domestic labour', *Sociology*, 37: 733–52.

Appendix

Table 4A.1: Working time among women (25–59 years), by occupation and region of origin (%)

	Norway/ Nordic	Asia	Africa	Eastern Europe	Western Europe	Other	Total
Trained nurse							
Short part-time	13.8%	12.0%	10.2%	9.1%	13.5%	12.6%	13.6%
Long part-time	31.4%	21.4%	27.4%	25.1%	29.0%	31.4%	30.9%
Full-time	54.8%	66.6%	62.4%	65.8%	57.5%	55.9%	55.5%
N	50,956	1,626	402	1,076	1,373	388	55,821
Auxiliary nurse							
Short part-time	24.2%	19.5%	25.7%	22.4%	21.1%	22.6%	24.0%
Long part-time	38.2%	28.9%	31.2%	27.8%	31.8%	36.8%	37.5%
Full-time	37.6%	51.7%	43.1%	49.8%	47.1%	40.6%	38.5%
N	58,514	2,435	1,021	424	1,522	584	64,500
Healthcare assistant							
Short part-time	46.0%	40.2%	43.8%	40.4%	41.6%	47.7%	45.2%
Long part-time	31.1%	29.7%	32.0%	33.7%	30.2%	31.6%	31.1%
Full-time	22.9%	30.0%	24.1%	26.0%	28.1%	20.7%	23.6%
N	21,766	1,682	1,143	627	992	392	26,602

Source: Register data for 2013, Statistics Norway.

PART TWO
The quality of working conditions and part-time work

5

Part-time working women's access to other types of flexible working-time arrangements across Europe

Heejung Chung

Introduction

One of the commonly used strategies for mothers to combine paid work with family life is to reduce their working hours and move to a part-time job (Stier et al, 2001; Visser, 2002). Part-time working allows mothers to address the demands of family life while maintaining their links to the labour market by reducing the demands coming from work. In addition to reducing hours, there are other flexible working arrangements that are increasingly being used to address work–family integration (Eurofound, 2015; Chung, 2018a). Of the various flexible working arrangements, this chapter focuses on the control that workers have over their work schedules to accommodate family demands, that is, flexitime, including flexibility in starting and ending the time of one's work, varying working hours across days or weeks, being able to accumulate hours to take days off (annualised hours), and time off work – the ability to take a couple of hours off work to tend to personal and family demands. Studies have shown that such schedule flexibility can allow workers a better balance between work and home life (Michel et al, 2011; Allen et al, 2013), as well as enable parents to extend their parenting time (Noonan et al, 2007; Craig and Powell, 2012).

Despite the large number of studies that deal with part-time working (O'Reilly and Fagan, 1998; Tomlinson, 2007; Connolly and Gregory, 2008) and schedule control (eg Chung, 2019b; Golden et al, 2018), rarely do studies examine the two together. Further, we have yet to see whether these arrangements are complementary or used as substitutions. In light of dualisation and the insider/outsider argument (Emmenegger et al, 2012; Schwander and Häusermann, 2013; see also Chapter 1, this volume), as well as the gendered high-status rewards argument (Schieman et al, 2013), we can assume that part-time workers, and especially women working part-time, will be less likely to gain access to and use flexible working arrangements (Swanberg et al, 2005). Also, flexible working can perhaps be used as a substitute for reduction of hours (Chung and Van der Horst, 2018a). In other words, when women are able to access other types of flexible working arrangements, they do not have to reduce their working hours to meet their family needs. On the other hand, there may be complementarity in the use of different types of flexible working arrangement, where part-time working is used alongside flexible work patterns to allow for a better work–life balance. This may be because reducing working hours or working part-time may already signal a person's need to adjust their work to meet family demands, making them less likely to fear the 'flexibility stigma' (Williams et al, 2013; Chung, 2018b) – ie the stigma workers face due to working flexibly for care purposes – as well as making employers more aware of their needs. We consider this the Matthew effect of flexible working, meaning that those who are working flexibly (through a reduction of hours) gain more flexibility in their work. Finally, the question arises as to whether the position of part-time working women is the same across different European countries. Dualisation theory scholars have argued that the strength of the barrier between the insider and outsider market, as well as the gaps in the labour conditions between insiders and outsiders, vary across countries (Schwander and Häusermann, 2013; Biegert, 2014; Chung, 2016). Thus, we can also expect that part-time working women's access to flexible working arrangements may vary across countries due to the differences in their relative position in the labour market.

These questions will be answered through the use of the European Working Conditions Survey of 2015 and a multilevel random slopes model focusing only on women. The reason why we focus on women is because the reasons for working part-time may be different for men and women, and part-time work is still a very female phenomenon (see also Chapter 1, this volume). The main question asked in this chapter is thus whether part-time working women are more likely to access other types of flexible working-time arrangements compared to their full-time counterparts, and whether their relative access varies across countries due to institutional contexts. The next section explains what is meant by flexible working-time arrangements and examines key literature and theories. The third section examines the data, the variables used and the methodologies applied in the chapter. The fourth section will present the analysis results, before making some final concluding remarks and suggestions for future studies.

Background

Definitions

Flexible schedules or schedule control is when employees are given control over *when* they work (Glass and Estes, 1997; Kelly et al, 2011) and is one of the most commonly used type of flexible working-time arrangements in Europe. This is to be distinguished from flexible working-time arrangements that allow changes in *how much* employees work, including part-time working and a temporary reduction of hours, which has been a main focus of working-time arrangements in the work–life balance literature. Flexitime entails workers' control over the timing of their work (ie to alternate the starting and ending times). Flexitime can potentially result in time banking, where workers can take days off due to accumulated overtime hours. Working-time autonomy is when workers are free to work whenever (and, in some cases, how long) they want. Time off work entails workers' ability to take time off during working hours to meet personal demands. Work–family border theory (Clark, 2000) and flexibility enactment theory (Kossek et al, 2005) suggest that having control over one's work schedule can help facilitate the integration of work and home roles (Golden, 2008). The flexibility in the border between work and family allows workers to adapt the borders of one domain around the demands of others – in this case, adapting the timing of work to fit around family and other personal demands. Due to this, having control over your schedule has been shown to relieve work–family conflict, that is, the conflict workers feel due to the competing demands coming from work and family (eg Chung, 2011; Kelly et al, 2014), although others have argued that the effect is rather minimal (for a review, see Allen et al, 2013; Michel et al, 2011; Chung, 2017).

Schedule control is used not only to increase the family-friendliness of a company, but also to enhance their performance outcomes (Ortega, 2009; Brescoll et al, 2013; Den Dulk et al, 2013). The high-performance or high-involvement strategy approach argues that when workers have more control or discretion over their work, this will increase their performance outcomes (Appelbaum, 2000; Davis and Kalleberg, 2006). Schedule control can be implemented as part of such a performance-enhancing strategy, especially when given to workers in higher-status positions (Schieman et al, 2013) and or to high-skilled/high-occupational groups, where employers expect more returns from their investment (Swanberg et al, 2005).

Part-time workers' access to flexible working-time arrangements

The link between part-time working status and access to other types of flexible working arrangements/schedule control will largely depend on the nature of part-time work, but also on the nature of flexible working arrangements. In particular, we can distinguish between three principles that employers may use to decide on who gets access to flexible working arrangements, namely, principles of need, equity and equality (Lambert and Haley-Lock, 2004; Swanberg et al, 2005). When employers are genuinely interested in addressing the work–life balance needs of workers, those with most family demands or most need for flexible working arrangements are most likely to get access. On the contrary, when employers are more interested in the enhanced performance outcomes gained from introducing schedule control (the principle of equity), those who are more likely to increase their productivity through schedule control, may it be through increasing their work intensity/hours (Lott and Chung, 2016; Chung and van der Horst, 2018b) or contributing to the organisation through other means, will have more access. Lastly, when the equality principle takes precedence, access to schedule control will be provided to all workers equally regardless of their care needs or anticipated performance outcomes.

When employers largely provide flexible working arrangements based on the need principle, part-time workers may be more likely to have access to flexible working arrangements (H1a). First, by reducing their working hours, part-time working women may already signal to employers their need to adjust their work to family demands, allowing employers to make such arrangements available to them. This may also make them less likely to fear the flexibility stigma (Williams et al, 2013), that is, the stigma faced by workers when they deviate from the ideal worker status of perpetually working and prioritising work first. In other words, part-time workers may not fear the further negative consequences of using flexible working arrangements in addition to the ones that they may already face by working part-time (see Chung, 2018b). Lastly, by working part-time, it may be easier to have varying shifts of work that are flexible, through flexitime, yet fit within the boundaries of the 'normal working hours' of their full-time co-workers. In other words, when a worker works four hours a day, it may not make a large difference whether they start at 9am or 10am since they will end before their full-time co-workers finish their work. This may not be the case for a full-time worker, where it may be more difficult to shift their start time to an hour earlier if it comes into conflict with the company's operating hours/core hours.

However, when companies mainly provide flexible working arrangements based on the principle of equity, we can assume that women working part-time will be less likely to gain access and use flexible working arrangements (H1b). The dualisation literature posits that part-time workers can be considered outsiders in the labour market (Rueda, 2005), working in 'dead-end' unstable jobs, with low-pay, bad working conditions, few career advancement prospects and frequent layoffs (Doeringer and Piore, 1975; Rueda, 2014). On the other hand, workers in the primary sector, the 'insiders', enjoy high wages, good working conditions, prospects for career advancement and, most importantly, job stability. In most cases across Europe, part-time work is more commonly found in the low-paid low-occupational groups (Connolly and Gregory, 2008). Thus, when the goal of providing flexible working arrangements is to increase performance outcomes, or is provided as a reward, part-time workers will be less likely to have access to such arrangements. We could, however, expect that once we control for occupations and education levels, this relationship will disappear somewhat.

Another reason why part-time workers may be less likely to have access to or use flexible working arrangements is because they may already be addressing their work–life balance need through reduced working hours. Chung and Van der Horst (2018a) provide evidence to show how flexible working arrangements may be used as substitutes for a reduction of hours by mothers, that is, women with flexible working arrangements are less likely to reduce their working hours post-childbirth. Putting it differently, those who have reduced their working hours may not need to work flexibly because their work–life balance needs have already been met by their reduction in hours.

Although the issue of the substitution and complementarity of part-time work and flexible working arrangements has not been examined, some studies link access to flexible working arrangements to working hours. Some cross-sectional studies have shown a U-shaped relationship between flexible working arrangements and working hours, that is, use of and access to flexible working arrangements are positively associated with both long hours (50/60+) (Drago et al, 2005; Lyness et al, 2012) and shorter hours (Golden, 2009; Chung, 2019b), while some studies show no clear relationship at all (Chung, 2019a). However, the majority of these studies have been based in the US and, to the author's knowledge, no study has examined cross-national variation in the relative access that part-time workers have to flexible working arrangements.

Cross-national variation in the position of part-time workers

Previous studies have shown that the level of dualisation of the labour market varies across countries, with the division between insiders and outsiders being larger and more pronounced in some countries and smaller in others (Schwander and Häusermann, 2013; Biegert, 2014; Chung, 2016). Similarly, part-time workers' relative access to flexible working arrangements, compared to full-time workers, should be expected to be different across different countries (H2). This is mainly because part-time work entails different labour market positions depending on the country, and the protective mechanisms provided by the legal system regarding the working conditions of part-time workers (again, relative to those of full-time workers) vary across different countries (see also Anxo et al, 2007).

Of the various relevant factors, three contextual factors may be of most relevance when examining the relative position of part-time workers in their access to flexible working-time arrangements. First, the division between part-time and full-time workers is expected to be lower in countries where part-time work is prevalent (H3.1). In countries where part-time work is a norm for most women, their relative position to full-time workers may not be as bad when compared to countries where part-time work is centred on a relatively specific proportion of the workforce. In other words, the more part-time work is normalised, the better the position of part-time workers may be (see also van der Lippe and Lippényi, 2018).

Second, union strength and centralisation may be of relevance. According to the power resource theory, the power that is mobilised by wage-earners can influence welfare state development (Korpi, 1989). Palier and Thelen (2010) argue that traditionally strong coordinated unions contribute to the diffusion, generalisation and institutionalisation of good working conditions within the wider population, reducing inequalities between different groups of workers. Similarly, the power resources of unions may influence employers in providing family-friendly benefits at the company level. Several studies have shown that collective bargaining coverage rates and union density is positively associated with the provision of flexible working-time arrangements at the company level (Berg et al, 2004; Chung, 2009; Lyness et al, 2012; Präg and Mills, 2014). From this, we can expect a smaller gap between part-time and full-time workers in their access to flexible working arrangements in countries with strong and centralised unions (H3.2a). However, other studies have also noted that it is especially in corporatist countries with strong and centralised unions that dualism in the labour market has developed. Strong centralised unions were successful in protecting insiders from the pressures of labour-shedding strategies through negotiations with employers while allowing them to increase flexibility on the secondary market in a so-called 'dual reform' (Ebbinghaus and Eichhorst, 2007; Palier and Thelen, 2010; Davidsson and Emmenegger, 2013). These countries are those where the gaps between different segments of the labour markets are more pronounced (Biegert, 2014; Chung, 2016). In this case, corporatist countries with stronger and more centralised unions may be where the position of part-time workers is also the weakest in relation to their access to better working conditions (H3.2b).

Third, family policies at the national level may also be relevant in explaining who gets access to flexible working arrangements. 'Crowding out' theory argues that national-level policies will crowd out lower-level welfare arrangements (Etzioni, 1995), in other words, companies will not provide company-level family-friendly policies when there are generous policies at the national level. The counter-argument to this comes from the 'crowding in' theory (eg Künemund and Rein, 1999; Van Oorschot and Arts, 2005; Chung, 2019a), arguing a positive, rather than negative, relationship between generous national-level policy and occupational welfare. This may be because institutions, laws and policies put pressure on organisations to become similar to national institutions (DiMaggio and Powell, 1983). Based on this theory, we can expect that when there are generous national-level family policies, this will raise the benchmark and change the culture that companies operate in, making them more likely to provide company-level family-friendly policies. Been et al (2017) argue that when generous national-level family policies exist, company-level family-friendly arrangements are also considered more as general terms of employment, and managers are more likely to provide them across the board to all workers equally. Following from this, we could expect that part-time workers will have equal access to flexible working-time arrangements in countries with generous family policies (H3.3a). On the other hand, Chung (2018a, 2019a) argues that companies 'crowd-in' occupational welfare more for the more profitable workers given the added incentive of keeping and recruiting these workers. In this case, we could expect employers to be more likely to provide these arrangements to full-time core workers, increasing the division between part-time and full-time working women in countries with generous family policy arrangements (H3.3b).

Data and methods

Data

The European Working Conditions Survey (EWCS) of 2015 is used for the purposes of this analysis. Individuals across the EU28 and five candidate countries are surveyed on a number of working conditions items. In this chapter, for comparability issues, the EU28 countries plus Norway and Switzerland are used. A random stratified sampling procedure was used to gather a representative sample of those aged 15 or over and in employment (a minimum of one hour a week) at the time of the survey, which was conducted through face-to-face interviews. Approximately 1,000 cases are included per country, with varying response rates. Of the total sample, I restrict the analysis to those in dependent employment, and further exclude those in the armed forces and agriculture/fishery due to the specific nature of these jobs. Flexible working-time arrangements are used by men and women for different purposes (Clawson and Gerstel, 2014), and can also lead to different outcomes (Lott, 2015; Chung and van der Lippe, 2018). Thus, I only focus on female workers. The analysis further excludes workers over the retirement age of 65 and all cases missing any one of the variables in the model, resulting in 13,283 cases across 30 countries (for more information, see: www.eurofound.europa.eu/surveys/european-working-conditions-surveys).

Dependent variable

The chapter examines workers' access to family-friendly working-time arrangements. The provision of flexitime was measured through the following question: 'How are your working-time arrangements set?'. Workers could answer 1 ('They are set by the company/organisation, with no possibility for changes'), 2 ('You can choose between several fixed working schedules determined by the company/organisation'), 3 ('You can adapt your working hours within certain limits [eg flexitime]') and 4 ('Your working hours are entirely determined by yourself'). Those who have answered 3 or 4 to this question are considered to have flexitime. Second, time off work for personal reasons was measured through the question 'Would you say that for you arranging to take an hour or two off during working hours to take care of personal or family matters is …', where respondents could answer 'very easy', 'fairly easy', 'fairly difficult' and 'very difficult'. Those who answered the first two categories are included as having the ability to take time off work.

Independent variables

The key independent variable is workers' part-time contract status. To distinguish between short and long part-time work, those working fewer than 20 hours a week are considered as short part-timers, those working between 20 and 34 hours a week as long part-time workers, those working between 35 and 47 hours a week as full-time workers, and anyone working longer than 48 hours a week as those working long hours.

Based on previous studies (eg Chung, 2018a, 2019a; Wiß, 2017), the following variables are included as controls: the respondent's age; whether the respondent lives with a partner; the respondent's parental status, that is, whether or not the respondent lives with a child under 18 years of age, as well as whether the respondent lives with a preschool child under six years of age; whether the respondent has care responsibilities for the elderly; the respondent's occupation; the respondent's education level; whether the respondent holds a supervisory role; the existence of an employee representative at the company; management support; the gender of the direct manager; the gender dominance of the post; whether the respondent has an open-ended contract, as well as their subjective job-insecurity perspective; and, finally, the size and sector of the company that the respondent works in (public versus private, as well as the line of business, with the reference group being 'commerce and hospitality').

At the national level, context variables include the size of the part-time employment of women (as a percentage of the total dependent employed). In order to measure union bargaining power and structure, union density and the collective bargaining coverage rate are used, both represented as a percentage of wage-earners – which indicate bargaining power and, to a certain degree, corporatism. These variables are derived from the ICTWSS data set 5.1 and are for 2013 or the closest year available due to the lack of data. Family policy is measured, first, through public expenditure on family policies as a percentage of gross domestic product (GDP) and, second, through the proportion of children (aged three and under) using formal childcare, indicating work-facilitating measures (Misra et al, 2011), which has been shown to be most important in determining workers' access to flexible working-time arrangements (see also Chung, 2018a, 2019a). All data are for 2015 or the closest year available. All context variables have been centred and standardised for the models.

Method

Random-slope multilevel regression models are used for the purposes of this chapter. Multilevel modelling assumes that the data are hierarchical and that individuals are subject to the influences of country-level characteristics. In this chapter, to test H1, the empty model is examined before moving on to the multivariate analysis to see the influence of the individual- (and company-)level characteristics that can explain part-time working women's access to flexible working arrangements. Next, random-slope models are used to test the varying impact of short and long part-time statuses across different countries (H2). A significant variance in the random slope entails that there are significant differences across countries in the relative access that short and long part-time workers have to flexible working arrangements compared to that of full-time workers. Finally, cross-level interaction terms with the five national-level variables and part-time contract status are included to test H3. STATA 15.0 meqrlogit is used for the analysis.

Results

Descriptive results

As shown in Figure 5.1, there are large variances across countries in the access that part-time women have to flexitime. In general, in Northern European countries, part-time women have good access to flexitime, while in some Southern European and Baltic countries, access is restricted. As for the European average, the gap between full-time and part-time working women in their access to flexitime is not very large, with part-time workers having a slight advantage (at 27%) compared to full-time workers (at 23%). However, the access gap between part-time and full-time workers varies significantly across countries – in Norway, Sweden and Denmark, although part-time working women have good access to flexitime, it is much lower than that for full-time working women. On the other hand, in Bulgaria, Lithuania, Romania, Greece and Cyprus, although part-time working women's access to flexitime is restricted, it is much better than that for their full-time working counterparts.

Examining women's access to time off work (see Figure 5.2), on average, full-time workers are much more likely to have access. However, again, the gap between full- and part-time working women varies across countries, although not as much as that for flexitime. The

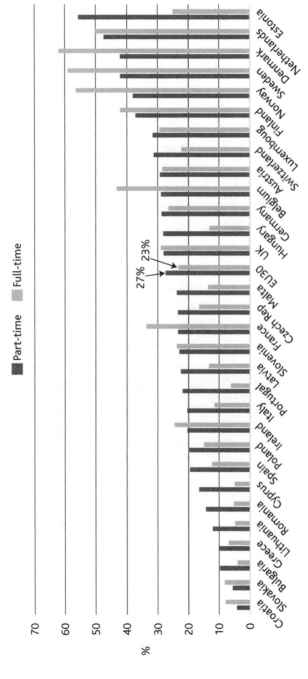

Figure 5.1: Part-time versus full-time working women's access to flexitime across 30 European countries

Note: Part-time = less than 35 hours a week.

Source: Weighted averages from the 2015 EWCS (available via the UK data archive: https://beta.ukdataservice.ac.uk/datacatalogue/systems-upgrade)

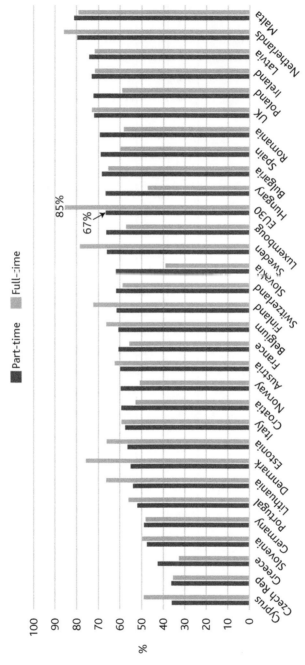

Figure 5.2: Part-time versus full-time working women's access to time off work across 30 European countries

Note: Part-time = less than 35 hours a week.

Source: Weighted averages from the 2015 EWCS (available via the UK data archive: https://beta.ukdataservice.ac.uk/datacatalogue/systems-upgrade)

country ranking in the access that women have to these arrangements is not as clear-cut as that shown for flexitime. Countries such as Malta, the Netherlands, Latvia, Ireland, Poland and the UK are where part-time working women have good access to time off work for personal issues. On the other hand, again, Cyprus and Greece, but now also including the Czech Republic and Germany, are the countries where part-time working women's access to time off work is restricted. However, these figures do not take other characteristics into account; thus, a multivariate analysis is needed.

Multivariate results

Part-time working women's access to flexible working-time arrangements

As shown in Table 5.1, when we control for a whole range of other factors, we generally find a U-shaped pattern in the access to flexitime and working hours. In general, those working part-time, especially those working shorter part-time (less than 20 hours a week), are more likely to have access to flexitime compared to those working full-time (ie 35–47 hours a week). However, those who work long hours (48 hours or more) are much more likely to have access to flexitime. In comparison, once other factors were taken into account, there were no significant differences between full-time and part-time working women in their access to time off work for personal reasons. Those working long hours were significantly less likely to have access to time off work.

Cross-national variance in part-time working women's access to flexible working-time arrangements

Hypothesis 2 expected that there to be cross-national variation in the degree to which part-time working women's access to flexible working-time arrangements were different to that of full-time working women. To test for this, random-slope models for the short and long part-time work variables were ran for each of the dependent variables, that is, access to flexitime and time off work. The results showed that there was no significant cross-national variance in the relative position of part-time working women's access to time off work (short part-time variance = 0.073, p = 0.285; long part-time variance = 0.028, p = 0.418). However, there was (marginally) significant cross-national variation in the relative position of short and long part-time workers in

Table 5.1: Explaining women's access to flexible working-time arrangements across 30 European countries in 2015

	Flexitime		Time off work	
	Coefficient	S.E.	Coefficient	S.E.
Working hours (ref: full-time 35–47)				
Short part-time (1–19)	0.404***	0.084	0.038	0.074
Long part-time (20–34)	0.177**	0.06	0.048	0.051
Long hours (48+)	0.715***	0.095	−0.345***	0.076
Age	0.006**	0.002	0.007***	0.002
Partner	0.005	0.051	0.038	0.042
Youngest child <6	0.298***	0.073	−0.068+	0.063
Youngest child 6–12	0.090	0.067	−0.100	0.056
Elderly care responsibility	0.155**	0.059	−0.059	0.049
Supervisory role	0.442***	0.07	0.103	0.066
Education level (ref: upper secondary)				
Lower secondary or below	−0.226**	0.088	−0.020	0.067
Tertiary educated	0.361***	0.059	−0.060	0.052
Employee rep in workplace	−0.013	0.060	−0.100*	0.049
Management support	0.279***	0.051	0.724***	0.041
Direct boss woman	0.013	0.051	−0.100*	0.042
Workplace composition (ref: equal share of men and women)				
Mostly men w/ same position	−0.102	0.086	0.157+	0.081
Mostly women w/ same position	−0.453***	0.053	−0.197***	0.046
Open ended contract	−0.132+	0.07	0.078	0.056
Job insecurity	−0.253***	0.071	−0.298***	0.055
Public company	−0.257***	0.066	−0.081	0.056
Size of company (ref: large companies 250+)				
Micro company <10	−0.021	0.076	0.214***	0.064
SME 10–249	−0.313***	0.056	0.090+	0.048
Occupational levels (ref: service and sales workers)				
Managers	1.264***	0.121	1.022***	0.129
Professionals	0.697***	0.085	0.236***	0.069
Associate professionals and technicians	0.633***	0.084	0.521***	0.071
Clerical support workers	0.552***	0.085	0.538***	0.072
Crafts and related trades workers	−0.035	0.188	0.127	0.126
Plant and machine operators	−0.465*	0.210	−0.046	0.131
Elementary occupations	0.051	0.102	0.485***	0.077
Sectors (ref: commerce and hospitality)				
Industry	0.126	0.098	0.339***	0.082
Transport	−0.302+	0.158	−0.327**	0.123
Financial services	0.516***	0.118	0.270*	0.112
Public administration	0.899***	0.117	0.653***	0.109

(continued)

Table 5.1: Explaining women's access to flexible working-time arrangements across 30 European countries in 2015 (continued)

	Flexitime		Time off work	
	Coefficient	S.E.	Coefficient	S.E.
Sectors (ref: commerce and hospitality) (continued)				
Education	–0.492***	0.111	–0.105	0.086
Health social services	–0.379***	0.091	–0.210**	0.072
Other services	0.578***	0.080	0.452***	0.068
Cons	–2.181***	0.235	–0.501***	0.153
Variance level 2	1.027***	0.275	0.297***	0.081
ICC	0.217		0.069	
Explained variance level 2 from the empty model	–12.40%		–22.20%	
Log likelihood	–5951.03		–8080.02	

Notes: N level 1 = 13,283, N level 2 = 30 countries. *** = $p < 0.001$; ** = $p < 0.010$; * = $p < 0.050$; + = $p < 0.100$.

Source: EWCS 2015 (available via the UK data archive: https://beta.ukdataservice.ac.uk/datacatalogue/studies/study?id=8098)

their access to flexitime (short part-time variance = 0.174, $p = 0.074$; long part-time variance = 0.263, $p = 0.025$). The rest of this chapter focuses on the results for longer part-time working women's position but the results are similar to those for shorter part-time working women (results available upon request).

Table 5.2 examines how country-level variables explain variation in part-time working women's relative access to flexitime across countries. As shown in Table 5.2, in countries where part-time contracts are prevalent among women, or there is high collective bargaining coverage, or there is high union density, or there are generous family policies, women generally have better access to flexitime. However, this increase in access is significantly lower for part-time working women. On average, women working long part-time have better access to flexitime compared to full-time working women. However, in countries with above average (about one standard deviation more) levels of any one of the context variables listed above, there is no gap between these two groups of workers. Again, this is largely due to the fact that as union strength, family policy generosity and the proportion of part-time working women increase, full-time working women's access to flexitime increases significantly, while this is not the case for part-time working women. In countries with very high levels of any one of these context variables, the relative gap flips over, so that full-time working women are more likely to have access to flexitime compared to part-time working women. Of the context variables, it is

Table 5.2: Multilevel results explaining the cross-national variance between part-time and full-time female workers in their access to flexitime across 30 European countries in 2015

Flexitime/model	2–1	2–2	2–3	2–4	2–5
Individual-level variable[a]					
Part-time	0.378***	0.339***	0.360***	0.371***	0.362***
Country-level variables[b]					
% of part-time workers	0.700***				
Collective bargaining coverage		0.657***			
Union density			0.517*		
Family policy expenditure				0.706***	
Childcare coverage (0–3)					0.770***
Interactions					
Part-time*% of part-time workers	−0.315***				
Part-time*collective bargaining coverage		−0.403***			
Part-time*union density			−0.303***		
Part-time*family expenditure				−0.343***	
Part-time*childcare coverage					−0.371***
Constant	−2.179***	−2.146***	−2.231***	−2.218***	−2.152***
Var. random slope	0.163*	0.110+	0.162*	0.101	0.097
R^2 random slope	38.1%	58.3%	38.4%	61.7%	62.9%
Log likelihood[c]	−5926.0891**	−5924.5614***	−5930.7149*	−5924.066***	−5920.0293***

Notes: N level 1 = 13,283; N level 2 = 30 countries. [a] The models include all variables included in Model 1 in Table 5.1. [b] All context variables have been standardised. [c] Significance symbols represents the significant increase in log likelihood scores from the nested model (random slopes without interactions). Part-time = Long part-time work (20–34h/w). *** = $p < 0.001$; ** = $p < 0.010$; * = $p < 0.050$; + = $p < 0.100$.

Source: EWCS 2015 (available via the UK data archive: https://beta.ukdataservice.ac.uk/datacatalogue/studies/study?id=8098)

collective bargaining coverage, family policy expenditure and childcare coverage that are most influential, each variable explaining up to two thirds of the total cross-national variance of part-time workers' relative access to flexitime.

Other factors explaining access to flexible working-time arrangements

In addition to working hours, we find that older workers (probably with more work experience), those with higher skills (higher education and higher occupational levels) and those in supervisory roles are more likely to have access to flexitime. Having preschool children and elderly care responsibilities increased women's access to flexitime. Interestingly, permanent contract status slightly reduced the likelihood of getting access to flexitime, while feeling job insecurity significantly reduced it (see also Chung, 2018a). Looking at company-level characteristics, those with supportive managers and those working in larger companies were more likely to have access to flexitime. Working in posts with mostly women, as well as working in public companies, also reduced the likelihood of having access to flexitime (see also Chung, 2019b), while the gender of the respondent's boss did not make a difference. The financial services and public administration sectors were the best in relation to access to flexitime, while mostly female-dominated sectors, such as education and health and social services, were the worst. With regards to time off work, older workers in higher occupational positions, as well as those with management support, were more likely to have access to this arrangement, while those with preschool children, those feeling job insecurity, those with a woman as a boss and those working in predominantly female-dominated jobs were less likely to have access (see also, Chung, 2019b). Strangely enough, companies with employee representatives were, on average, less likely to have access to time off work for personal issues and those in micro-companies were more likely to have access. There were sectoral variances similar to that of flexitime, but in this case, those in manufacturing sectors were more likely to have access compared to the commerce and hospitality sector, while transport sectors were significantly less likely to have access.

Conclusion and discussion

This chapter examined the relative position part-time working women had in their access to other types of flexible working arrangements, namely, schedule control. Two hypotheses were set up. First, it was expected that part-time working women would have worse access to flexible working arrangements given their relatively poor positions in the labour market. On the other hand, it was also expected that part-time women would have better access due to the signalling effect of part-time work, or the ease of changing schedules due to shorter working hours per day, which can allow for more flexibility. The analysis results based on 30 European countries in 2015 show that the latter is more likely to be the case. In the case of flexitime, that is, the ability of workers to adapt their work schedules to personal preferences, part-time working women, especially shorter part-time working women, had better access compared to full-time working women. Those who worked longer part-time also had better access, as did those who worked long working hours of 48+ hours a week compared to those who worked the typical full-time contract. With regards to time off work for personal issues, part-time workers were in as good a position as full-time workers.

The chapter further examined whether this relative access of part-time workers varied across different countries. A random-slope model showed that there were no significant differences across countries in the relative position of part-time workers in their access to time off work. However, for flexitime, part-time workers' positions varied for both shorter and longer part-time workers, that is, in most but not all countries, part-time workers were better off in their access to flexitime. Examining the context variables, the countries with higher shares of women working part-time, with stronger and more centralised unions, and with generous family and work-facilitating policies were the ones where the gap between part-time and full-time workers was smaller or the latter had slightly better access. This was due to the fact that full-time workers in these countries were much more likely to gain access to flexitime compared to countries without such institutional contexts. The results at the country level were similar to those found in previous studies (Chung, 2016, 2018a, 2019a), where countries with strong centralised unions or generous family policies were those where insiders gain relatively better access to better working conditions. However, in this case, this meant that there were no differences in the access to flexitime between workers on different working hour contract statuses, or that full-time workers had a slight advantage.

The results of the chapter show that, unlike our expectations, part-time working women were not worse off in their access to flexible working arrangements. In other words, there were no clear signs that due to the relative bad position of part-time working women in the labour market, they are unable to access good family-friendly working practices such as flexitime or time off work for personal issues. However, we need to be aware that this analysis controls for a wide range of factors, including occupational levels – one of the most important factors in explaining access to flexible working arrangements (Chung, 2019a) – which may distort the results somewhat given that part-time jobs are usually prevalent in low-occupational jobs in most countries (Connolly and Gregory, 2008). Thus, future studies should try to look at part-time not as a variable in itself, but more holistically, taking into account other crucial aspects of the job that may be important in understanding part-time workers' position. Furthermore, the consequences of flexible working and the discrepancies in these outcomes for full- and part-time workers need to be examined (see Chung and van der Lippe, 2018). It may be the case that although flexitime may be used to complement part-time work for many women to better balance work with family life, there is evidence that they may be more likely to face further stigma when using flexitime compared to their full-time working counterparts (Chung, 2018b). In other words, rather than access to flexible working, the real dualisation patterns may be found in the outcomes of flexible working, that is, in pay and career patterns (see also Glass and Noonan, 2016; Lott and Chung, 2016). In sum, although we find that part-time workers have as good, or even in some cases better, access to other types of flexible working-time arrangements when compared with full-time workers, it would be unwise to use this as evidence to reject the idea that part-time working women are outsiders in Europe.

Acknowledgement

This chapter was made possible due to generous funding by the Economic and Social Research Council (grant ES/K009699/1) for the project 'Work autonomy, flexibility and work–life balance' (see: www.wafproject.org).

References

Allen, T.D., Johnson, R.C., Kiburz, K.M. and Shockley, K.M. (2013) 'Work–family conflict and flexible work arrangements: deconstructing flexibility', *Personnel Psychology*, 66(2): 345–76.

Anxo, D., Fagan, C., Cebrian, I. and Moreno, G. (2007) 'Patterns of labour market integration in Europe – a life course perspective on time policies', *Socio-Economic Review*, 5(2): 233–60.

Appelbaum, E. (2000) *Manufacturing advantage: why high-performance work systems pay off*, Ithaca, NY: Cornell University Press.

Been, W.M., Van der Lippe, T., Den Dulk, L., Guerreiro, M.D.D.H., Mrčela, A.K., Kanjuo Mrčela, A. and Niemistö, C. (2017) 'European top managers' support for work–life arrangements', *Social Science Research*, 65(July): 60–74.

Berg, P., Appelbaum, E., Bailey, T. and Kalleberg, A.L. (2004) 'Contesting time: international comparisons of employee control of working time', *Industrial & Labor Relations Review*, 57(3): 331–49.

Biegert, T. (2014) 'On the outside looking in? Transitions out of non-employment in the United Kingdom and Germany', *Journal of European Social Policy*, 24(1): 3–18.

Brescoll, V.L., Glass, J. and Sedlovskaya, A. (2013) 'Ask and ye shall receive? The dynamics of employer-provided flexible work options and the need for public policy', *Journal of Social Issues*, 69(2): 367–88.

Chung, H. (2009) *Flexibility for whom? Working time flexibility practices of European companies*, Ridderkerk: Ridderprint.

Chung, H. (2011) 'Work–family conflict across 28 European countries: a multi-level approach', in S. Drobnic and A. Guillén (eds) *Work–life balance in Europe: the role of job quality*, Hampshire: Palgrave Macmillan, pp 42–68.

Chung, H. (2016) 'Dualization and subjective employment insecurity: explaining the subjective employment insecurity divide between permanent and temporary workers across 23 European countries', *Economic and Industrial Democracy*. Available at https://doi.org/10.1177/0143831X16656411

Chung, H. (2017) *Work autonomy, flexibility and work–life balance final report*, Canterbury: University of Kent. Available at: http://wafproject.org/research-outputs/final-report/

Chung, H. (2018a) 'Dualization and the access to occupational family-friendly working-time arrangements across Europe', *Social Policy and Administration*, 52(2): 491–507.

Chung, H. (2018b) 'Gender, flexibility stigma, and the perceived negative consequences of flexible working in the UK', *Social Indicators Research*. Available at: https://doi.org/10.1007/s11205-018-2036-7

Chung, H. (2019a) 'National-level family policies and the access to schedule control in a European comparative perspective: crowding out or in, and for whom?', *Journal of Comparative Policy Analysis*, 21(1): 25–46.

Chung, H. (2019b) '"Women's work penalty" in the access to flexible working arrangements across Europe', *European Journal of Industrial Relations*, 25(1): 23–40.

Chung, H. and Van der Horst, M. (2018a) 'Women's employment patterns after childbirth and the perceived access to and use of flexitime and teleworking', *Human Relations*, 71(1): 47–72.

Chung, H. and Van der Horst, M. (2018b) 'Flexible working and unpaid overtime in the UK: The role of gender, parental and occupational status', *Social Indicators Research*. Available at: https://doi.org/10.1007/s11205-018-2028-7

Chung, H. and Van der Lippe, T. (2018) 'Flexible working work life balance and gender equality: Introduction', *Social Indicators Research*. Available at: https://doi.org/10.1007/s11205-018-2025-x

Clark, S.C. (2000) 'Work/family border theory: a new theory of work/family balance', *Human Relations*, 53(6): 747–70.

Clawson, D. and Gerstel, N. (2014) *Unequal time: gender, class, and family in employment schedules*, New York, NY: Russell Sage Foundation.

Connolly, S. and Gregory, M. (2008) 'Moving down: women's part-time work and occupational change in Britain 1991–2001', *The Economic Journal*, 118(526): F52–F76.

Craig, L. and Powell, A. (2012) 'Dual-earner parents' work–family time: the effects of atypical work patterns and non-parental childcare', *Journal of Population Research*, 29(3): 229–47.

Davidsson, J.B. and Emmenegger, P. (2013) 'Defending the organisation, not the members: unions and the reform of job security legislation in Western Europe', *European Journal of Political Research*, 52(3): 339–63.

Davis, A.E. and Kalleberg, A.L. (2006) 'Family-friendly organizations? Work and family programs in the 1990s', *Work and Occupations*, 33(2): 191–223.

Den Dulk, L., Groeneveld, S., Ollier-Malaterre, A. and Valcour, M. (2013) 'National context in work–life research: a multi-level cross-national analysis of the adoption of workplace work–life arrangements in Europe', *European Management Journal*, 31(5): 478–94.

DiMaggio, P.J. and Powell, W.W. (1983) 'The iron cage revisited: institutional isomorphism and collective rationality in organizational fields', *American Sociological Review*, 48(2): 147–60.

Doeringer, P.B. and Piore, M.J. (1975) 'Unemployment and the dual labor market', *The Public Interest*, 38: 67–79.

Drago, R.W., Black, D. and Wooden, M. (2005) 'The existence and persistence of long work hours', IZA Discussion Paper No. 1720.

Ebbinghaus, B. and Eichhorst, W. (2007) *WP 52 – the distribution of responsibility for social security in Germany*, Amsterdam: Amsterdam Institute for Advanced Labour Studies (AIAS).

Emmenegger, P., Häusermann, S., Palier, B. and Seeleib-Kaiser, M. (2012) *The age of dualisation: the changing face of inequality in Europe*, Oxford: Oxford University Press.

Etzioni, A. (1995) *The spirit of community: the reinvention of American society*, London: Fontana Books.

Eurofound (2015) *Third European company survey – overview report: workplace practices – patterns, performance and well-being*, Luxembourg: Publications Office of the European Union.

Glass, J.L. and Estes, S.B. (1997) 'The family responsive workplace', *Annual Review of Sociology*, 23: 289–313.

Glass, J.L. and Noonan, M.C. (2016) 'Telecommuting and earnings trajectories among American women and men 1989–2008', *Social Forces*, 95(1): 217–50.

Golden, L. (2008) 'Limited access: disparities in flexible work schedules and work-at-home', *Journal of Family and Economic Issues*, 29(1): 86–109.

Golden, L. (2009) 'Flexible daily work schedules in US jobs: formal introductions needed?', *Industrial Relations: A Journal of Economy and Society*, 48(1): 27–54.

Golden, L., Chung, H. and Sweet, S. (2018) 'Positive and negative application of flexible working time arrangements: comparing the United States and the EU countries', in E. Farndale, C. Brewster and W. Mayrhofer (eds) *The handbook of comparative human resource management*, Northampton, MA: Edward Elgar, pp 237–56.

Kelly, E.L., Moen, P. and Tranby, E. (2011) 'Changing workplaces to reduce work–family conflict schedule control in a white-collar organization', *American Sociological Review*, 76(2): 265–90.

Kelly, E.L., Moen, P., Oakes, J.M., Fan, W., Okechukwu, C. et al (2014) 'Changing work and work–family conflict: evidence from the Work, Family, and Health Network', *American Sociological Review*, 79(3): 485–516.

Korpi, W. (1989) 'Power, politics, and state autonomy in the development of social citizenship: social rights during sickness in eighteen OECD countries since 1930', *American Sociological Review*, 54(3): 309–28.

Kossek, E.E., Lautsch, B.A. and Eaton, S.C. (2005) 'Flexibility enactment theory: implications of flexibility type, control, and boundary management for work–family effectiveness', in E.E. Kossek and S.J. Lambert (eds) *Work and life integration: organizational, cultural, and individual perspectives*, Mahwah, NJ: Lawrence Erlbaum Associates Publishers, pp 243–61.

Künemund, H. and Rein, M. (1999) 'There is more to receiving than needing: theoretical arguments and empirical explorations of crowding in and crowding out', *Ageing and Society*, 19(1): 93–121.

Lambert, S.J. and Haley-Lock, A. (2004) 'The organizational stratification of opportunities for work–life balance: addressing issues of equality and social justice in the workplace', *Community, Work & Family*, 7(2): 179–95.

Lott, Y. (2015) 'Working-time flexibility and autonomy: a European perspective on time adequacy', *European Journal of Industrial Relations*, 21(3): 259–74.

Lott, Y. and Chung, H. (2016) 'Gender discrepancies in the outcomes of schedule control on overtime hours and income in Germany', *European Sociological Review*, 32(6): 752–65.

Lyness, K.S., Gornick, J.C., Stone, P. and Grotto, A.R. (2012) 'It's all about control: worker control over schedule and hours in cross-national context', *American Sociological Review*, 77(6): 1023–49.

Michel, J.S., Kotrba, L.M., Mitchelson, J.K., Clark, M.A. and Baltes, B.B. (2011) 'Antecedents of work–family conflict: a meta analytic review', *Journal of Organizational Behavior*, 32(5): 689–725.

Misra, J., Budig, M. and Boeckmann, I. (2011) 'Work-family policies and the effects of children on women's employment hours and wages' *Community, Work & Family*, 14(2): 139–57.

Noonan, M.C., Estes, S.B. and Glass, J.L. (2007) 'Do workplace flexibility policies influence time spent in domestic labor?', *Journal of Family Issues*, 28(2): 263–88.

O'Reilly, J. and Fagan, C. (1998) *Part-time prospects: an international comparison of part-time work in Europe, North America and the Pacific Rim*, London: Routledge.

Ortega, J. (2009) 'Why do employers give discretion? Family versus performance concerns', *Industrial Relations: A Journal of Economy and Society*, 48(1): 1–26.

Palier, B. and Thelen, K. (2010) 'Institutionalizing dualism: complementarities and change in France and Germany', *Politics & Society*, 38(1): 119–48.

Präg, P. and Mills, M. (2014) 'Family-related working schedule flexibility across Europe', *Short statistical report no. 6*, Brussels: European Commission.

Rueda, D. (2005) 'Insider-outsider politics in industrialized democracies: the challenge to social democratic parties', *American Political Science Review*, 99(1): 61–74.

Rueda, D. (2014) 'Dualization, crisis and the welfare state', *Socio-Economic Review*, 12(2): 381–407.

Schieman, S., Schafer, M.H. and McIvor, M. (2013) 'The rewards of authority in the workplace: do gender and age matter?', *Sociological Perspectives*, 56(1): 75–96.

Schwander, H. and Häusermann, S. (2013) 'Who is in and who is out? A risk-based conceptualization of insiders and outsiders', *Journal of European Social Policy*, 23(3): 248–69.

Stier, H., Lewin-Epstein, N. and Braun, M. (2001) 'Welfare regimes, family-supportive policies, and women's employment along the life-course 1', *American Journal of Sociology*, 106(6): 1731–60.

Swanberg, J.E., Pitt-Catsouphes, M. and Drescher-Burke, K. (2005) 'A question of justice disparities in employees' access to flexible schedule arrangements', *Journal of Family Issues*, 26(6): 866–95.

Tomlinson, J. (2007) 'Employment regulation, welfare and gender regimes: a comparative analysis of women's working-time patterns and work–life balance in the UK and the US', *The International Journal of Human Resource Management*, 18(3): 401–15.

Van der Lippe, T. and Lippényi, Z. (2018) 'Beyond formal access: Organizational context, working from home, and work–family conflict of men and women in European workplaces', *Social Indicators Research*. Available at: https://doi.org/10.1007/s11205-018-1993-1

Van Oorschot, W. and Arts, W. (2005) 'The social capital of European welfare states: the crowding out hypothesis revisited', *Journal of European Social Policy*, 15(1): 5–26.

Visser, J. (2002) 'The first part-time economy in the world: a model to be followed?', *Journal of European Social Policy*, 12(1): 23–42.

Williams, J.C., Blair-Loy, M. and Berdahl, J.L. (2013) 'Cultural schemas, social class, and the flexibility stigma', *Journal of Social Issues*, 69(2): 209–34.

Wiß, T. (2017) 'Paths towards family-friendly working time arrangements: comparing workplaces in different countries and industries', *Social Policy & Administration*, 51(7): 1406–30.

6

Part-time work in Danish private services: a (mis)match between wage flexibility and living hours

Trine P. Larsen, Anna Ilsøe and Jonas Felbo-Kolding

Introduction

Part-time employment is often considered beneficial to both sides of industry by facilitating employees' work–life balance (Warren, 2004), while securing flexibility and cost curbing for employers (Atkinson, 1987). However, ample research questions how genuine this 'win–win' situation is for employees and employers alike. Part-time work is associated with increased risks of high employee turnover, less committed workers and precariousness for employees (Walsh, 1990). In-work poverty, earnings inequalities, high job insecurities and restricted access to social protection are only some of the risks associated with part-time work that have triggered distinct scholarly debates. Such debates stress that national welfare and industrial relations institutions cushion, to varying degrees, the risks of precarious part-time work (Campbell and Price, 2016). With its universal welfare protection, strong unions and densely regulated labour market, Denmark is often considered to provide a good example of such support (Esping-Andersen, 1999). Thus, Denmark appears well-suited to examine whether distinct part-time jobs increase dualisation, even in sectors where part-time contracts and low-wage work are widespread, like private services.

The key question is how the institutional framework for regulating working time and wages affects the levels of marginal part-time employment (less than 15 working hours per week) and its implications for men's and women's hourly earnings within private services (industrial cleaning, retail and hotels/restaurants). To address these issues, we draw on Danish register data for all employees and build on the concept of living hours (Ilsøe et al, 2017). We assume that the institutional framework for wage and working-time regulations within distinct sectors influences the prevailing types of part-time service work. However, we also include employees' family situation, ethnicity and age, and further posit the combined effects of these characteristics as affecting the composition of the part-time workforce and marginal part-time workers' risks of an earnings penalty and struggle to secure living hours. Part-time work is often considered an employer strategy of wage flexibility, where employers utilise employment regulation to curb costs and secure flexibility by offering contracts for few hours and replacing older workers with cheap young labour or migrants willing to work for low wages (Grimshaw et al, 2014). Others point to part-time work being a work–life strategy for employees, especially mothers wishing to combine paid work with child-rearing responsibilities (Lyonette, 2015). Thus, the analysis contributes to a research area where few studies have explicitly examined the combined effects of wage and working-time regulations on part-time employment practices and employees' earnings. We specifically explore whether such regulations may add another layer of institutionalised dualisation to the labour market, particularly as working hours – similar to wages – are regulated differently across European countries and sectors (Eichhorst, 2017).

The next section introduces the concept of living hours and the institutional factors that may influence part-time work and affect wage levels, such as wage and working-time regulations. We then present the data and methods used before outlining how wages and working conditions are regulated in Denmark. Thereafter, we examine the characteristics of part-time service work and the effects of part-time work on hourly wages.

Introducing the concept of living hours

Part-time employment has been subject to extensive research (Atkinson, 1987; Mateazzi et al, 2018). However, the different strands of the literature on part-time work rarely incorporate findings beyond their own discrete area and may therefore overlook important aspects that are highlighted in other parts of the literature (Warren, 2004). Here, we start from the discussions in the literature on living wages and labour market segmentation, where we mainly concentrate on the role of collective bargaining, though we are aware that other streams of literature also engage with these issues and include other interesting aspects related to part-time work.

Much of the literature on living wages is organised around various wage indicators, particularly the effects of minimum wages and national wage-setting systems on employment (Manning, 2016) and their importance for securing reasonable income levels (Grimshaw et al, 2014). Variables other than pay, such as weekly working hours and working-time regulations, are often overlooked in such calculations as they are typically built around the notion of full-time work and the male worker. However, early living wage research and more recent studies stress that full-time employment is no guarantee of decent income levels for many workers, particularly women, young people and migrants (Anker, 2011; Rubery, 2015). To meet these shortcomings within the literature, we draw on the concept of living hours (Ilsøe, 2016; Ilsøe et al, 2017). The concept considers not only the hourly wage, the number of weekly working hours and the suitability of the work schedule with regard to issues like unsocial work hours, but also the importance of the institutional framework for wage and working-time regulations in assessing the take-up of part-time work and its implications for individual earnings. However, we extend the original model to encompass employees' family situation, ethnicity and age, along with collectively agreed wages for distinct employee groups like young people. This allows us to explore the characteristics of marginal part-time workers and thus to infer whether distinct forms of part-time work involve a win–win situation for employers and employees alike or whether they lead to increased labour market dualisation.

The impact of institutional factors: wage-setting and working-time regulations

The living wage literature and much segmentation research often deal with working time in relation to how statutory minimum wages and wage-setting systems affect employment. Some studies report reduced earnings inequalities, particularly for part-timers and low-wage workers in countries with centralised wage-setting systems and statutory minimum wages as they secure a wage floor and limit a race to the bottom (Rubery et al, 2005; Garnero et al, 2014; Matteazzi et al, 2018). Others document that employers adjust employment practices to counteract minimum wage increases. They do so by relying, among others things, on contracts for few hours (Schulten, 2016), casual employment (Arpaia et al, 2017), the outsourcing of services (Bell and Machin, 2016) and cheaper young labour and migrants rather than older workers (Neumark and Wascher, 2006). Such research suggests a close link between wages and working time, where, in particular, the interplay between wage and working-time regulations seems pivotal as to how distinct employment practices unfold. Generous minimum wage and working-time floors are assumed to reduce the likelihood of (in)voluntary and 'poor' part-time work (Rubery and Grimshaw, 2015; Warren, 2015). Therefore, the institutional framework appears to be critical in securing living hours and a flexible workforce, especially when employers and employees opt for part-time work for various reasons (Ilsøe et al, 2017). The institutional framework may also narrow the gender pay gaps that arise, among other reasons, from the fact that mothers are typically the main caregiver (Rubery and Grimshaw, 2015; Matteazzi et al, 2018). However, the combined effects of wage and working-time regulations on employees' earnings are less researched. Such regulations may add another layer of institutionalised dualisation to the labour market, particularly as working hours – like wages – are regulated differently across countries and sectors (Eichhorst, 2017).

The role of working-time regulations for employees' employment and wages, and thus, implicitly, their ability to secure living hours, is highly dependent on institutional settings. Most national working-time regulations set a strict threshold for the maximum length of the working week and include various regulations on work scheduling and the distribution of working time (Berg et al, 2004; Seifert, 2005). Cross-national and inter-sectoral variations also exist with regard to working-time regulations (Eurofound, 2016). Denmark belongs to the so-called 'negotiated working-time regime', where working time (like wages) is primarily regulated through sectoral collective agreements, which can be further complemented by company-based bargaining (Eurofound, 2016). The Danish institutional setting gives social partners considerable latitude to adjust working-time standards in terms of the length, scheduling and distribution of working hours at sectoral and company levels. In fact, unlike most wage-setting systems, which set strict wage floors for the minimum hourly pay rate, few working-time regimes guarantee a minimum threshold for weekly working hours (Grimshaw et al, 2014). The national or sectoral working-time regimes thus appear more flexible than the wage-setting systems, which may also explain the rapid growth in marginal part-time work (Rubery, 2015; Warren, 2015).

To curb costs and secure flexibility, employers may utilise the wage and working-time regulations, with the inherited trade-offs that workers may (in)voluntarily opt for reduced hours as a work–life balance strategy or, in some instances, struggle to accrue enough hours, forcing them to hold multiple jobs to secure living hours (Walsh, 1990; Warren, 2015). Therefore, working-time regulations, including weekly working hours, in combination with wage regulations, seem pivotal to the scope of part-time work and earnings inequalities, and thus implicitly affect living hours and a flexible workforce across distinct sectors. We assume that the cross-sectoral variations in wage floors and working-time regulations can be attributed to employment practices that present particular difficulties for young people, migrants and (to a lesser extent) women in securing living hours (Grimshaw et al, 2014; McCollum and Findlay, 2015). The institutional framework often provides some leeway that, in some instances, allows young people and migrants to be offered lower wages and less generous social protection, while equal pay laws secure de jure equal pay and treatment for men and women (Grimshaw et al, 2014; Mailand, 2017). Such regulatory variations may, therefore, narrow the gender pay gaps and gender differences in the take-up of marginal part-time work, but they may also contribute to increased dualisation, where young people and migrants are particularly at risk. Therefore, the combined effects of the wage and working-time regulations are deemed to be pivotal in securing a flexible workforce and living hours, and thus a win–win situation for employers and employees alike.

Methods and data set used

This chapter draws on Danish register data covering all employees within private services from 2015. We define private services using the European Classification of Economic Activities (the NACE classification), as employment relationships in retail (47.00–48.99), hotels/restaurants (55.00–56.99) and industrial cleaning (81.21–81.23).

The register data cover everyone on the Danish labour market with any form of official taxable income in a Danish company. By drawing on information from the tax filings of the individual employers, the data provide detailed information on individuals' employment relationships at individual workplaces in terms of the length of employment, monthly income, monthly working hours and demographic characteristics. Employment in specific sectors is often estimated based on the primary job, like the Labour Force Survey, which thus underestimates the number of employment relationships. This is especially the case in private services, where most service workers hold more than one job (Ilsøe et al, 2017).

We include indicators like average hourly wages and weekly working hours. We distinguish between three *working hour categories* by using the average weekly working hours in all industry jobs in periods of employment, such as the total number of working hours in one or more jobs in the industry divided by the number of weeks worked.

The three working hour categories are: full-time (30+ weekly working hours); part-time (16–30 weekly working hours); and marginal part-time (15 weekly working hours or less). In the regression models, we include the following control variables: gender, ethnicity, age, educational attainment, multiple jobs, family situation, occupational groups and information on study activities and primary jobs. *Ethnicity* is defined by country of origin and distinguishes between Danish, EU15/EEA/Malta/Cyprus, EU11 and individuals coming from countries outside the European Union (EU). *Age* is grouped into seven groups (employee aged 15–17, 18–25, 26–35, 36–45, 46–55, 56–65 and 65+) to take account of the provisions specified in the relevant agreements. *Educational attainment* is defined using the International Standard Classification of Education (the ISCED classification) (0–9). *Multiple jobs* are defined as individuals who during the year, on average, hold more than one job for at least two months. *Family situation* is defined using two variables: partnership status, defining whether the individual has a partner or not and the employment status of the partner; and whether the individual has one or more dependent children aged 0–11 in the household. Finally, *occupational groups* are defined using the International Standard Classification of Occupations (ISCO-08) (0–11).

This chapter builds on a three-stage analytical strategy. In the first stage, we examine the main characteristics of the workforce within Danish private services and the collectively agreed wage and working-time regulations within industrial cleaning, retail and hotels/restaurants. In the second analytical stage, we focus on private service workers. Here, we apply a linear probability model with the aim of modelling the probability of working marginal part-time hours. Marginal part-time work is more widespread in private services than elsewhere, but not everyone works reduced hours. We therefore explore which groups are over-represented in these specific private services jobs.

In the third analytical stage, we examine the potential earnings penalties for working marginal part-time. We use a linear regression model to model the logged hourly wages of individuals in order to examine whether certain individual and job characteristics influence the wages of marginal part-time workers. Doing the analysis in these three steps allows us to separate the selection processes from possible discrimination processes. We are thereby in a better position to explain potential earnings differences and variations in part-time employment, and thus, implicitly, the (mis)match between wage flexibility and living hours across the sectors.

Analyses

The workforce and industrial relations settings within Danish private services

Danish private services employ 28% of the Danish workforce, mostly in retail (see Table 6.1). The three sectors are highly labour-intensive and dominated by fierce price competition. They include a high proportion of small companies, notably, those comprised of self-employed people without employees (Statistics Denmark, 2017). They also have a relatively high employee and company turnover, and industrial cleaning, in particular, has witnessed an increase in the outsourcing of cleaning services to private contractors (DI, 2016). Furthermore, young people (typically students), women, migrants and low-skilled workers are over-represented within private services

Table 6.1: Key features of Danish private services, percentages, 2015

	Total private sector	Industrial cleaning	Retail	Hotels/ restaurants
Share of total employment in private sector	100	3	16	9
Share of women	40	59	57	55
Share of migrants	13	52	10	23
Share of young people aged 15–25	24	17	57	54
Share of employees with lower-secondary schooling as highest level of education	27	39	44	40
Share of active students	25	18	56	53
Share of young people aged 15–25 not being students	18	35	22	18
Share of employees with dependent children aged 11 or less	27	26	23	18
Average working hours per week:				
Less than 15 hours	26	42	54	63
16–30 hours	16	31	15	18
30+ hours	58	27	31	20
Average hourly wages (DKK)	214	170	143	143
Share of employees with multiple jobs	35	57	47	62
Share of marginal part-timers with multiple jobs	46	70	53	69

Source: Authors' own calculations based on data from Statistics Denmark.

compared to the rest of the Danish labour market, although the figures vary across the three service sectors (see Table 6.1).

Part-time employment, especially marginal part-time, is widespread within private services: 42% of the employees within industrial cleaning, 54% in retail and 63% in hotels/restaurants work, on average, less than 15 hours per week (see Table 6.1). These figures are considerably higher than the general average for the Danish private sector, and the implications of working marginal part-time are many. For example, marginal part-time workers often hold multiple jobs and many also work unsocial hours, in shifts and (particularly in the case of industrial cleaners) on their own at multiple workplaces (Ilsøe, 2016; Mailand and Larsen, 2018). This, along with the fact that parents are less likely to work within private services (see Table 6.1), suggests that the high levels of marginal part-time service work may not necessarily be down to work–life balance concerns, or that it may not be without problems regarding securing living hours.

The institutional framework for regulating wages and working time may provide some leeway for flexibility that considers the needs of both employers and employees, and thus contribute to part-time work being a win–win situation for both parties. Danish wage and working conditions (including working time) are primarily regulated through collective agreements signed by social partners at sectoral and company levels. However, union densities, collective agreement coverage and workplace representation are lower within private services than in other sectors (see Table 6.2). In areas of private services without collective agreement coverage, wages and working conditions are either regulated by Danish labour law or the individual arrangements of the private company, which may not necessarily offer similar wages and conditions to those outlined in the collective agreements (Andersen and Felbo-Kolding, 2013).

The collective agreements covering private services allow for company-based bargaining but are more detailed with regards to wages and working conditions than agreements in other sectors, such as manufacturing (Larsen and Ilsøe, 2017). When looking at specific aspects of wages and working time, the collective agreements within private services differ depending on the sector and employee group under consideration. For example, the wage-setting system within the industrial cleaning sector follows the so-called standardised wage-setting system, where social partners set fixed hourly levels and outline specific rates for annual hourly pay increments, wage supplements, overtime payments and so on (Larsen and Mailand, 2018). Within the retail and hotels/restaurants sectors, the wage-setting system is, in principle, the so-called minimum wage-setting system, which leaves considerable latitude for company-based bargaining. However, it has developed into a de facto standardised wage-setting system since the wage pool for company-based bargaining is rather small (Larsen and Ilsøe, 2017). In addition, the collectively agreed minimum wages are less generous in retail, followed by hotels/restaurants and industrial cleaning (see Table 6.2). Moreover, the collectively agreed wages often differ according to age, with the agreed hourly wages for young people within retail being nearly half the rate paid to older co-workers, while the wage gap is slightly smaller in the hotels/ restaurants sector and somewhat narrower within industrial cleaning (see Table 6.2).

The cross-sectoral variations in terms of differentiated wages for young people are historically rooted, reflecting the compromises by

Table 6.2: Wage and working time regulations in selected collective agreements covering Danish private services, 2018

	Industrial cleaning	Retail	Hotels/ restaurants
Union density	54%	32%	33%
Collective agreement coverage	Estimated 40–50%	57%	Estimated 40–50%
Local wage bargaining	No[a]	Yes	Yes
Collectively agreed minimum hourly wages:			
General:	124.08kr	114.42kr	122.77kr
Young people:	106.58kr	65.01kr	72.96kr
Minimum wage supplements for unsocial hours:			
General:	14.51kr	25.20kr	18.37kr
Young people:		12.60kr[b]	13.20kr
Maximum weekly working hours:			
General:	48 hours per week	45 hours per week	48 hours per week
Young people:	2 hours per day[b]	2 hours per day[b]	2 hours per day[b]
Full-time work	30 hours per week	37 hours per week	37 hours per week
Guaranteed working hours:			
General:	15 hours per week		2–5 hours per week
Young people:		None	2 hours per day

Notes: Young people are defined as employees aged under 18 years – except in retail, which also covers students under 25 with a maximum of 15 weekly working hours. [a] Company-based wage bargaining allowed since 2018. [b] Only employees aged under 18 years.

Source: Larsen et al (2010), Horesta and 3F (2017a, 2017b), DI et al (2017) and Danish Chamber of Commerce and HK Retail (2017).Authors' own calculations based on data from Statistics Denmark

Danish social partners during distinct collective bargaining rounds. For example, Danish unions within industrial cleaning have historically opposed the very idea of introducing lower hourly wages for young people due to concerns about unleashing unfair competition, as well as for health and safety reasons. By opposing an age-related wage, the unions implicitly prevented 16–17 year olds working as cleaners in hospitals and thus dealing with toxic chemicals and so on. In retail, the unions agreed to lower wages for young people and students during the 1988 bargaining round, partly because Danish labour law at the time only allowed young people aged under 18 years working as trainees to take up employment in retail. Another important factor was that the unions favoured stronger protection for workers with a retail job as the main source of securing their livelihood. However, it is doubtful whether Danish unions would have agreed to differentiated age-related wages if they had known that the government would later abolish the restrictions on young retail workers. Moreover, the Danish government and social partners recently introduced differentiated hourly wages for new labour market entrants in order to ease refugees' labour market integration (Mailand, 2017).

The collective agreements also include various working-time regulations regarding the length (weekly working hours, part-time work, overtime, etc), scheduling (shift work, weekend work, on-call duties, etc) and distribution of work hours (flexi-time, annualised hours, time off). It is only industrial cleaning that guarantees all employees, including young people, a minimum number of weekly working hours, and secures overtime payment, even if it is voluntary and exceeds 7.5 working hours per day. In the retail and hotels/restaurants sectors, overtime payment only applies when employers request overtime and the work hours exceed a specific threshold of weekly working hours, which is less restrictive than the one applied within industrial cleaning. However, derogations are allowed, which may explain why marginal part-time employment is also widespread within industrial cleaning despite the collectively agreed threshold of a guaranteed minimum of 15 working hours (see Table 6.1). It is also important to note that, in principle, Danish agreements guarantee all workers similar rights to the collectively agreed benefits, irrespective of their employment contract and age. It is mainly regarding wages that some collective agreements differentiate according to age, while eligibility criteria are otherwise typically linked to employment records (Mailand and Larsen, 2018).

Characteristics of marginal part-time service workers

Within Danish retail, 69% of employees work part-time, and the share is higher within industrial cleaning (73%) and hotels/restaurants (80%). In fact, most private service employment relationships are less than 15 hours per week (see Table 6.1). Marginal part-time workers are often young people – typically students – with 76% being young students within retail. These figures are somewhat lower in the industrial cleaning and hotels/restaurants sectors (see Figure 6.1).

Migrant workers are also common within industrial cleaning, and many hold contracts for few hours. By contrast, migrant workers are less likely to work within the retail and hotels/restaurants sectors, and they rarely hold marginal part-time positions (see Table 6.1 and Figure 6.1). Our regression results echo the descriptive statistics and suggest that the characteristics of marginal part-time workers vary across the three service sectors, and thus point to different employment practices. Age, like study activities, is positively associated with

Figure 6.1: Characteristics of marginal part-time service workers (%)

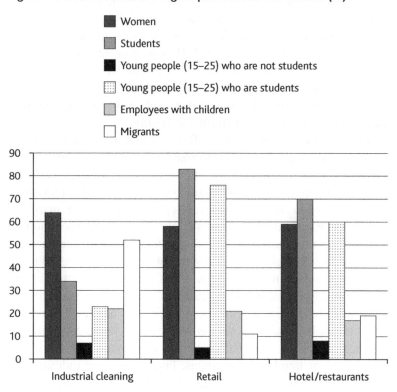

Source: Authors' own calculations based on data from Statistics Denmark

marginal part-time employment, particularly within retail and hotels/ restaurants, but less so in industrial cleaning (see Table 6.3).

Young people aged under 18 years are more likely to hold marginal part-time jobs than even their older peers aged 18–25 years across the three sectors. They often combine such part-time jobs with their studies, indicating that a slightly different work–life balance situation than that of juggling paid work and child-rearing is at play. The high share of young people among marginal part-time workers also suggests that employers, especially within retail and hotels/restaurants, rely on cheap young labour to secure a flexible workforce and reduce costs, particularly as the collectively agreed wages are lower for young people under 18 (and in the case of retail, also for students aged 18–25 years). Moreover, the collective agreements guarantee few (hotels/restaurants), if any (retail), weekly working hours for young people and students. Marginal part-time employment thus seems to provide a 'win–win' situation for both employers and most young people in retail and hotels/restaurants – especially students. It allows them to combine paid work with their studies, while employers gain access to highly flexible and cheap labour as young people also appear willing to work unsocial hours, according to recent studies (Westergaard-Nielsen, 2008; Ilsøe, 2016). However, young people not engaged in study activities, but working reduced hours (see Figure 6.1), may struggle to secure living hours, which questions how genuine the win–win situation is for employees other than students.

Our regression results also suggest that while young people continue to be over-represented in marginal part-time employment, when controlling for other factors, the effects of ethnicity seem to reduce, even if migrants seem more likely to take up marginal part-time service jobs (see Table 6.3). By contrast, the impact of gender, parenthood and partnership status is less than expected from the literature, although women are slightly over-represented among marginal part-timers. Parenthood seems to slightly decrease the likelihood of marginal part-time employment within industrial cleaning and hotels/ restaurants, while slightly increasing the likelihood of marginal part-time employment in retail (see Table 6.3). Other family-related factors like partnership status, including partners' employment patterns, are also negatively associated with the incidence of marginal part-time employment. In fact, employees whose partner works full-time are less likely to be in marginal part-time employment, particularly within retail or hotel and restaurants. Further analyses indicate that the gender differences among marginal part-time workers are limited, if not diminishing, when controlling for such factors. Therefore, many

Table 6.3: Linear probability estimates (dependent variable: marginal part-time work within private services), base and full models compared

	Base – private sector	Full – private sector	Base – cleaning	Full – cleaning	Base – retail	Full – retail	Base – hotels / restaurants	Full – hotels / restaurants
Under 18	0.422***	0.315***	0.192***	0.098***	0.301***	0.167***	0.222***	0.136***
	(0.001)	(0.001)	(0.011)	(0.012)	(0.002)	(0.002)	(0.002)	(0.003)
Age 26–35	-0.337***	-0.129***	-0.293***	-0.143***	-0.365***	-0.131***	-0.241***	-0.105***
	(0.001)	(0.001)	(0.006)	(0.009)	(0.002)	(0.003)	(0.003)	(0.004)
Age 36–45	-0.437***	-0.135***	-0.400***	-0.207***	-0.525***	-0.142***	-0.401***	-0.150***
	(0.001)	(0.001)	(0.007)	(0.010)	(0.002)	(0.003)	(0.004)	(0.005)
Age 46–55	-0.437***	-0.125***	-0.416***	-0.212***	-0.495***	-0.101***	-0.387***	-0.123***
	(0.001)	(0.001)	(0.007)	(0.010)	(0.003)	(0.004)	(0.004)	(0.005)
Age 56–65	-0.403***	-0.087***	-0.426***	-0.214***	-0.442***	-0.055***	-0.358***	-0.093***
	(0.001)	(0.001)	(0.008)	(0.011)	(0.004)	(0.004)	(0.006)	(0.007)
Over 65	-0.038***	0.276***	-0.089***	0.188***	-0.035***	0.349***	-0.034***	0.252***
	(0.002)	(0.002)	(0.017)	(0.019)	(0.006)	(0.007)	(0.009)	(0.010)
Male		-0.090***		-0.090***		-0.029***		-0.040***
		(0.001)		(0.005)		(0.001)		(0.002)
Partner with no labour market income		-0.014***		-0.037***		-0.024***		-0.013*
		(0.001)		(0.008)		(0.004)		(0.005)
Partner employed part-time		-0.030***		-0.015*		-0.035***		-0.019***
		(0.001)		(0.008)		(0.003)		(0.004)

(continued)

Table 6.3: Linear probability estimates (dependent variable: marginal part-time work within private services), base and full models compared (continued)

	Base – private sector	Full – private sector	Base – cleaning	Full – cleaning	Base – retail	Full – retail	Base – hotels / restaurants	Full – hotels / restaurants
Partner employed full-time		-0.069***		-0.071***		-0.087***		-0.082***
		(0.001)		(0.006)		(0.002)		(0.003)
Dependent child aged 0–11 in household		0.003***		-0.004		0.009***		-0.005
		(0.001)		(0.006)		(0.002)		(0.003)
EU15/EEA+Malta+Cyprus		0.013***		0.029		0.009		-0.068***
		(0.002)		(0.019)		(0.008)		(0.008)
EU11		0.034***		0.030*		-0.044***		-0.019*
		(0.003)		(0.012)		(0.010)		(0.009)
Countries outside the EU		0.072***		0.035***		0.013***		0.052***
		(0.001)		(0.006)		(0.003)		(0.003)
Multiple jobs		0.082***		0.198***		0.092***		0.163***
		(0.001)		(0.005)		(0.001)		(0.002)
Active student		0.328***		0.289***		0.389***		0.271***
		(0.001)		(0.008)		(0.003)		(0.003)
Primary education		0.091***		-0.018		0.137***		0.103***
		(0.002)		(0.016)		(0.011)		(0.012)
Lower secondary		0.052***		0.022***		0.127***		0.092***
		(0.001)		(0.005)		(0.002)		(0.003)

(continued)

Table 6.3: Linear probability estimates (dependent variable: marginal part-time work within private services), base and full models compared (continued)

	Base – private sector	Full – private sector	Base – cleaning	Full – cleaning	Base – retail	Full – retail	Base – hotels / restaurants	Full – hotels / restaurants
Short-cycle tertiary		-0.030***		0.035**		0.000		0.037***
		(0.001)		(0.012)		(0.004)		(0.006)
Bachelor's		0.064***		0.063***		0.164***		0.137***
		(0.001)		(0.010)		(0.004)		(0.005)
Master's		-0.011***		0.022		0.060***		0.117***
		(0.001)		(0.015)		(0.005)		(0.009)
PhD		0.049***		-0.039		0.261***		0.304***
		(0.004)		(0.128)		(0.067)		(0.053)
Other		0.077***		-0.006		0.149**		0.107**
		(0.015)		(0.033)		(0.053)		(0.040)
Constant	0.527***	0.264***	0.720***	0.449***	0.664***	0.256***	0.666***	0.398***
	(0.001)	(0.001)	(0.005)	(0.009)	(0.001)	(0.003)	(0.001)	(0.004)
R squared	0.321	0.409	0.105	0.234	0.345	0.444	0.008	0.263
Observations	1,995,353	1,888,423	52,765	36,967	314,965	309,110	185,088	165,661

Notes: Standard errors in parentheses. * $p < 0.05$; ** $p < 0.01$; *** $p < 0.001$.

Source: Authors' own calculations based on data from Statistics Denmark

Danish parents, including mothers, seem to work long part-time hours or full-time during periods of child-rearing within private services. This indicates that factors other than work–life balance for child-rearing purposes are at play when trying to explain the high levels of marginal part-time service work – findings that are supported when controlling for age, study activities and ethnicity (see Table 6.3).

The fact that multiple jobs are widespread among marginal part-timers suggests that for many service workers, such jobs are merely a necessity to make ends meet, which is thus symptomatic of a struggle to secure living hours rather than a choice to ease their work–life balance. The institutional framework regulating wage and working conditions appears to influence how employment practices unfold across the sectors. The collective agreements covering industrial cleaning guarantee a minimum of 15 weekly working hours and have no specific collectively agreed wage rate for young people. This may explain the lower incidence of marginal part-time work within industrial cleaning and the effects of age and ethnicity on the take-up of marginal part-time jobs, particularly as the share of young people under 18 is lower compared to retail and hotels/restaurants (see Table 6.3). The combined effects of allowing cheap young labour within the retail and hotels/restaurants sectors without any, or very low, guaranteed working hours seem to account for the high levels of marginal part-time employment, particularly among young people and students. Therefore, the overall institutional framework for regulating wage and working conditions within these sectors may affect employment practices, including the scope of marginal part-time positions. Such forms of employment are more widespread in sectors without specific working-time guarantees and in sectors where the sectoral agreements operate with age-differentiated wage floors.

The earnings penalty

The earnings penalties for part-time workers are well researched, and women often face greater risks of lower wages (Matteazzi et al, 2018). Working as a marginal part-time service worker also entails lower hourly wages, though their average hourly wages – similar to their peers in full-time and long part-time positions – are higher than the collectively agreed minimum wages and have increased in recent years (Ilsøe et al, 2017). The wage gap between full-time and marginal part-time workers is somewhat narrower in industrial cleaning (13%) than hotels/restaurants (22%) and retail (29%), where the wage-setting systems – unlike industrial cleaning – allow for company-based wage bargaining and differences between employee groups. The importance of the sector-specific wage-setting system seems even more evident when examining distinct groups of marginal part-timers' exposure to earnings penalties when working few hours.

Women, young people under the age of 18, low-skilled workers and migrants, particularly from outside the EU, earn less, though wide cross-sector variations exist and the earnings penalty varies considerably among the distinct groups of marginal part-time workers (see Table 6.4). Young people aged under 18 receive considerably lower wages than their peers in other marginal, full-time and long part-time positions. However, the average earnings penalty suffered by young people is lower within industrial cleaning compared to retail and hotels/restaurants. In fact, the wage gap between marginal part-time workers and their peers in full-time and long part-time employment diminishes considerably in all three sectors when controlling for age and student activity, but even more so within retail and hotels/restaurants. This underlines not only the importance of the institutional framework in terms of differentiated wages for young people aged under 18 (retail and hotels/restaurants) and students under 25 (retail), but also suggests that employers utilise the opportunities within the collective agreements to employ cheap young labour (see Table 6.4).

While age, ethnicity and study activities seem strongly associated with lower wages within private services, the impact of gender, parenthood and partnership status on marginal part-time workers' average hourly wages is not always negative, as assumed within much work–life balance and equal pay literature. Within industrial cleaning and retail, marginal part-timers with dependent small children have slightly higher earnings. Likewise, the average hourly wages among marginal part-timers are often slightly higher among employees with a partner in full-time and part-time employment. However, men's earnings appear slightly higher than women's, indicating that a small gender wage gap exists among marginal part-timers. The gender pay gap increases slightly when controlling for other indicators, such as educational attainment, partnership status, ethnicity and age, in all three sectors. However, parenthood does not seem to affect women's hourly wage in the three sectors – women with children earn similar hourly wages to those without children. Further analyses suggest that gender pay gaps continue to persist but remain marginal, even when running separate regressions for male and female marginal part-timers. This suggests that although industrial cleaning has the most centralised wage-setting system and would thus be in a better

Table 6.4: Ordinary Least Squares (OLS) estimates of logged hourly wages for employed individuals in private services, base and full models compared

	Base – private sector	Full – private sector	Base – cleaning	Full – cleaning	Base – retail	Full – retail	Base – hotels / restaurants	Full – hotels/ restaurants
Marginal part-time	0.000	0.000	0.000	0.000	0.000	0.000	0.000	0.000
	(.)	(.)	(.)	(.)	(.)	(.)	(.)	(.)
Part-time	0.197***	−0.005***	0.040***	0.003	0.220***	−0.034***	0.134***	0.013***
	(0.001)	(0.001)	(0.002)	(0.004)	(0.002)	(0.002)	(0.002)	(0.002)
Full-time	0.304***	0.021***	0.139***	0.067***	0.360***	−0.016***	0.257***	0.050***
	(0.001)	(0.001)	(0.003)	(0.005)	(0.002)	(0.002)	(0.002)	(0.003)
Male		0.045***		0.059***		0.062***		0.016***
		(0.001)		(0.003)		(0.001)		(0.001)
Under 18		−0.349***		−0.260***		−0.326***		−0.365***
		(0.001)		(0.013)		(0.001)		(0.002)
Age 26–35		0.073***		0.029***		0.063***		0.083***
		(0.001)		(0.005)		(0.002)		(0.002)
Age 36–45		0.163***		0.081***		0.168***		0.152***
		(0.002)		(0.006)		(0.003)		(0.003)
Age 46–55		0.178***		0.095***		0.182***		0.159***
		(0.002)		(0.006)		(0.003)		(0.003)
Age 56–65		0.178***		0.101***		0.173***		0.172***
		(0.003)		(0.006)		(0.004)		(0.005)
Over 65		0.134***		0.090***		0.116***		0.159***
		(0.005)		(0.012)		(0.006)		(0.008)

(continued)

Table 6.4: OLS estimates of logged hourly wages for employed individuals in private services, base and full models compared (continued)

	Base – private sector	Full – private sector	Base – cleaning	Full – cleaning	Base – retail	Full – retail	Base – hotels/restaurants	Full – hotels/restaurants
Partner with no labour market income		0.009***		0.008		0.017***		-0.005
		(0.002)		(0.005)		(0.003)		(0.004)
Partner employed part-time		0.038***		0.017***		0.046***		0.022***
		(0.002)		(0.004)		(0.002)		(0.002)
Partner employed full-time		0.053***		0.028***		0.058***		0.050***
		(0.001)		(0.004)		(0.002)		(0.002)
Dependent child aged 0–11 in household		0.012***		0.015***		0.015***		0.001
		(0.001)		(0.004)		(0.001)		(0.002)
EU15/EEA+Malta+Cyprus		-0.025***		-0.045***		-0.018**		-0.026***
		(0.004)		(0.013)		(0.006)		(0.006)
EU11		-0.051***		-0.077***		-0.047***		-0.066***
		(0.004)		(0.006)		(0.008)		(0.007)
Countries outside the EU		-0.062***		-0.078***		-0.017***		-0.132***
		(0.001)		(0.003)		(0.002)		(0.002)
Multiple jobs		0.000		-0.033***		0.018***		0.004*
		(.)		(0.003)		(0.001)		(0.002)
Active student		-0.084***		-0.045***		-0.095***		-0.069***
		(0.001)		(0.005)		(0.002)		(0.002)

(continued)

Table 6.4: OLS estimates of logged hourly wages for employed individuals in private services, base and full models compared (continued)

	Base – private sector	Full – private sector	Base – cleaning	Full – cleaning	Base – retail	Full – retail	Base – hotels/restaurants	Full – hotels/restaurants
Primary education		-0.168***		-0.045***		-0.243***		-0.178***
		(0.006)		(0.009)		(0.012)		(0.010)
Lower secondary		-0.138***		-0.045***		-0.173***		-0.111***
		(0.001)		(0.003)		(0.002)		(0.002)
Short-cycle tertiary		0.056***		-0.000		0.076***		0.033***
		(0.002)		(0.008)		(0.003)		(0.004)
Bachelor's		0.031***		0.028***		0.036***		0.016***
		(0.002)		(0.007)		(0.003)		(0.003)
Master's		0.151***		0.035***		0.216***		0.059***
		(0.005)		(0.012)		(0.007)		(0.007)
PhD		0.099**		-0.090*		0.305***		0.006
		(0.038)		(0.035)		(0.080)		(0.035)
Other		-0.145***		-0.074***		-0.193***		-0.181***
		(0.013)		(0.012)		(0.038)		(0.023)
Constant	4.804***	4.951***	5.044***	5.073***	4.719***	4.950***	4.812***	4.949***
	(0.001)	(0.001)	(0.002)	(0.006)	(0.001)	(0.002)	(0.001)	(0.003)
R squared	0.116	0.470	0.045	0.140	0.165	0.501	0.089	0.423
Observations	519,558	481,763	52,764	36,967	314,963	309,108	185,086	165,659

Notes: Standard errors in parentheses. * $p < 0.05$; ** $p < 0.01$; *** $p < 0.001$.

Source: Authors' own calculations based on data from Statistics Denmark

position to eliminate the gender pay gap according to much equal pay literature (Matteazzi et al, 2018), this is not always the case, at least in Denmark. The collective agreements covering retail and hotels/restaurants appear more successful in eliminating the gender pay gap compared to industrial cleaning, though their wage-setting systems allows for differentiated wages and company-based wage bargaining (see Table 6.4). Therefore, the institutional framework for regulating wage and working conditions may, in some instances, limit the gender wage gap (retail and hotels/restaurants), while in others, the same collective agreements appear to contribute to increased dualisation by offering lower wages to young people and migrants (see Table 6.4).

Discussion and conclusion

Marginal part-time work is widespread within industrial cleaning, retail and hotels/restaurants – sectors that are also dominated by low-wage work and an over-representation of women, young people, migrants and low-skilled workers. Furthermore, most marginal part-time service workers hold multiple jobs to secure living hours and often experience a significant earnings gap compared to their peers in long part-time and full-time employment. The wage gap seems to correspond with the regulation of average hourly wages in the collective agreements, especially in retail and hotels/restaurants, where young workers and, in the case of retail, also students aged 25 or younger are guaranteed significantly lower hourly wages than their older peers. However, we also find that the very same agreements narrow the gender pay gap in retail and hotels/restaurants, though less so within industrial cleaning. Therefore, the institutional framework may facilitate as well as limit wage gaps and thus echo other studies exploring the importance of wage-setting systems for earnings penalties experienced by part-time workers (Matteazzi et al, 2018).

Our analyses indicate that private service workers are often young people – typically students – just entering the labour market. Many combine a marginal part-time job with their studies. Thus, our findings point to a possible win–win situation for both sides of industry, where students wishing to supplement their student allowances with earnings from a marginal part-time job are matched by the employers' needs for highly flexible and cheap labour to match the changing business cycles. This is further underpinned by the fact that young people and students are not only over-represented among marginal part-time service workers, but are also exposed to an earnings penalty, with their wages being only about half of their older peers in retail and hotels/

restaurants. This implies that employers utilise the overall institutional framework for regulating wages and working time. The combined effects of the collective agreements covering retail and hotels/restaurants may facilitate these employment practices by allowing lower collectively agreed wages for young people (retail and hotels/restaurants) and students aged 25 or less (retail), as well as offering very low thresholds (hotels/restaurants), if any (retail), for guaranteed weekly working hours. The findings within industrial cleaning support this notion as marginal part-time work is less widespread and young people and students are also less likely to take up employment within industrial cleaning – a sector where the collective agreements guarantee 15 weekly working hours and do not operate with a specific wage rate for young people. Therefore, the wage gap and employment practices in private services should be characterised as an 'age gap' rather than a gender gap, even if one can talk of a genuine win–win situation for both employers and some employee groups, and this 'age gap' seemingly corresponds with the regulatory setting, that is, the collective agreements' content.

Our findings also suggest that some marginal part-time workers – young as well as older workers – are not engaged in any study activities. The fact that many marginal part-time workers (70% in cleaning, 53% in retail and 69% in hotels/restaurants) hold multiple jobs indicates that contracts for few hours may not necessarily be voluntary and seem inadequate to secure living hours, especially for employee groups other than students. This questions the idea of the genuine win–win situation for employers and employees alike with respect to marginal part-time employment. Indeed, our findings demonstrate that although Denmark has some of the most extensive work–life balance policies in Europe (Larsen and Navrbjerg, 2018), parents, including mothers, are less likely to work within retail or hotels/restaurants than other sectors. Therefore, the often-assumed match with part-time employment facilitating the interests of employers and employees seems highly questionable for some groups of marginal part-timers. Marginal part-time work primarily appears to deliver flexibility for employers but is often associated with risks of lower wages for individual employees and for many seems to be a necessity to secure living hours rather than a choice to improve employees' (other than students') work–life balance. The working-time and wage regulations appear detrimental with regard to the high share of marginal part-time work. The recent rule changes for new labour market entrants like migrants and refugees may contribute to wider wage gaps among these groups vis-à-vis other workers as they allow employers to pay new labour market entrants even lower wages. Thus, the dualisation seen within private services, where young people, migrants and, to a lesser extent, women appear to become risk-bearers, may be facilitated by the combined effects of working-time and wage regulations within the sampled sectors.

In sum, our analysis implies that even in Denmark, where comparatively generous collectively agreed wage floors and strong welfare and industrial relations institutions are assumed to cushion the effects of precariousness, we find dualisation within private services. Marginal part-timers are particularly at risk as they are often exposed to lower hourly wages and struggle to secure living hours, which may also have negative implications for their income security in the short and long term. For example, they may have difficulties in meeting the eligibility criteria for unemployment benefits and accruing enough pension savings to secure their livelihood in old age (Mailand and Larsen, 2018). Therefore, many marginal part-time service workers seem to be the risk-bearers of a highly flexible labour market, notwithstanding that win–win situations and cross-sectoral variations exist regarding their characteristics. Therefore, our analyses point to the importance of considering the joint effects of wage-setting systems and working-time regulations, as well as weekly working hours and thus living hours, when examining the risks of precariousness. By considering working time and its regulations, it becomes evident that dualisation is also often embedded in trade-offs, even regarding distinct forms of part-time work.

References

Andersen, S.K. and Felbo-Kolding, J. (2013) *Danske virksomheders brug af østeuropæisk arbejdskraft*, Copenhagen: FAOS.

Anker, R. (2011) *Estimating a living wage*, Conditions of Work and Employment Series No. 29, Geneva: International Labour Organisation.

Arpaia, A., Cardoso, P., Kiss, A., Van Herck, K. and Vandeplas, A. (2017) *Statutory minimum wages in the EU*, IZA Policy Paper 124, Bonn: IZA.

Atkinson, J. (1987) 'Flexibility or fragmentation?', *Labour and Society*, 12(1): 86–105.

Bell, B. and Machin, S. (2016) *Minimum wages and firm value*, CEP Discussion Paper No. 1404, London: London School of Economics.

Berg, P., Appelbaum, E., Bailey, T. and Kalleberg, E.L. (2004) 'Contesting time', *Industrial Labor Relations Review*, 57(3): 331–49.

Campbell, I. and Price, R. (2016) 'Precarious work and precarious workers', *The Economic and Labour Relations Review*, 37(3): 314–32.

Danish Chamber of Commerce and HK Retail (2017) *Butiksoverenskomsten 2017–2020*, Copenhagen: HK Retail.

DI (Danish Industries) (2016) *Servicebranchens årsrapport*, Copenhagen: DI.

DI, 3F and Serviceforbundet (2017) *Serviceoverenskomsten 2017–2020*, Copenhagen: DI.

Eichhorst, W. (2017) *Labour market institutions and the future of work*, IZA Working Paper No. 122, Bonn: IZA.

Esping-Andersen, G. (1999) *Social foundations of post-industrial economics*, Oxford: Oxford University Press.

Eurofound (2016) *Working time developments in the 21st century*, Luxembourg: Publications Office of the European Union.

Garnero, A., Kampelmann, S. and Ryck, F. (2014) *Minimum wage systems and earnings inequalities*, IZA Working Paper 8419, Bonn: IZA.

Grimshaw, D., Bosch, G. and Rubery, J. (2014) 'Minimum wages and collective bargaining', *British Journal of Industrial Relations*, 52(3): 470–98.

Horesta and 3F (2017a) *Restaurantoverenskomsten 2017–2020*, Copenhagen: Horesta.

Horesta and 3F (2017b) *Hoteloverenskomsten 2014–2020*, Copenhagen: Horesta.

Ilsøe, A. (2016) 'From living wage to living hours', *Labour and Industry*, 26(1): 40–57.

Ilsøe, A., Larsen, T.P. and Felbo-Kolding, J. (2017) 'Living hours under pressure', *Employee Relations*, 39(6): 888–902.

Larsen, T.P. and Ilsøe, A. (2017) 'Varieties of organised decentralisation: country or sector', Paper presented at SASE conference, Lyon, 29 June–1 July.

Larsen, T.P. and Mailand, M. (2018) 'Lifting wage and working conditions for atypical workers', *Industrial Relations Journal*, 49(2): 88–108.

Larsen, T.P. and Navrbjerg, S.E. (2018) 'Bargaining for equal pay and work–life balance in Danish companies: does gender matter?', *Journal of Industrial Relations*, 60(2): 176–200.

Larsen, T.P., Navrbjerg, S.E. and Johansen, M.M. (2010) *Tillidsrepræsentanten og arbejdspladsen*, Rapport 1, Copenhagen: LO.

Lyonette, C. (2015) 'Part-time work, work–life balance and gender equality', *Journal of Social Welfare and Family Law*, 37(3): 321–33.

Mailand, M. (2017) 'The European refugee crisis in the reaction of labour market actors', *Global Labour Journal*, 8(1): 90–8.

Mailand, M. and Larsen, T.P. (2018) *Hybrid work: Social protection of atypical employment in Denmark*, Research Report 000, Berlin: WSI.

Manning, A. (2016) *The elusive employment effect of the minimum wage*, CEP Discussion Paper No. 1428, London: London School of Economics.

Matteazzi, E., Pailhë, A. and Solaz, A. (2018) 'Part-time employment, the gender wage gaps and the role of wage-setting institutions', *European Journal of Industrial Relations*, 24(3): 221–41.

McCollum, D. and Findlay, A. (2015) '"Flexible" workers for "flexible" jobs?', *Work, Employment and Society*, 29(3): 427–43.

Neumark, D. and Wascher, W. (2006) *Minimum wages and employment*, Working Paper 12663, Cambridge: National Bureau of Economic Research.

Rubery, J. (2015) 'Change at work', *Employee Relations*, 37(6): 633–44.

Rubery, J. and Grimshaw, D. (2015) 'The 40-year pursuit of equal pay', *Cambridge Journal of Economics*, 39(2): 319–43.

Rubery, J., Ward, K., Grimshaw, D. and Beynon, H. (2005) 'Working time, industrial relations and the employment relationship', *Time and Society*, 14(1): 89–111.

Schulten, T. (2016) 'Danish, German and European perspective on statutory minimum wages', in T.P. Larsen and A. Ilsøe (eds) *Den danske model set udefra*, Copenhagen: DJØF Publishing.

Seifert, H. (ed) (2005) *Flexible Zeiten in der Arbeitswelt*, Frankfurt: Campus Verlag.

Statistics Denmark (2017) *Firmastatistikken*, Copenhagen: Statistics Denmark.

Walsh, T.J. (1990) 'Flexible labour utilisation in the private sector', *Work Employment and Society*, 4(4): 517–30.

Warren, T. (2004) 'Working part-time', *British Journal of Sociology*, 55(1): 99–122.

Warren, T. (2015) 'Work-time underemployment and financial hardship', *Work, Employment and Society*, 29(2): 191–212.

Westergaard-Nielsen, N. (eds) (2008) *Low wage work in Denmark*, New York, NY: Russell Sage Foundation.

7

Stepping in, stepping out or staying put? Part-time work and immigrant integration in Norway

Hanne Cecilie Kavli and Roy A. Nielsen

Introduction

Increased migration has put the economic integration of immigrants high on the agenda in Western Europe. A large number of studies have shown that immigrants are often at a disadvantage in the labour market (Heath and Cheung, 2007; European Commission, 2008). This has led to a strong focus on integration policy that can facilitate rapid employment. In this perspective, part-time work is often viewed as a stepping stone to full-time employment, and the workplace as an arena where immigrants can acquire skills and contacts that will enable upwards mobility in the labour market (Becker, 1993 [1964]; Granovetter, 1995; Friedberg, 2000). However, is this a valid assumption?

Part-time work departs from the standard employment relationship, as described by Bosch (2004), and is often used as an indicator of a precarious labour market position. The 'full-time nature of the job, its stability, and the social standards linked with permanent full-time work' are key elements in Bosch's (2004: 619) definition. Part-time work is linked to a higher risk of unstable employment, wage penalties, less career opportunities and less opportunity to participate in skill-enhancing activities at the workplace (Messenger and Ray, 2015). Nevertheless, it would be a mistake to reduce part-time work to a singular type of labour market phenomenon as the extent, organisation, causes and consequences of part-time work vary between different contexts. The risk that part-time workers run of being in a precarious or marginalised position is influenced by the country's institutional arrangements (Gash, 2008b; Vosko, 2010). In Norway, part-time work underwent a process of normalisation during the 1980s. Part-time workers increased their hours of work, improved their contracts and grew their union membership; moreover, wage differences between part- and full-time workers were limited (Hardoy and Schøne, 2006; Ellingsæter, 2017).

However, although institutional regulations improved the position of part-time workers in general, there may still be differences within the overall category of part-time workers. In this chapter, we set out to examine the extent to which part-time work facilitates labour market integration for immigrants. To what degree do immigrants transition from part- to full-time jobs? Do they display higher or lower levels of upwards mobility in working time compared to natives? What separates part-time workers who are stepping further into the labour market in terms of a full-time job from workers who either 'stay put' in a part-time position or who exit the labour market? By analysing Norwegian register data, we outline the changing labour market characteristics of part-time employees and investigate the degree to which different categories of workers display different patterns of transition. We conclude by assessing the implications of the various types and patterns of part-time work for debates on the dualisation of part-time work.

The integration scenario: part-time work as a stepping stone

Is part-time employment a path towards full integration in the labour market for immigrants or a sign of a precarious labour market position? A central assumption in the literature, which we have labelled 'the integration scenario', is that employment, even if it is non-standard, represents an opportunity for employees to secure a better position in the labour market. According to Gash (2008a: 652), this scenario postulates a 'win–win' situation, with employers benefitting from greater flexibility and employees from a more open labour market with increased opportunities for transition from atypical to standard employment. In countries where job security is high, employing workers on fixed-term contracts or in (short) part-time positions might reduce the perceived risks of employing workers who signal low productivity. Immigrants may have more to gain compared to natives in this regard as foreign educational credentials and foreign work experience can set off risk-averse behaviour among employers. Being in employment may signal ability and skills (Waldman, 1984). Furthermore, with increased tenure, such signals may become more reliable, and, in addition, a transition to more work hours would signal ability even more. Thus, immigrants who lack either formal qualifications or the documents to prove their qualifications may benefit from on-the-job screening.

Human capital theory (Becker, 1993 [1964]) assumes that competence increases with employment. A premise is that through their work, employees are able to acquire skills and contacts that will make them more attractive to employers and more eligible for a full-time job. Whether being in employment is a signal of innate skills or leads to increased skills is of secondary importance as both should be conducive to further employment. Having a job can also equip the employee with a network that might provide information about and access to jobs (Granovetter, 1995), while unemployment may produce scarring effects that further reduce employment opportunities (Eriksson and Rooth, 2014). In line with this reasoning, we might assume that while atypical employment can be hard to move beyond, it will still provide better opportunities than a position of unemployment (Giesecke and Groß, 2003). In particular, in regulated labour markets with high levels of employment protection, workers who are seen as uncertain investments in terms of productivity may have greater chances of gaining employment if employers are able to 'test' them.

Formal education and work experience are central to what workers have to offer employers. A person's national origin can, however, significantly impact the value of their human capital. While empirical analyses have shown a correlation between education and immigrants' economic integration (see, eg, Bratsberg et al, 2012), immigrants have lower returns from their education than non-immigrants, both in terms of their pay (Brekke and Mastekaasa, 2008) and their position (Hardoy and Schøne, 2014). Migration researchers have looked for explanations within theories of 'country-specific human capital', emphasising that human capital is not easily transferable across borders (Borjas, 1995). Limited knowledge of the new country's language and labour markets, as well as different formal demands regarding occupational competence, can reduce the value of education and experience acquired abroad (Chiswick et al, 2005; Kanas and Van Tubergen, 2009). Also, uncertainties about the labour market value of immigrants' educational credentials could lead employers to place less emphasis on education as a signal of the productivity of immigrant workers (Bratsberg and Ragan, 2002). However, as immigrants gradually acquire more country-specific skills and networks, these reduce disadvantages and employment levels rise (Friedberg, 2000; Chiswick and Miller, 2010). The 'integration scenario' thus predicts that part-time employment can be a stepping stone to full-time employment. As immigrants have less 'documented' qualifications to help signal their attractiveness to employers, we would, in fact, expect immigrants to benefit more from the opportunity to 'prove themselves' through part-time employment. Furthermore, this may imply that immigrants in part-time positions are more interested in transitioning to full-time employment.

The dualised scenario: part-time work as an end station for immigrants

As pointed out in the Introduction to this volume, recent decades have seen an increase in atypical employment across countries. The 'dualisation scenario' describes a process where this is leading to a dualised labour market with a growing divide between 'insiders' and 'outsiders'. 'Insiders' are protected through stable and well-regulated employment and enjoy full rights to benefits. 'Outsiders' are in more precarious positions, with higher risks of unemployment and underemployment, lower levels of protection and employment rights, lower salaries, and limited rights to benefits (Kalleberg, 2009; Palier and Thelen, 2010; Emmenegger et al, 2012; Rueda et al, 2015). The degree to which part-time work increases the risk of being an 'outsider' is likely to vary by country of origin and occupation. Short and/or involuntary part-time work is often considered an indication that the worker is in an outsider position (Kalleberg, 2000; Bosch, 2004; Standing, 2011). Of course, the gravity of being in an outsider position will depend on its permanency. Broadly speaking, 'the dualised scenario' argues that non-standard employment is not a stepping stone, but rather a 'trap' or an 'end station'. Once workers have entered the secondary labour market, they have limited opportunities to transition to the primary labour market.

Several studies have addressed the question of mobility out of part-time work. O'Reilly and Bothfeld (2002) found that in Britain and Germany in the early 1990s, only a small number of part-time workers transitioned to full-time employment, while a substantial proportion exited the labour market. They concluded that while part-time work served as a route from unemployment to employment, the evidence that part-time work can lead to further integration into full-time work was 'very thin' (O'Reilly and Bothfeld, 2002: 434). In a comparative analysis including Denmark, France and the UK, Gash (2008b) links differences in part-time workers' transition to full-time work to policies supporting maternal employment. She concludes that Danish and French policies, to a larger degree than British policies, enable women to work their preferred hours, and that this consequently makes women in the UK more 'constrained' to part-time work. Like Denmark, Norway has well-developed policies enabling parents to combine work and family. Even so, low education, young children and employment in typical 'part-time industries' still constrain women's transitions from part- to full-time work and increase the risk of labour market exit (Kitterød et al, 2013).

Immigrants are over-represented among the low-skilled part of the labour market, as well as in part-time industries (European Commission, 2008; Rubin et al, 2008; Vrålstad and Wiggen, 2017). As these jobs require limited training, workers are easy to replace. More job experience will therefore not necessarily give the employee an advantage. Upwards mobility from the secondary sector would require an increase in formal education rather than more work experience in that sector. Muñoz-Comet (2016) argues that this is an important reason why work experience does not seem to protect immigrants from becoming unemployed in times of downscaling. While more years in the labour market reduced the risk of becoming unemployed among Spanish-born workers, the protective effect was far more limited for Africans, Latin Americans and Eastern Europeans.

In contrast to the integration scenario, the dualised scenario predicts limited upwards mobility and high exit risk for workers in part-time employment. As immigrants are over-represented in the low-skilled part of the labour market and in typical part-time industries, this perspective also suggests that, in general, immigrants are less able than others to use part-time work as a stepping stone to full-time employment.

Immigrants, part-time employment and gender

Finally, yet importantly, part-time employment is a highly gendered phenomenon. Compared to men, women have lower levels of employment and take up part-time work to a larger extent, over longer periods and often in the middle of their careers (O'Reilly and Fagan, 1998; Ellingsæter, 2017). The literature on women's work orientation has dedicated much attention to the question of individual preferences versus structural constraints. On the one hand, a lack of mobility from part- to full-time employment may indicate that the worker is 'stuck' in involuntary, part-time employment. On the other hand, part-time work can be a preferred way to facilitate a work–life balance. 'Stable' part-time work can be both 'good' and 'bad' in this regard.

Involuntary part-time work is more common among female immigrants than among non-immigrants (Rubin et al, 2008). We would therefore expect female immigrants to strive for upwards mobility in working time to a greater extent than non-immigrants. In this case, the integration perspective would predict higher upwards mobility in working time among immigrant women than among non-immigrant women. On the other hand, both male and female immigrants are over-represented in part-time-dominated sectors (European Commission, 2008; Hussein and Christensen, 2017). According to the dualisation perspective, employment in these sectors may limit workers' options and reduce their ability to transition from part- to full-time positions.

Providing work is available, the share of men who take on part-time jobs in their prime working years is low. Those who do may therefore differ from other men in ways that will also affect their working-time mobility. Poor health, for example, may increase the likelihood of part-time employment while also reducing the probability of transitioning to full-time work and increasing the likelihood of labour market exit. Male immigrants may differ from male non-immigrants in at least two ways. First, they may need to take on a part-time job in the middle of their careers as a way of (re-)entering the labour market after migration. While the integration scenario would predict this to be temporary, the dualisation scenario would argue that further 'integration' from part- to full-time work can be hard to achieve. Second, male immigrants are over-represented in sectors otherwise dominated by female and part-time workers (European Commission, 2008; Hussein and Christensen, 2017). In these sectors, the number of full-time positions tends to be limited. On the one hand, this might reduce immigrant men's opportunities to increase their working time compared to other men. On the other, they might gain advantages from their gender status in female-dominated industries and thus be able to move more effectively from part- to full-time positions (Hussein and Christensen, 2017).

The Norwegian context

Modern migration to Norway is characterised by four phases. During the economic upturn of the late 1960s, there was a considerable inflow of labour migrants from Morocco, Yugoslavia, Pakistan and Turkey. By 1975, the economy had shifted and labour migration halted. In the second phase, migration continued as family members came to reunite with former labour migrants. The third phase started in the mid-1980s with a rapid increase in asylum seekers. The fourth phase is dominated by new labour migration, this time from European Union

(EU) countries, in particular, from Poland and Lithuania. In 2017, the immigrant share of the population was 16.8%. Between 1990 and 2016, 36% secured residency through family reunification, 33% as labour migrants, 20% as refugees and 10% on student visas (Vrålstad and Wiggen, 2017).

Immigrants' economic integration in Norway takes place in a context of high employment among both men and women, but also a gendered labour market with high degrees of segregation by occupation and in part-time employment (Ellingsæter, 2017). The employment rate in 2008, the year in which we start our analyses, for the age group 20–66 years was 82.1% among men and 76.2% among women.[1] Overall, immigrants' employment rates are about 10 percentage points below those of non-immigrants. However, employment rates for immigrants from Europe and the US are close to the rate for the overall population. Meanwhile, employment rates among immigrants from Africa and Asia are closer to 20 percentage points below that of non-immigrants. Working time also varies according to regional origin, with part-time employment more common among immigrants from regions with low employment levels. Compared to the overall population, male and female immigrants from Europe are less likely to work part-time (defined as less than 30 hours per week) than non-immigrants. Among immigrants from Asia and Africa, part-time employment rates for both men and women are almost eight percentage points higher than among non-immigrants (Olsen, 2017).

Data and methods

This study employed Norwegian register data from several sources linked via a unique personal identification number. The data cover more than 90% of all employees in Norway[2] and include information on, for example, establishment characteristics and contractual work hours, as well as demographics. The sample consists of all prime working-age (25–54 years) employees who had a part-time job at T_0 in 2008. Part-time is defined as less than 30 hours per week (agreed in the employment contract), which is the definition used by Statistics Norway and the Organisation for Economic Co-operation and Development (OECD). Actual working hours can be somewhat higher or somewhat lower than agreed. A full-time position usually corresponds to 37.5 hours per week, which means that our full-time category (30+ hours) encompasses individual workers with 80–90% positions. Employees with more than one part-time job were excluded as several part-time jobs may equal full-time work in total. Since most student work is transitory in nature, we also excluded students in part-time employment. Employees with a single part-time job in the third week of November 2008 were chosen for follow-up. In total, 177,046 part-time employees were followed up for 61 months, through to 2013.

There were two endpoints in the analyses: either a transition to full-time work or an exit from the labour market.[3] The purpose of the analyses was to estimate the cumulative incidence of either transition. To estimate the probability of a transition to full-time work, exits could not be treated as censored, and to estimate the exit probability, transitions to full-time work could not be treated as censored. The probability of a transition to full-time employment (or exit) is both a function of the hazard of a transition to full-time work (or exit) and the hazard of an exit (or transition to full-time work). Thus, using Kaplan–Meier plots or Cox regression would yield biased estimates (Andersen et al, 2012; Noordzij et al, 2013). Transitions to full-time work or exit are competing events; thus, we employed a sub-distributions hazards approach proposed by Fine and Gray (1999) and implemented in Stata software (Cleves et al, 2016).

We estimated two models: one unadjusted model containing only regional immigrant origin; and a second model adjusted by both individual and employment covariates.[4] We follow the definition of an immigrant by Statistics Norway (born abroad to two foreign-born parents). Individual covariates were age (and age squared), education level, marital status and the presence of children. There is a lack of register information on immigrants' education levels, particularly for the newest groups of refugees. Education was therefore only divided into five levels: long tertiary, short tertiary, secondary, primary and unknown. Covariates regarding employment included tenure (in months) at the start of the follow-up, the share of women and share of part-time employees at the workplace, the number of employees at the workplace (1–19, 20–99, 100+), contractual working hours (short part-time: 4–14 hours per week; long part-time: 15–29 hours per week), and occupational groups. All analyses are performed separately for men and women.

Descriptive statistics

When we exclude students, older workers and workers with more than one job, 32,000 men and 145,000 women were in a single part-time occupation in 2008 when our follow-up period began. Among men (see Table 7.1a), our four regional groups differ in terms of education, family status, occupation and tenure. The lowest education level is among immigrants from Africa and Asia – 60% had either unknown or only primary education. Among part-timers from Europe, North America and Australia, however, the share with long tertiary education is higher than among Norwegians. In terms of family status, more immigrant men, in particular, from Asia, Africa and Central and South America, are married and have young children than among Norwegian men. Also, the distribution across occupations varies substantially, with migrants from Eastern Europe, Africa, Asia and Central and South America strongly over-represented within services and sales and in unskilled occupations. Norwegian and Western European, North American and Australian (henceforth also referred to as 'Western') part-timers are distributed quite evenly between occupations, with the largest share in services and sales. The distribution across establishment sizes does not vary substantially, but there are more Norwegians in small companies, whereas migrants are more evenly distributed. The average tenure is substantially longer among Norwegians and immigrants from Western countries compared to other immigrants.

Among female part-timers (see Table 7.1b), we find some, but not all, of the same differences according to regional origin. Education levels are somewhat higher for women than for men in all regional groups, but the general differences follow the same patterns. A total of about 60% of African, Asian and Central and South American women have either unknown or primary education. Female immigrants from Eastern Europe have a large share with tertiary education, only surpassed by immigrants from Western countries. The average age varied from slightly below 36 among African immigrants to well over 41 among non-immigrants. A large number of female part-timers have small children under the age of six, varying from 29% among non-immigrants to almost 43% among African immigrants. Short part-time work is relatively uncommon among non-immigrant women (at 18%), whereas the share is substantially higher among African/Asian immigrants (at over 30%). Women are evenly distributed across establishment sizes, except for African/Asian immigrants, who have a small share in the smallest establishments. Among Norwegians and Western immigrants, about 40% work as a nurse or personal care worker. Personal care work is substantial among immigrants as well, with 40% among female African immigrants. Among Eastern Europeans, Africans and Asians, about a third work as a cleaner.

Table 7.1a: Descriptive statistics, male part-time employees, November 2008

		Region of origin		
	Norway	Western Europe, North America, Australia	Eastern Europe	Africa, Asia, Central and South America
Average age	40.4	40.1	38.0	37.5
No/unknown education	0.5	17.5	18.3	18.1
Primary education	36.8	19.0	22.9	41.8
Secondary education	34.8	19.4	29.6	18.7
Tertiary education, short	19.5	22.7	17.5	14.4
Tertiary education, long	8.5	21.3	11.8	7.1
Unmarried	52.8	47.5	26.6	23.4
Married/partner	36.9	41.7	62.3	64.1
Divorced/separated/widowed	10.3	10.9	11.1	12.5
No children <18 years	50.8	48.2	46.4	38.7
Youngest child <7 years	21.9	30.2	30.7	41.4
Youngest child 7–18 years	27.3	21.5	22.9	19.9
Tenure (in months at T_o)	55.2	38.1	29.8	26.7
Short part-time (<15 hours/week)	32.3	34.3	32.2	36.7

(continued)

Table 7.1a: Descriptive statistics, male part-time employees, November 2008 (continued)

		Region of origin		
	Norway	Western Europe, North America, Australia	Eastern Europe	Africa, Asia, Central and South America
Share of women within establishment	38.5	45.5	38.9	41.8
Share in part-time within establishment	50.5	52.3	57.8	56.7
1–19 employees within establishment	39.5	35.8	33.1	33.5
20–99 employees within establishment	32.5	33.2	31.6	30.4
100+ employees within establishment	28.0	31.0	35.3	36.1
Managers and professionals (1, 2)	12.1	18.8	6.1	5.0
Technicians & associate professionals (3)	14.1	15.1	6.6	4.6
Clerical support & machine operators (4, 8)	18.4	10.1	14.9	12.7
Services & sales (5)	27.9	31.2	26.3	34.2
Skilled workers (6, 7, 0)	18.4	14.8	13.9	6.9
Unskilled workers (9)	9.1	10.0	32.2	36.6
N	32,897	1,577	1,217	5,102

Source: Register data 2013, Statistics Norway

Table 7.1b: Descriptive statistics, female part-time employees, November 2008

		Region of origin		
	Norway	Western Europe, North America, Australia	Eastern Europe	Africa, Asia, Central and South America
Average age	41.4	40.9	38.0	37.7
No/unknown education	0.1	9.7	14.8	18.4
Primary education	36.8	20.9	24.0	39.3
Secondary education	32.8	21.4	28.1	19.6
Tertiary education, short	27.2	37.6	20.4	18.3
Tertiary education, long	3.0	10.3	12.8	4.5
Unmarried	29.2	28.0	13.1	8.7
Married/partner	59.0	62.4	74.2	75.8
Divorced/separated/widowed	11.8	9.6	12.7	15.5
No children <18 years	30.1	27.9	34.2	27.8
Youngest child <7 years	29.3	34.8	34.0	40.4
Youngest child 7–18 years	40.6	37.3	31.8	31.8
Tenure (in months at T_0)	56.6	39.8	27.1	26.5
Short part-time (<15 hours/week)	17.4	21.2	28.8	30.8

(continued)

Table 7.1b: Descriptive statistics. Female part-time employees, November 2008 (continued)

		Region of origin		
	Norway	Western Europe, North America, Australia	Eastern Europe	Africa, Asia, Central and South America
Share of women within establishment	77.3	75.0	72.2	72.5
Share in part-time within establishment	53.7	52.1	54.4	53.8
1–19 employees within establishment	32.7	31.3	33.6	27.2
20–99 employees within establishment	34.7	33.2	36.2	35.9
100+ employees within establishment	32.6	35.5	30.2	36.9
Managers & professionals (1, 2)	6.8	13.7	4.2	2.4
Technicians & associate professionals (3)	20.6	26.3	11.0	7.6
Clerical support & machine operators (4, 8)	9.7	7.9	7.8	6.2
Services & sales (5)	47.9	37.8	39.9	43.2
Skilled workers (6, 7, 0)	8.1	7.2	6.6	7.1
Unskilled workers (9)	6.9	7.1	30.5	33.6
N	130,198	3,462	3,332	8,039

Source: Register data 2013, Statistics Norway

Findings

The overall transition rates of male part-time employees are illustrated in Figure 7.1, which figure shows that non-immigrant males are most likely to remain in part-time work, while Africans, Asians and immigrants from Central and South America are least likely to remain in part-time positions. After 60 months, the estimated transition to full-time work (based on Model 1 in Table 7.2) among males varies from 31% among non-immigrants to almost 39% among immigrants from Africa, Asia and Central and South America, while exit rates vary between 11% and 18%, respectively. This implies that about 58% of non-immigrants remain in part-time work, whereas this only applies to 43% of immigrants from Africa, Asia and Central and South America.

Thus, among male part-timers, immigrants have a higher probability of transition to full-time employment than non-immigrants (see Model 1, Table 7.2). Adjusting for individual and employment covariates reduces country group differences (see Model 2). After adjustment, male Eastern European and Western part-time employees are not significantly different from non-immigrants. Relative differences between non-immigrants and immigrants from Asia/Africa are reduced but still significant. Most included covariates have an impact on transition rates. Transition to full-time employment decreases monotonically with increasing age, and individuals with secondary or tertiary education have higher transition rates. Marital status does not impact transition rates to full-time employment among men, but having children increases transition rates somewhat. Working in female-dominated establishments increases the likelihood of transitioning to full-time positions among male part-timers, whereas working in establishments with a high share of part-timers reduces transition rates. Transition rates to full-time employment are highest among males in large establishments. Male employees in short part-time positions have substantially lower transition rates to full-time employment compared to males in long part-time positions. Transition rates are highest among those with short tenure, indicating either that if part-time work is used as a way to 'test' employees, then this testing does not take too long, or that workers who want more hours are prone to change jobs in order to secure them (see, eg, Böheim and Taylor, 2004). Separate analyses without non-immigrants yield similar results, but among immigrants, age is insignificant and the impact of short part-time work is not quite as strong.

On the other hand, all male immigrant groups have a higher risk of exit from the labour market than non-immigrants. The overall exit

Figure 7.1: Overall male transitions from part-time to full-time work or exit, stacked cumulative incidence, by region of origin

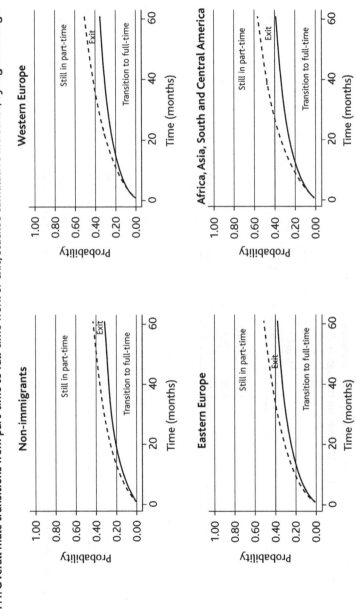

Source: Estimated from Model 1 in Table 7.2

Table 7.2: Sub-distribution hazard ratios (SHRs) of the transition to full-time work and exit from the labour market for males in a single part-time occupation in November 2008 followed up through to 2013

| | Transition to full-time | | | | Exit | | | |
| | Model 1 | | Model 2 | | Model 1 | | Model 2 | |
	SHR	95% CI	SHR	95% CI	SHR	95% CI	SHR	95% CI
Norway (=ref)								
Western Europe, N. America and Australia	1.14	(1.03–1.27)	1.00	(0.90–1.11)	1.34	(1.15–1.57)	1.18	(1.00–1.39)
Eastern Europe	1.26	(1.12–1.41)	1.11	(0.99–1.25)	1.19	(0.98–1.44)	0.93	(0.77–1.14)
Africa, Asia, Central & South America	1.29	(1.22–1.37)	1.15	(1.08–1.23)	1.63	(1.49–1.77)	1.18	(1.07–1.30)
Age			0.97	(0.95–0.99)			0.97	(0.93–1.01)
Age*age			1.00	(1.00–1.00)			1.00	(1.00–1.00)
No/unknown education (=ref)								
Primary education			0.99	(0.88–1.11)			0.93	(0.79–1.09)
Secondary education			1.19	(1.06–1.34)			0.87	(0.74–1.02)
Tertiary education, short			1.44	(1.28–1.62)			0.93	(0.78–1.10)
Tertiary education, long			1.30	(1.14–1.47)			0.91	(0.75–1.10)
Unmarried (=ref)								
Married/partner			1.03	(0.98–1.08)			0.97	(0.89–1.06)
Divorced/separated/widowed			1.05	(0.97–1.13)			1.05	(0.93–1.19)

(continued)

Table 7.2: Sub-distribution hazard ratios (SHRs) of the transition to full-time work and exit from the labour market for males in a single part-time occupation in November 2008 followed up through to 2013 (continued)

	Transition to full-time				Exit			
	Model 1		Model 2		Model 1		Model 2	
	SHR	95% CI	SHR	95% CI	SHR	95% CI	SHR	95% CI
No children (=ref)								
Youngest child <7 years			1.19	(1.13–1.26)			1.01	(0.93–1.10)
Youngest child 7–18 years			1.09	(1.03–1.15)			1.06	(0.96–1.16)
Tenure (in months at T_0)			1.00	(1.00–1.00)			0.98	(0.98–0.98)
Tenure*tenure			1.00	(1.00–1.00)			1.00	(1.00–1.00)
Short part-time (<15 hours/week)			0.63	(0.60–0.66)			1.23	(1.16–1.32)
Share of females within establishment			1.53	(1.41–1.66)			1.22	(1.07–1.38)
Share in part-time within establishment			0.72	(0.67–0.77)			0.77	(0.68–0.87)
1–19 employees within establishment (=ref)								
20–99 employees within establishment			1.54	(1.46–1.62)			1.04	(0.96–1.13)
100+ employees within establishment			1.98	(1.88–2.08)			0.86	(0.79–0.94)
Occupational groups			(6)				(6)	
N			32,015				32,105	

Source: Register data 2013, Statistics Norway

175

risk can largely be explained by the covariates included in Model 2, but a difference remains between non-migrants and immigrants from Asia/Africa. Exit risk decreases with increased age. Education only has a minor impact on exit rates, and secondary and tertiary education have very similar exit rates. Marital status and having children does not impact male exit rates. What matters most (in Model 2) is working short part-time and establishment size. In a separate regression including only male immigrants, we find that education does not have a measurable influence on exit rates, and a tendency for working short part-time has less impact among immigrants.

Overall, male transition to full-time employment or exit is, in part, explained by age, education and having parental responsibilities, but mostly by contractual work hours and establishment size. Immigrants from Africa/Asia have an increased rate of both transition to full-time employment and of exit from the labour market. Older workers have lower transition rates to both full-time employment and exit. Tertiary education increases the likelihood of transition to full-time employment but has no measurable impact on exit risk. Males in short part-time positions have substantially lower transition rates to full-time employment and higher exit risks compared to males in long part-time positions. The included covariates only partly explain male immigrants' increased likelihood of transition to full-time employment and risk of exit from the labour market.

Estimated transition rates of female part-timers from the various immigrant groups are illustrated in Figure 7.2 (based on Model 1 in Table 7.3). Overall transition rates to full-time positions are very similar among the different immigrant groups, with female immigrants from Africa, Asia and Central and South America having a slightly higher likelihood of making the transition. In terms of labour market exits, however, immigrant women have a higher risk compared to non-immigrants. After five years, overall transition rates to full-time positions vary between 42% and 44% among the different regional groups, while exit rates vary between 10% among non-immigrants to 16% among immigrants from Africa and Asia. Consequently, the share remaining in part-time work only varies between 40% and 48%, respectively, and is somewhat lower than the share among men who are employed in what we have categorised as 'stable part-time' positions.

Among women, regional groups differ very little in terms of transition rates from part- to full-time employment. However, when adjusting for the same covariates as applied to the male regression model, that is to say, comparing more similar individuals, we find that

Figure 7.2: Overall female transitions from part-time to full-time work or exit, stacked cumulative incidence, by region of origin

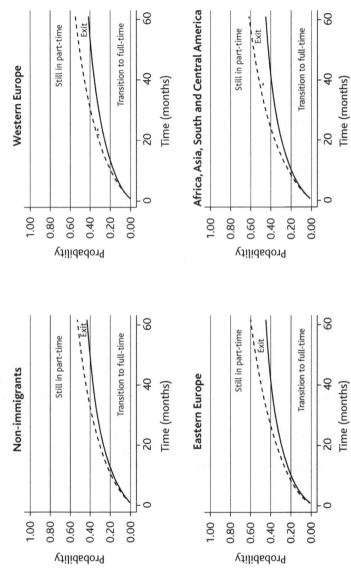

Source: Estimated from Model 1 in Table 7.3

most immigrants have higher transition rates to full-time positions, with the exception of immigrants from Western countries. Transition to a full-time position initially increases with age among female part-timers but subsequently levels off. Transition to full-time work is more common among women with a tertiary education. Unmarried women have higher transition rates to full-time positions compared with married, divorced, separated or widowed women. Having children, particularly older children, increases transition to full-time work; women without children have the lowest transition rates. A high share of women at the establishment also increases transition to full-time work, while a high share of part-timers reduces the transition rate. Female part-timers with low tenure have the highest transition rates. As was the case among men, working hours and establishment size have a large impact on the rate of transition to full-time positions. Separate analyses without non-immigrants yield similar results.

Overall, exit rates from the labour market are much higher among immigrant women than among non-immigrant women, particularly among non-Western women. However, when adjusting for demographics and work-related variables, exit rates between the different immigrant groups become more similar. That said, after adjustment, immigrants from Africa, Asia and Central and South America still have higher exit rates than non-immigrants. Exit rates decrease monotonically with increasing age, whereas education has very little impact in our model, which also controls for occupation. Divorcees have high exit rates but having children only has a minor impact. Similar to what we found among male part-timers, exit rates among women are (in our model) mostly impacted by working short part-time and establishment size.

Overall, female transition to full-time work and exit is, in part, explained by age, education and having parental responsibilities, but mostly by contractual hours and establishment size. Immigrant women from Africa/Asia in part-time positions are both more likely to experience a transition to full-time work and to experience an exit from the labour market. The included covariates seem to explain immigrant women's likelihood of transition to full-time work and risk of exit from the labour market slightly more than in the male analyses. Generally, the various covariates influence male and female transition rates in a similar way.

Table 7.3: Sub-distribution hazard ratios (SHRs) and standard errors of the transition to full-time work and exit from the labour market for females in a single part-time occupation in November 2008 followed up through to 2013

| | Transition to full-time | | | | Exit | | | |
| | Model 1 | | Model 2 | | Model 1 | | Model 2 | |
	SHR	95% CI	SHR	95% CI	SHR	95% CI	SHR	95% CI
Norway (=ref)								
Western Europe, N. America and Australia	0.97	(0.92–1.02)	0.95	(0.90–0.99)	1.23	(1.12–1.35)	1.09	(0.99–1.20)
Eastern Europe	1.04	(0.98–1.09)	1.16	(1.09–1.22)	1.38	(1.26–1.51)	0.92	(0.84–1.02)
Africa, Asia, Central & South America	1.04	(1.00–1.08)	1.15	(1.11–1.20)	1.61	(1.52–1.71)	1.07	(1.01–1.15)
Age			1.04	(1.03–1.05)			0.94	(0.92–0.96)
Age*age			0.99	(0.99–0.99)			1.00	(1.00–1.00)
No/unknown education (=ref)								
Primary education			1.08	(1.01–1.17)			1.00	(0.89–1.11)
Secondary education			1.20	(1.11–1.29)			0.97	(0.87–1.08)
Tertiary education, short			1.34	(1.25–1.45)			1.00	(0.90–1.12)
Tertiary education, long			1.32	(1.21–1.43)			1.15	(1.01–1.31)
Unmarried (=ref)								
Married/partner			0.92	(0.91–0.94)			0.98	(0.94–1.02)
Divorced/separated/widowed			0.95	(0.93–0.98)			1.23	(1.16–1.30)

(continued)

Table 7.3: Sub-distribution hazard ratios (SHRs) and standard errors of the transition to full-time work and exit from the labour market for females in a single part-time occupation in November 2008 followed up through to 2013 (continued)

| | Transition to full-time | | | | Exit | | | |
| | Model 1 | | Model 2 | | Model 1 | | Model 2 | |
	SHR	95% CI	SHR	95% CI	SHR	95% CI	SHR	95% CI
No children (=ref)								
Youngest child <7 years			1.09	(1.06–1.12)			1.02	(0.97–1.07)
Youngest child 7–18 years			1.18	(1.16–1.21)			1.05	(0.99–1.10)
Tenure (in months at T_0)			0.99	(0.99–0.99)			0.99	(0.99–0.99)
Tenure*tenure			1.00	(1.00–1.00)			1.00	(1.00–1.00)
Short part-time (<15 hours/week)			0.56	(0.55–0.57)			1.49	(1.44–1.55)
Share of females within establishment			1.62	(1.55–1.70)			0.83	(0.77–0.91)
Share in part-time within establishment			1.01	(0.97–1.05)			0.99	(0.92–1.07)
1–19 employees within establishment (=ref)								
20–99 employees within establishment			1.65	(1.62–1.68)			0.88	(0.85–0.92)
100+ employees within establishment			1.94	(1.90–1.98)			0.76	(0.73–0.79)
Occupational groups			(6)				(6)	
N	145,031				145,031			

Source: Register data 2013, Statistics Norway

Discussion and conclusion

This chapter sought to reveal whether immigrants' part-time work is likely to provide a stepping stone to full-time employment or is more of an 'end station' with greater precariousness and risk of labour market exit. We also investigated whether the mobility patterns among part-timers differ between immigrants and non-immigrants, according to immigrants' regional origin and gender. By means of register data comprising virtually all part-time employees in Norway, we have followed individuals in a single part-time position for five years, and we have investigated transitions into full-time work as well as transitions out of employment.

Comparing the relative rate of transitions from part-time employment, we found that while stable part-time work is the most common trajectory among both men and women, transitions to full-time work are more widespread than employment exits. This is true for immigrants as well as for non-immigrants. However, in general, immigrants have the same or higher likelihood of transition from part-time to full-time work when compared to non-immigrants. This suggests that while immigrants may have a hard time entering the Norwegian labour market, for some, a part-time position may be a stepping stone to a full-time job. This finding is in line with the assumption that workers with 'foreign' human capital may benefit more than natives from the opportunity to demonstrate their ability and competence to employers.

While part-time employment is a stepping stone for some, it can be an end station for others, either through labour market exit or in terms of a stable, but marginal, part-time job with short agreed hours. Immigrants, particularly from Africa, Asia and Central and South America, have an increased risk of employment exit as well as of short agreed hours. Contrary to the analysis of transitions to full-time work, it is mainly among the workplace variables that we find significant impacts on transitions from part-time work to unemployment. Working less than 15 hours per week increases the exit risk, with an increased (sub)hazard of more than 20% among men and close to 50% among women. Thus, short part-time work seems to be less of a stepping stone and more of an end station. Since we do not know whether short part-time work is voluntary or not, or if adverse working conditions are more widespread in such positions, we can only speculate regarding the extent to which such positions are 'bad' jobs or if such jobs are more often populated by unfavourable (to the employer) employees. However, short hours will have negative implications for social benefits and statutory entitlements, potentially placing the worker in a more precarious position.

There are some limitations to our analyses. First, we use only part-time work and mobility out of part-time work to distinguish between potential labour market insiders and outsiders. This is only one of many aspects relevant to measuring dualisation in the labour market. Results may change – or become clearer – if other measures are included and examined. Second, while we show variations in mobility patterns among immigrants according to region of origin, there are likely to also be substantial differences among immigrants within regions. By investigating immigrants from selected countries and in different receiving contexts in more detail, we may gain additional knowledge of the intersections between migration and labour market integration. Third, while five years in part-time work may be considered a stable part-time position, we do not know the longevity of the full-time positions or the length of exit spells. Given current knowledge on immigrants' employment rates and work hours, future research could investigate whether transitions to full-time positions are transitory or stable, and whether employment exits are temporary setbacks or the beginning of a path into welfare dependency.

That said, the study also provides new knowledge on the relation between part-time work and the economic integration of immigrants. Empirically, the limited movement of outsiders into insider positions has been used as evidence for a dual or segmented labour market (see, eg, Palier and Thelen, 2010; Emmenegger et al, 2012). Within our five-year time frame, part-time work is the final destination among a substantial share of part-timers, but less so for immigrants than for non-immigrants. If part-time work is voluntary and with equal social rights and working conditions as full-timers, it is no surprise that it is also quite stable. Further studies are needed to investigate in more depth if, and to what degree, stable part-time work among immigrants is, indeed, voluntary and has equal conditions to full-time work. Among immigrants who leave part-time work, transitions into full-time work are more common than labour market exits. As such, our findings are in line with the 'integration perspective', with its notion of one labour market providing flexibility for employers and opportunities for upwards mobility for employees. However, male immigrants from Western countries and Africa, Asia and Central and South America also show a significantly higher risk of labour market exit. While the Norwegian institutional configuration is protective of part-time workers, employees in short part-time positions still face a higher risk of labour market exit and reduced opportunities in terms of upwards mobility to full-time work.

Acknowledgement

The project is funded by the Research Council of Norway's programme on welfare, working life and migration (VAM), grant number 237031.

Notes

[1] Statistics Norway, Statistikkbanken.

[2] All employees are present in the AA register (State Register of Employers and Employees), but variables concerning work and work hours are deemed more reliable when linked to the LTO register (Register of Certificates of Pay and Tax Deductions), for example, by removing 'inactive' employees (see Aukrust et al, 2010).

[3] Analyses of exit rates help identify individuals in precarious positions. However, precariousness in the form of frequent job changes is not addressed in our analyses.

[4] Analyses including only migrants and various subgroups of migrants gave very similar results (not shown).

References

Andersen, P.K., Geskus, R.B., De Witte, T. and Putter, H. (2012) 'Competing risks in epidemiology: possibilities and pitfalls', *International Journal of Epidemiology*, 41: 861–70.

Aukrust, I., Aurdal, P.S., Bråthen, M. and Køber, T. (2010) *Registerbasert sysselsettingsstatistikk. Dokumentasjon*, Notater 8/2010, Oslo: Statistics Norway.

Becker, G.S. (1993 [1964]) *Human capital. A theoretical and empirical analysis, with special reference to education*, Chicago, IL, and London: The University of Chicago Press.

Böheim, R. and Taylor, M.P. (2004) 'Actual and preferred working hours', *British Journal of Industrial Relations*, 42: 149–66.

Borjas, G.J. (1995) 'Assimilation and changes in cohorts revisited: what happened to immigrants' earnings during the 1980s?', *Journal of Labour Economics*, 13(2): 201–45.

Bosch, G. (2004) 'Towards a new standard employment relationship in Western Europe', *British journal of industrial relations*, 42: 617–36.

Bratsberg, B. and Ragan, J.F., Jr (2002) 'The impact of host-country schooling on earnings: a study of male immigrants in the United States', *Journal of Human Resources*, 37(1): 63–105.

Bratsberg, B., Raaum, O. and Røed, K. (2012) 'Educating children of immigrants: closing the gap in Norwegian schools', *Nordic Economic Policy Review*, 3: 211–51.

Brekke, I. and Mastekaasa, A. (2008) 'Highly educated immigrants in the Norwegian labour market: permanent disadvantage?', *Work, Employment and Society*, 22: 507–26.

Chiswick, B.R. and Miller, P.W. (2010) 'Occupational language requirements and the value of English in the US labor market', *Journal of Population Economics*, 23: 353–72.

Chiswick, B.R., Lee, Y.L. and Miller, P.W. (2005) 'Immigrant earnings: a longitudinal analysis', *Review of Income and Wealth*, 51: 485–503.

Cleves, M., Gould, W.W. and Marchenko, Y.V. (2016) *An introduction to survival analysis using Stata*, College Station, TX: Stata Press.

Ellingsæter, A.L. (2017) *Vår tids moderne tider: det norske arbeidstidsregimet*, Oslo: Universitetsforlaget.

Emmenegger, P., Häusermann, S., Palier, B. and Seeleib-Kaiser, M. (2012) 'How we grow unequal', in P. Emmenegger, S. Häusermann, B. Palier and M. Seeleib-Kaiser (eds) *The age of dualization: the changing face of inequality in deindustrializing societies*, New York, NY: Oxford University Press.

Eriksson, S. and Rooth, D.-O. (2014) 'Do employers use unemployment as a sorting criterion when hiring? Evidence from a field experiment', *The American Economic Review*, 104: 1014–39.

European Commission (2008) *Employment in Europe 2008*, Brussels: Directorate-General for Employment, Social Affairs and Equal Opportunities.

Fine, J.P. and Gray, R.J. (1999) 'A proportional hazards model for the subdistribution of a competing risk', *Journal of the American Statistical Association*, 94: 496–509.

Friedberg, R.M. (2000) 'You can't take it with you? Immigrant assimilation and the portability of human capital', *Journal of Labor Economics*, 18: 221–51.

Gash, V. (2008a) 'Bridge or trap? Temporary workers' transitions to unemployment and to the standard employment contract', *European Sociological Review*, 24: 651–68.

Gash, V. (2008b) 'Preference or constraint? Part-time workers' transitions in Denmark, France and the United Kingdom', *Work, Employment and Society*, 22: 655–74.

Giesecke, J. and Groß, M. (2003) 'Temporary employment: chance or risk?', *European Sociological Review*, 19: 161–77.

Granovetter, M. (1995) *Getting a job: a study of contacts and careers*, Chicago, IL: University of Chicago Press.

Hardoy, I. and Schøne, P. (2006) 'The part-time wage gap in Norway: how large is it really?', *British Journal of Industrial Relations*, 44: 263–82.

Hardoy, I. and Schøne, P. (2014) 'Returns to pre-immigration education for non-Western immigrants: why so low?', *Education Economics*, 22: 48–72.

Heath, A. and Cheung, S.Y. (2007) *Unequal chances: ethnic minorities in Western labour markets*, Oxford: Oxford University Press.

Hussein, S. and Christensen, K. (2017) 'Migration, gender and low-paid work: on migrant men's entry dynamics into the feminised social care work in the UK', *Journal of Ethnic and Migration Studies*, 43: 749–65.

Kalleberg, A.L. (2000) 'Nonstandard employment relations: part-time, temporary and contract work', *Annual Review of Sociology*, 26: 341–65.

Kalleberg, A.L. (2009) 'Precarious work, insecure workers: employment relations in transition', *American Sociological Review*, 74: 1–22.

Kanas, A. and Van Tubergen, F. (2009) 'The impact of origin and host country schooling on the economic performance of immigrants', *Social Forces*, 88: 893–915.

Kitterød, R.H., Rønsen, M. and Seierstad, A. (2013) 'Mobilizing female labour market reserves: what promotes women's transitions between part-time and full-time work?', *Acta Sociologica*, 56: 155–71.

Messenger, J.C. and Ray, N. (2015) 'The "deconstruction" of part-time work', in J. Berg (ed) *Labour markets, institutions and inequality: building just societies in the 21st century*, Cheltenham: Edward Elgar Publishing.

Muñoz-Comet, J. (2016) 'Potential work experience as protection against unemployment: does it bring equal benefit to immigrants and native workers?', *European Sociological Review*, 32: 537–51.

Noordzij, M., Leffondré, K., Van Stralen, K.J., Zoccali, C., Dekker, F.W. and Jager, K.J. (2013) 'When do we need competing risks methods for survival analysis in nephrology?', *Nephrology Dialysis Transplantation*, 28: 2670–7.

Olsen, B. (2017) 'Innvandrere i og utenfor arbeidsmarkedet', Statistics Norway, Innvandrere i Norge.

O'Reilly, J. and Bothfeld, S. (2002) 'What happens after working part time? Integration, maintenance or exclusionary transitions in Britain and Western Germany', *Cambridge Journal of Economics*, 26: 409–39.

O'Reilly, J. and Fagan, C. (eds) (1998) *Part-time prospects: an international comparison of part-time work in Europe, North America and the Pacific Rim*, London and New York: Routledge.

Palier, B. and Thelen, K. (2010) 'Institutionalizing dualism: complementarities and change in France and Germany', *Politics & Society*, 38: 119–48.

Rubin, J., Rendall, M.S., Rabinovich, L., Tsang, F., Van Oranje-Nassau, C. and Janta, B. (2008) *Migrant women in the European labour force. Current situation and future prospects*, Cambridge: RAND Europe.

Rueda, D., Wibbels, E. and Altamirano, M. (2015) 'The origins of dualism', in H. Kriesi, H. Kitschelt, P. Beramendi and S. Häusermann (eds) *The politics of advanced capitalism*, Cambridge: Cambridge University Press.

Standing, G. (2011) *The precariat: the dangerous new class*, London: Bloomsbury Academic.

Vosko, L.F. (2010) *Managing the margins: Gender, citizenship, and the international regulation of precarious employment*, New York: Oxford University Press.

Vrålstad, S. and Wiggen, K.S. (2017) *Living conditions among immigrants in Norway in 2016* (in Norwegian), Rapporter 2017/13, Oslo/Kongsvinger: Statistics Norway.

Waldman, M. (1984) 'Job assignments, signalling, and efficiency', *The RAND Journal of Economics*, 15: 255–67.

8

How good is half a job?
Part-time employment and
job quality in the US

Kenneth Hudson and Arne L. Kalleberg

Introduction

Part-time employment – usually defined in the US as working less than 35 hours a week – characterises a sizeable portion of the US labour force.[1] In January 2018, the part-time workforce comprised about 17% of all American workers. From 1955 to the mid-1970s, part-time employment increased dramatically as the American economy shifted from manufacturing to services, and women entered the workforce in large numbers.[2] Part-time employment is especially common among women. About a quarter of working-age women in wage and salary jobs work part-time and two thirds of the part-time workforce is female. In the past, the rate of part-time employment in the US was high relative to other countries (Kalleberg, 2000), but in 2016, the percentage of workers employed part-time was comparatively lower than in most other developed countries (OECD, 2017).

Part-time work arrangements can offer important advantages to both organisations and their employees. They are a major way by which organisations manage their workforces. In the 1990s, nearly half of all US establishments employed part-time workers (Kalleberg et al, 2003) and over 70% of private establishments with five or more employees used 'direct hire' part-time employees, that is, those not hired through temporary agencies or other intermediaries (Houseman, 2001). Part-time jobs can give employers the numerical and work-time flexibility they need to adjust to changes in demand for their goods and services. Employers can also vary the number of hours that employees work and arrange their schedules so that they are at work when they are most needed (Rosenberg, 1989).

Part-time employment can also serve useful purposes for workers, especially parents and family caretakers. It gives many people the flexibility to juggle other life activities, such as going to school and caring for children. Workers in dual–earner and single–headed families are especially likely to seek flexible jobs in order to balance their paid work outside the home with caregiving (Blossfeld and Hakim, 1997; Glass and Estes, 1997). Part-time work also provides jobs for many retirees who need to supplement the income they receive from their pensions.

Despite these advantages, part-time employment also has a dark side. Tilly (1996) described part-time employment as 'half a job'. Part-time jobs are cheaper for employers because they are generally able to pay lower wages and provide fewer benefits than for comparable full-time jobs (Blank, 1990; Callaghan and Hartmann, 1991; Tilly, 1996; Kalleberg et al, 2000; Hudson, 2007). Employers also have more control over part-time workers because they are less likely to be unionised, and part-time jobs are often exempt from many personnel regulations. In addition, part-time jobs are more apt to involve shift work or irregular schedules (Negrey, 1993; Tilly, 1996). Some scholars and policymakers have claimed that the growth in the number of 'bad' part-time jobs is a factor in rising income inequality and the deepening race/ethnicity and gender divisions within the US labour market (Peck, 1996; Rosenfeld, 1997).

However, some part-time jobs in the US are better than others, and a small percentage provide health insurance, pension benefits and wages that are adequate to keep a family out of poverty. Tilly (1996) theorised that in some situations, employers create these high-quality part-time jobs to retain workers with highly valued job skills and knowledge. He hypothesised that these jobs would be instrumental in retaining female employees with children who need to balance their time between work and family. Unfortunately, most studies have not examined differences among part-time jobs, but have simply compared part-time to full-time employment (Feldman, 1990). In this chapter, we compare the quality of full-time and part-time jobs in the US and analyse the differences in job quality within the part-time workforce.

Important issues about part-time employment

Our study addresses several important issues related to part-time employment. First, in our descriptive analysis, we examine the evidence for claims in the popular media that the rate of part-time employment is climbing and that the US is becoming a 'part-time nation' (Phillips, 1997; De Rugy, 2013; *Guardian*, 2016). Some of these reports have also attributed rising income inequality to an increase in the utilisation of part-time workers. Others claim that the rate of part-time employment spiked after the implementation of the Patient Protection and Affordable Care Act, which requires firms to offer insurance to employees who work 30 or more hours a week (Fox News, 2013; Turner, 2013). Second, we examine the distribution of part-time and full-time employment for women and men and the different reasons why women and men work part-time. Third, we examine the distribution of 'bad job' characteristics for women and men in full- and part-time jobs. Based on our prior research on dual labour markets, we use the clustering of good and bad characteristics in different sets of jobs to identify discrete segments of the labour market (Doeringer and Piore, 1971; Hudson, 2007). Fourth, we examine the evidence for Tilly's theory of retention part-time employment, which predicts that employers create part-time jobs to avoid losing valued employees. Fifth, we draw on 'dualisation' theory (Emmenegger et al, 2012) and utilise data on race/ethnicity and citizenship to examine the relationship between part-employment and the 'insider–outsider' divide in the US.

In the last part of our analysis we use multivariate hierarchical models (Raudenbush and Bryk, 2002) to estimate the effect of part-time employment on the likelihood that workers will have a job in the secondary or intermediary labour market (versus the primary labour market), controlling for a variety of relevant demographic and labour market characteristics. We also use these models to estimate the likelihood that part-time workers live in families with incomes below the US poverty threshold. Finally, we examine the effect of part-time employment on individual bad job characteristics, net of the effects of union coverage and other relevant variables.

We begin with an overview of the literature that relates differences in the quality of part-time jobs to a variety of structural and individual characteristics. Next, we discuss our data and variables, and the results of our analysis. We end with a summary of our findings and conclusions.

Job quality and part-time employment

In their theory of the dual labour market, Doeringer and Piore (1971) argued that the labour market consists of two segments: the primary labour market, where jobs have good pay, health and retirement benefits and opportunities for advancement, and the secondary labour market, where jobs have low pay, no benefits and few opportunities to move into better jobs (see also Bluestone, 1970; Reich et al, 1973; Osterman, 1975; for a review, see Kalleberg and Sørensen, 1979). In our previous work on non-standard work arrangements in the US, we found that workers in part-time jobs have more 'secondary' or 'bad' characteristics than full-time workers, even when controlling for important labour-related variables (Kalleberg et al, 2000). We also show that although there are many jobs that combine primary and secondary characteristics (ie there is an intermediary labour market), the good (primary) characteristics cluster together, and the same is true for job characteristics that are bad (secondary) (Hudson, 2007).

In his theory of retention part-time employment, Tilly (1996) predicts the existence of a dual labour market among part-time workers. While part-time jobs are generally worse than full-time jobs, some part-time jobs are good and some are bad. Drawing on Doeringer and Piore's (1971) classical conception of the dual labour market, he identified four sets of job characteristics that differentiate primary and secondary jobs: (1) skill, training and responsibility; (2) pay and benefits; (3) turnover; and (4) promotion ladders. Tilly used these characteristics to distinguish *secondary* part-time jobs (which he called 'half-jobs') that have low wages, low skills, low fringe benefits, few or no job ladders, low productivity, and high turnover, from *primary* or *retention* part-time jobs that have better pay and benefits. He argued that in some situations, primary part-time jobs might be better than comparable full-time jobs because they afford workers the flexibility to attend to other things.

Tilly's distinction between secondary and retention jobs parallels Kahne's (1992) division between 'old concept' and 'new concept' part-time jobs. Old concept part-time jobs are temporary, relatively low paying and have few fringe benefits. New concept part-time jobs are good jobs that are filled by permanent workers who have career potential. Both Tilly (1996) and Kahne (1992) hypothesised that employers create good (or retention) part-time jobs to motivate and retain valued employees. Employees who fill these jobs are likely to be 'permanent' workers, not temporaries, that value and desire part-time work. The combination of predictable, regular but reduced hours with good pay enables some workers to combine employment with other activities, such as family responsibilities, community work or further schooling (Negrey, 1993; Wickham, 1997). Employers create secondary or 'old concept' part-time jobs to accomplish low-skill tasks at a minimal cost. Workers that fill these jobs, such as homemakers, students and moonlighters, often have limited employment aspirations, at least in the short term (Tilly, 1996).

Our explanation of the inequality within the part-time workforce incorporates both supply-side and demand-side factors. While demographic and human capital characteristics (such as gender, race/ethnicity, age and education) are likely to be salient in allocating workers to segments within the part-time labour market, we have found that the structural characteristics associated with the job also play an equal, if not more important, role. Unionisation, the industrial context and other aspects of the structure of the employment relationship have an impact on job quality that is independent of worker characteristics (Kalleberg et al, 1981, 2000). Non-firm-specific occupational skills are another important source of human capital (Becker, 1964; Mincer, 1974), and are likely to play a role in generating job-quality differences among part-time workers.

Prior research shows that different industries affect a worker's earnings independently of their individual characteristics and occupations (Beck et al, 1978, 1980; Oster, 1979; Kalleberg et al, 1981). Tilly (1996) argued that decisions on the part of employers to adopt a 'low-road' cost-cutting strategy have increased the use of part-timers in virtually all industries. The growth in part-time work that has occurred since the late 1950s is due, in part, to the increased size of the service sector. Nardone (1995) found that the increase in part-time work during the period 1979–90 was primarily due to the growth of industries that employ part-time workers (business, medical and personal services; finance, insurance and real estate [FIRE]; and retail trade), rather than an increase in part-time employment within industries.

One reason why industries differ in the quality of part-time jobs is their level of unionisation and collective bargaining. Unionisation constitutes a major source of collective power for workers vis-à-vis employers, but, overall, unionisation in the US is very low (Rosenfeld, 2014). In our sample of wage and salary workers aged 24–60, almost 14% of workers belong to a labour union or participate in a collective bargaining agreement. Among part-time workers, however, union membership and collective bargaining is lower (at 11.5%).

Perhaps the most important factor affecting the quality of a worker's job is their occupation. A worker's occupation often determines whether a job is in the primary or secondary labour market, and occupational differences help explain the existence of primary and secondary jobs within the same industry or even the same firm (for a review of this literature, see Hudson, 2007). Prior research has found that as the percentage of women in an occupation increases, the average earnings in that occupation decrease for all workers in that occupation (England, 1992). Bergman (1974, 1986) and Sorensen (1989a, 1989b) argued that the negative relationship between the share of an occupation that is female and its mean wage occurs because women are excluded from 'male' occupations. Consequently, they are 'crowded' into a limited number of occupations, driving down the wages of workers in those occupations. England (1992) and other researchers (Acker, 1989; Baron and Newman, 1989, 1990; Tomaskovic-Devey, 1993; England et al, 2000) attribute this occupational status composition effect to the devaluation of women, suggesting that if men did the same work, it would pay more. Tam (1997), however, argued that these studies did not adequately control for the workers' level of human capital, and none of the studies, including Tam, have used multilevel models to control for the prevalence of part-time employment at the occupational level. In our analysis we revisit this issue in the context of part-time employment.

Data and methods

Our analyses use data from the 2015 March Current Population Survey (CPS, 2015), Annual Social and Economic Survey (ASEC).[3] These data are uniquely suited for our purposes for several reasons. The ASEC provides annual earnings and information for the longest job held in the previous year. It also provides information on employer-provided health insurance and pensions. Lastly, the 2015 ASEC occurred after the Great Recession of 2008 and the implementation of the Patient Protection and Affordable Care Act in 2014.

We base our study on the characteristics of the longest job held in the previous year, which was 2014. The data analysis is restricted to employed wage and salary workers who were aged 24–60 years of age (inclusive) at the time of the survey. Our measures of job quality include information on earnings, employer-provided health insurance and employer-provided retirement benefits. In keeping with our previous research on bad jobs (eg Kalleberg et al, 2000), we use binary measures of poverty-level earnings, the absence of employer-provided health insurance and the absence of pension or retirement benefits to measure the quality of both full-time and part-time jobs and to identify the segments of the labour market.

Part-time work

Economists generally classify part-time work according to whether persons work part-time for 'non-economic' or 'economic' reasons. The majority of people who work part-time do so for non-economic reasons, such as family obligations or attending school. This category also includes those for whom a short schedule is 'full-time' for their job (Nardone, 1995). We often assume that these workers do not want a full-time job or are not available for full-time work. In contrast, workers classified as working part-time for economic reasons are those who want a full-time job and would accept one if it were offered, but they cannot find a full-time job because one is not available. Their work may also be seasonal, or they may not have the job skills required to qualify for the available full-time jobs.[4] Female part-time workers who are married and have children are more likely to work part-time for non-economic reasons than part-time workers who are single and have no children (Nardone, 1995; Tilly, 1996). Stratton (1996) and Tilly (1996) reported that part-time employment for economic reasons accounted for most of the growth in part-time work between the late 1960s and mid-1990s, reflecting the demand-side needs of employers rather than the supply-side considerations of workers (Callaghan and Hartmann, 1991).[5] However, time-series data on part-time employment over the long term, from the 1950s to the present, show that this increase resulted mainly from the growth in part-time employment for non-economic reasons.

Job quality, labour market segmentation and poverty

Poverty-level earnings refer to individuals in families with wage and salary earnings that are below a particular threshold. The federal poverty threshold for a family comprised of a single adult and two children in 2014 was US$19,073. The thresholds used to compute the poverty measure vary depending on the family's income and composition. Individuals may have poverty-level earnings and yet are not be classified as 'poor' because of their combined family income (and vice versa). We use the poverty measure of family income from the March 2015 CPS to measure the poverty status of individuals and their family members. Our other measures of 'bad jobs' are the absence of employer-provided health insurance and the absence of pension or retirement benefits.

We use the three bad job indicators and their combinations to measure job quality and to identify three distinct segments of the labour market. Jobs in the primary labour market (good jobs) are jobs without any of the three bad job characteristics, and jobs in the secondary labour market (bad jobs) are jobs that have all three. Jobs that have just one or two of the bad job characteristics constitute the 'intermediary labour market'.

Demographic and labour market variables

Our multivariate analyses include measures of race/ethnicity, citizenship, highly detailed measures of educational attainment, a variable indicating whether the respondent is a public sector employee and 12 fixed-effects dummy variables that designate major industrial categories. We use random intercept hierarchical linear models (Raudenbush and Bryk, 2002) to measure the effects of the respondents' detailed occupational status. These models also estimate the effects of three important occupational characteristics in our models: the percentage of workers in detailed-level occupations that have a bachelor's or advanced degree; the percentage of workers in each occupation that are women; and the percentage of workers in each occupation that are employed part-time. We hypothesise that the percentage of part-time workers in an occupation is an important causal mechanism that explains or accounts for all or most of the effect of occupational sex composition on the quality of jobs.

Our models estimate the effects of both individual and occupational-level variables on the odds that a part-time employee works in the secondary labour market versus the primary labour market, and the odds that a part-time employee works in the intermediary versus the primary labour market. We estimate these models separately for men and women. The multinomial hierarchical logistic regression models are represented by the following set of multilevel equations. The individual (level 1) model is given in equation 1:

$$\ln\left(\frac{P(Y_{ij} = m)}{P(Y_{ij} = M)}\right) = \beta_{0j(m)} + \sum_{q=1}^{Q_m}\beta_{qi(m)}X_{qij} \tag{1}$$

The term $P(Y_{ij} = m)/P(Y_{ij} = M)$ is the probability that the ith worker within the jth detailed-level occupation is employed in labour market m relative to labour market M (the reference category). The multinomial model ensures that the probability estimates associated with each of the labour market outcomes will sum to unity (Long, 1997). The equation intercept $\beta_{0j(m)}$ is a random variable that varies across detailed-level occupations, $\beta_{qi(m)}$ is the set of individual-level regression coefficients, and X_{qij} represents the set of individual-level predictors.

In equation 2, the intercept, $\beta_{0j(m)}$, is expanded in a second (level 2) equation:

$$\beta_{0j(m)} = \gamma_{00(m)} + \sum_{s=1}^{S}\gamma_{0s(m)}W_{sj} + u_{0j(m)} \tag{2}$$

where $\gamma_{00(m)}$ represents the grand mean of the dependent variable across all occupations when the value of each of the level 1 and level 2 variables is 0, W_{sj} represents occupational-level (level 2) variables, and $u_{0j(m)}$ is an occupational-level error term. The $u_{0j(m)}$ term represents the residual effect of occupation after controlling for the percentage of the occupation that is female, the percentage of the occupation that has a bachelor's or advanced degree, and the percentage of the occupation that is employed part-time. The effects of the individual (level 1) predictors in equation 2 are fixed across all occupations. This implies that, for all q:

$$\beta_{qj(m)} = \gamma_{q0(m)}. \tag{3}$$

In each of the equations, the subscript m refers to the mth labour market.

The occupational variables in these models provide an important test of our hypothesis that the prevalence of part-time jobs within occupations explains some or all of the variance in job quality between occupations previously attributed to their sex composition (England et al, 2000).

Next, we use hierarchical logistic regression to examine the likelihood that employment in a part-time job increases the odds that the worker and their family are poor. We estimate these models separately for women and men, and control for the each of the demographic and labour market variables that are included in the multinomial hierarchical logistic regression model. The equations for these models are the same as those for the multinomial model except for the dependent variable, which is $\ln(p/1 - p)$, where p represents the probability that the individual and his or her family are poor.

Because the March CPS only provides information on union membership and collective bargaining for the outgoing rotation groups (one fourth of the CPS sample), we estimate separate logistic regression models with smaller samples. These models estimate the effect of part-time employment, net of union membership or coverage, on each of the three 'bad job' indicators previously mentioned: poverty earnings, no health insurance and no pension benefits. These models include the same demographic and labour market variables used in the other models, with one exception: they include fixed-effect variables for each of the major occupational categories in lieu of the random effects used in the hierarchical linear models.

Analysis and results

Figure 8.1 presents trend data on part-time employment in the US from May 1955 through January 2018. The line graphs depict the percentage of workers employed part-time, the percentage employed part-time for non-economic reasons and the percentage employed part-time for economic reasons (for a description of the non-economic and economic reasons for part-time employment, see Table 8.2).

We find that beginning in the 1950s, part-time employment increased as share of all employment until the early 1980s. This period also coincided with a substantial increase in female labour force participation. Since then, part-time employment has ranged between 15% and 20%, with transient increases during periods of high unemployment (especially for 'economic' part-time employment). Part-time employment increased abruptly during the recession of the early 1980s and during the Great Recession of 2008 but declined afterwards. However, there does not appear to be any long-term trend in the economic part-time employment series. The rise of part-time employment from the 1950s to the early 1980s resulted almost entirely from the increase in part-time employment for non-economic reasons. Thus, these data do not support Tilly's (1996) claim that the increasing part-time employment between 1969 and 1993 resulted from increasing part-time employment for involuntary or economic reasons. Moreover, contrary to media reports, there is no evidence that part-time work as a share of total employment is increasing over the long term. Although the average level of part-time employment since the early 1980s has fluctuated, there is no indication of an upward trend.

Descriptive analysis

In Table 8.1, we use cross-sectional data from the 2015 ASEC on the respondent's longest job in 2014. The first panel shows that female workers were twice as likely as male workers to work part-time. Almost a quarter of female wage and salary employees worked part-time. The second panel also shows that about two thirds of all part-time workers were women. Most part-time workers were part-time for non-economic reasons, and women were more than two times as likely as men to work part-time for non-economic reasons.

In Table 8.2, we find that the most frequent reasons reported by women for working part-time were family responsibilities. When we combine this category with those who report that they worked part-time because of 'childcare problems', we find that about 36% of

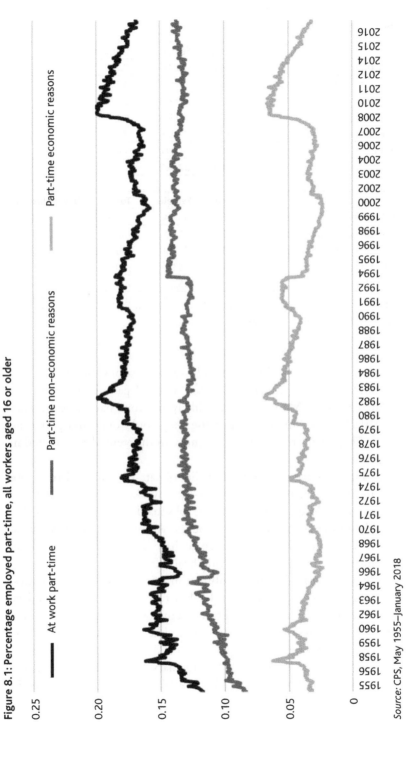

Figure 8.1: Percentage employed part-time, all workers aged 16 or older

At work part-time — Part-time non-economic reasons — Part-time economic reasons

Source: CPS, May 1955–January 2018

Table 8.1: Full-time and part-time employment, by sex, among wage and salary workers aged 24–60

	Male	Female	All workers
Full-time	88.2%	75.4%	82.2%
Part-time economic reasons	3.8%	4.5%	4.1%
Part-time non-economic reasons	7.7%	19.2%	13.2%
Part-time, not at work	0.3%	0.9%	0.6%
Part-time, all reasons	11.8%	24.6%	17.8%
Total	100%	100%	100%
Unweighted N	34,817	32,582	67,399

	Male	Female	Total	*Unweighted N*
Full-time	56.6%	43.4%	100%	55,198
Part-time economic reasons	48.3%	51.7%	100%	2,613
Part-time non-economic reasons	31.0%	69.0%	100%	9,196
Part-time, not at work	24.1%	75.9%	100%	392
Part-time, all reasons	34.8%	65.2%	100%	12,201
All workers	52.7%	47.3%	100%	67,399

Note: All percentages are weighted.

Source: ASEC 2015

women worked part-time for family-related reasons. In contrast, less than 11% of men reported that they worked part-time for family-related reasons. Men were most likely to work part-time because of a slack labour market or because they could only find part-time jobs. These data are highly consistent with the trend data depicted in Figure 8.1.

In Table 8.3, we compare the quality of part-time and full-time jobs for male and female workers. Part-time workers are more likely to have poverty-level earnings and have jobs that lack employer-provided health insurance and pension benefits. Among part-time workers, women are more likely than men to have a job with poverty-level earnings and that does not provide health insurance.

When we consider the combination of 'bad job' characteristics, part-time workers are far more likely to have jobs in the secondary and intermediary labour markets than employees that work full-time, and female part-time workers are more likely than male part-timers to have a 'bad' or 'mediocre' job. Almost 84% of women who work part-time are in secondary or intermediary jobs. Contrary to Tilly's theory that employers create primary labour market jobs to retain women who wish to work part-time, we find that males are more likely to have primary part-time jobs.

Table 8.2: Reasons for part-time employment, by sex, among part-time wage and salary workers aged 24–60

Economic reasons	Male	Female	Total
Slack work or business conditions	25.6%	11.3%	16.1%
Could only find part-time work	11.6%	8.8%	9.7%
Seasonal work	1.7%	0.5%	0.9%
Job started or ended during the workweek	0.6%	0.3%	0.4%
Total economic reasons	39.5%	20.9%	27.1%
Non-economic reasons			
Other family or personal obligations	9.1%	29.3%	22.6%
Workweek less than 35 hours	11.4%	14.8%	13.7%
Illness, injury, medical appt, health, medical limitations	15.0%	11.9%	12.9%
School, training	9.1%	6.9%	7.6%
Other reasons	6.8%	6.8%	6.8%
Childcare problems	1.5%	6.8%	5.1%
Weather affected job	5.8%	1.3%	2.8%
Retired, social security limit on earnings	1.6%	1.2%	1.3%
Civic or military duty	0.3%	0.0%	0.1%
Total non-economic reasons	60.6%	79.0%	72.9%
All part-time workers	100%	100%	100%
Unweighted N	3,166	7,087	10,253

Note: All percentages are weighted.
Source: ASEC 2015

Table 8.3: Job quality and labour market segmentation, by sex, among part-time and full-time workers, wage and salary workers aged 24–60

	Full-time			Part-time		
	Male	Female	Total	Male	Female	Total
Poverty earnings	10.0%	15.2%	12.2%	38.5%	51.2%	46.8%
No pension	55.4%	52.3%	54.1%	72.6%	72.1%	72.3%
No health	33.5%	35.8%	34.5%	60.6%	66.9%	64.7%
Unweighted N	30,842	24,356	55,198	3,975	8,226	12,201
Labour market segments						
Primary	36.1%	35.5%	35.8%	19.2%	14.9%	16.4%
Intermediary	57.8%	55.7%	56.9%	49.5%	46.3%	47.4%
Secondary	6.1%	8.8%	7.3%	31.3%	38.9%	36.2%
Total	100%	100%	100%	100%	100%	100%
Unweighted N	30,842	24,356	55,198	3,975	8,226	12,201

Note: All percentages are weighted.
Source: ASEC 2015

In Table 8.4, we provide a more specific test of Tilly's theory. We use the household and family structure of the CPS to create variables that indicate whether respondents have children and an employed spouse. We combine this information with the respondents' sex and level of education attainment (a post-secondary degree) to test Tilly's theory of retention part-time employment. In the first panel of Table 8.4, we find that employees that match Tilly's demographic description of retention part-timers are, indeed, much more likely to work part-time than all other wage and salary employees that are within the age range of our study. Women with small children, that have a bachelor's or advanced degree, and that have an employed spouse are much more likely to work part-time than all other employees. Although Tilly did not stipulate the employed spouse criterion, our research indicates that it is necessary to differentiate this group from the other workers.[6]

In our test of Tilly's hypothesis that employers offer retention part-timers jobs in the primary labour market, we also restricted the group to those who indicated that they were working part-time for family-related reasons. This subset of part-time workers is very small, only 7.4% of the part-time workers who report the reason why they work part-time. Among part-time employees, we find that although retention part-timers are less likely to have jobs in the secondary labour market than other part-time workers, they are also less likely to have jobs in the primary labour market.

Table 8.4: Test of Tilly's theory of retention part-time employment, wage and salary workers aged 24–60

Hours usually worked	Retention group*	All other workers	All workers		
Full-time	72.6%	82.4%	82.2%		
Part-time	27.4%	17.6%	17.8%		
Total	100%	100%	100%		
Unweighted N	2,356	65,043	67,399		
Labour market segments	Full-time	Retention part-time*	Other part-time	Not at work part-time	All workers
Primary	35.8%	14.7%	16.7%	9.4%	32.4%
Intermediary	56.9%	55.1%	46.9%	44.0%	55.2%
Secondary	7.3%	30.2%	36.4%	46.6%	12.5%
Total	100%	100%	100%	100%	100%
Unweighted N	55,198	1,054	10,755	392	67,399

Note: All percentages are weighted. *Includes women with small children and an employed spouse, and that have a bachelor's or advanced degree.

Source: ASEC 2015

In the last part of our descriptive analyses, we examine the relationship between 'dualisation' and part-time employment in the US. The concept of dualisation encompasses previous theory and research on labour market segmentation but extends the concept of inequality beyond the labour market to state social welfare arrangements and the political arena (Emmenegger et al, 2012). The extent to which there are consistent insider–outsider 'divides' in all three spheres is highly salient in the US context. In the US, we find that when workers in different segments of the labour market retire, become disabled or lose their jobs, they are typically not eligible for the same social welfare programmes or the same levels of support. Workers who are employed part-time in their prime working years are more likely to rely on Supplemental Security Income and Medicaid, programmes that are less generous than regular Social Security benefits and Medicare. However, the extent to which these differences are associated with divides in the political arena depends on how we define and operationalise insiders and outsiders.

Previous research on dualisation (Emmenegger et al, 2012; Häuserman and Schwander, 2012) has developed operational measures of 'insiders' and 'outsiders' in the labour market by combining information on occupational groups, gender, non-standard work arrangements and unemployment. The level of dualisation at the national level depends on the extent to which insiders and outsiders participate in different social welfare programmes, and the degree to which insiders and outsiders consistently affiliate with different political parties.

Defining labour market insiders and outsiders in this way, however, is problematic in several respects. First, it mirrors some of the same problems with causality that characterised some of the early research on dual labour market theory in the US (Kaufman et al, 1981). Are individuals 'outsiders' because they are in 'bad jobs', or are they in 'bad jobs' because they are 'outsiders'? This is an important question in both the European and the American contexts. We address this problem by defining insider and outsider groups sociologically. For example, in France, it is quite clear that African immigrants are an 'outsider community' and that their status as outsiders leads *a priori* to their participation in a secondary labour market. Regardless of whether their immigration and citizenship status enable them to participate in the electoral process, it seems unlikely that they support conservative, anti-immigrant political parties. We have remarkably similar divides in the US between African-Americans, Hispanic immigrants and native-born white people. In the area of social welfare, however, there are important cross-national differences. In education, health care and public assistance, Europeans countries are less likely to means test these services, making them more accessible to low-income and minority communities.

In the analysis presented in Tables 8.5a and 8.5b, we use race/ethnicity and citizenship status to define insiders (white people) and outsiders (black people, mixed-race people and Hispanic non-citizens) in the US. In Table 8.5a, we show the rate of part-time employment for each of these groups; in Table 8.5b, we examine the distribution of each group across the three segments of the labour market. We find that the outsider groups are more likely to work in part-time jobs than white people. We also find that among part-time employees, the outsider groups are more likely to have jobs in the secondary labour market. Finally, we see that the greatest degree of disadvantage in the labour market falls upon Hispanic non-citizens, whose outsider status is reinforced by the combination of their race/ethnicity and nativity status.

Table 8.5a: Race/ethnicity and part-time status, wage and salary workers aged 24–60

	White	Black only	Mixed race	Non-citizen Hispanics	All groups
Full-time	82.4%	81.2%	78.8%	79.0%	81.9%
Part-time	17.6%	18.8%	21.2%	21.0%	18.1%
Total	100%	100%	100%	100%	100%
	41,916	7,187	963	4,130	54,196

Note: All percentages are weighted.
Source: ASEC 2015

Table 8.5b: Part-time employees, race/ethnicity and labour market segment, wage and salary workers aged 24–60

	White	Black only	Mixed race	Non-citizen Hispanics	All groups
Primary	18.8%	15.6%	15.4%	3.0%	17.0%
Intermediary	48.6%	46.9%	46.0%	39.4%	47.5%
Secondary	32.6%	37.4%	38.6%	57.7%	35.4%
Total	100%	100%	100%	100%	100%
Unweighted N	7,612	1,310	207	863	9,992

Note: All percentages are weighted.
Source: ASEC 2015

Multivariate models

The analysis in Tables 8.6a and 8.6b presents results from two hierarchical multinomial logistic regression models. The dependent variable is a measure of labour market segmentation with categories for the primary (the reference category), intermediary and secondary labour markets. These models estimate the effect of part-time employment on the odds of having a job in the secondary and intermediary labour market versus the primary labour market. Each of the models controls for the effects of age, race/ethnicity, citizenship status, educational attainment, student status and public employment. The models also include a set of dummy variables for each of the major industry categories. We use random intercept models to estimate the effect of the worker's occupation (at the detailed level) and the effect of the occupation's characteristics on the dependent variable. We estimate separate models for women and men.

The results show that in each of the models, working part-time increases the odds of employment in both the secondary labour market and the intermediary labour market, versus the primary labour market. The effects of part-time employment are statistically significant, even when we control for the effects of all of the other variables in the model. This is true for all the models in Tables 8.6a and 8.6b. The relative magnitude of the odds ratios indicates that part-time employment has a greater effect on increasing the odds of secondary labour market employment (versus the primary labour market) than it has on the odds of working in the intermediary labour market (versus the primary labour market). Overall, these results show that the negative effects of part-time employment cannot be attributed to covariation with the demographic characteristics of workers, their occupation, their industry or other relevant labour market variables.

The occupational characteristics include the share of workers in an occupation that are female, the share that work part-time and the share that have a bachelor's or advanced degree. We estimate models with and without the variable for the percentage of workers in an occupation that work part-time. In Table 8.6a, Models 1 and 3 show the well-known gender status composition effect on job quality. As the percentage of women in occupations increases, the odds of having a job in the secondary and the intermediary labour market (versus the primary labour market) increase. However, when we add the variable for the percentage of workers employed part-time in Model 2 and Model 4, the effect of the percentage of women decreases and is no longer statistically significant. The models for men reveal the same

Table 8.6a: Hierarchical multinomial logistic regression of secondary and intermediary labour market employment on part-time employment and labour market variables, female wage and salary workers aged 24–60

Individual level variables	Secondary labour market[a]		Intermediary labour market[a]	
	Model 1	Model 2	Model 3	Model 4
	Exp (b)	Exp (b)	Exp (b)	Exp (b)
Age	0.9632***	0.9630***	0.9818***	0.9817***
Black	0.8540*	0.8568*	1.0281	1.0295
Native	1.0823	1.0822	1.1591	1.1590
Asian	0.9837	0.9830	1.1485	1.1466
Pacific	0.4458**	0.4429**	0.7064*	0.7028*
Mixed	1.0404	1.0400	1.0764	1.0770
Hispanic	1.2708***	1.2731***	1.1939***	1.1942***
Citizen	0.5078***	0.5075***	0.6511***	0.6512***
Less than high school	2.1973***	2.2047***	1.4922***	1.4951***
Some college	0.8410*	0.8419*	0.8670**	0.8677***
Two year college, trade	0.7577**	0.7582**	0.8895	0.8887
Two year college, academic	0.7660***	0.7651***	0.8505**	0.8495**
Bachelor's	0.4957***	0.4947***	0.7182***	0.7177***
Master's	0.3488***	0.3463***	0.6067***	0.6040***
Professional degree	0.4470**	0.4267**	0.6923*	0.6708**
PhD	0.2362***	0.2228***	0.6783**	0.6628**
In school	1.2536	1.2511	1.0502	1.0485
Part-time	8.4266***	8.2478***	1.8301***	1.8028***
Public employee	0.3676***	0.3647***	0.4607***	0.4610***

(continued)

Table 8.6a: Hierarchical multinomial logistic regression of secondary and intermediary labour market employment on part-time employment and labour market variables, female wage and salary workers aged 24–60 (continued)

	Secondary labour market[a]			Intermediary labour market[a]		
	Model 1	Model 2		Model 3	Model 4	
Individual level variables	Exp (b)	Exp (b)		Exp (b)	Exp (b)	
Agriculture, forestry, fishing and hunting	2.4133*	2.2772*		1.3341	1.2607	
Mining	0.1979***	0.2092***		0.4815**	0.4932**	
Construction	0.7197	0.7157		0.9048	0.9034	
Manufacturing	0.2441***	0.2658***		0.5372***	0.5594***	
Wholesale and retail trade	0.7091**	0.6937**		0.7829**	0.7682**	
Transportation and utilities	0.3601***	0.3624***		0.4616***	0.4613***	
Information	0.3856***	0.3825***		0.5457***	0.5424***	
Financial	0.2857***	0.2976***		0.5605***	0.5692***	
Educational and health services	0.4486***	0.4463***		0.6478***	0.6437***	
Leisure and hospitality	1.0995	1.0239		0.9714	0.9210	
Other services	1.7137*	1.6591*		1.1318	1.1024	
Public administration	0.3104***	0.3222***		0.5328***	0.5434***	
Occupational level variables						
Intercept	1.0424	1.0502		5.0562***	5.1456***	
Percent female	1.0069**	0.9984		1.0045***	1.0003	
Percent part-time		**1.0391**			**1.0199***	
Percent Bachelor's or Advanced	0.9776	0.9838		0.9934	0.9964**	
Occupational-level N	431	431		431	431	
Individual-level N	32,571	32,571		32,571	32,571	

Note: All percentages are weighted. [a] The reference group is the primary labour market. *$p < .05$; **$p < .01$; ***$p < .000$.

Source: ASEC 2015

Table 8.6b: Hierarchical multinomial logistic regression of secondary and intermediary labour market employment on part-time employment and labour-related variables, male wage and salary workers aged 24–60

	Secondary labour market[a]			Intermediary labour market[a]		
	Model 5	Model 6		Model 7	Model 8	
Individual level variables	Exp (b)	Exp (b)		Exp (b)	Exp (b)	
Age	0.9638***	0.9634***		0.9858***	0.9857***	
Black	1.4929***	1.4800***		1.1342**	1.1297**	
Native	3.4212***	3.4120***		1.4641**	1.4614**	
Asian	1.3533**	1.3553**		1.1729**	1.1718**	
Pacific	0.8204	0.8056		0.9166	0.9014	
Mixed	1.0191	1.0211		0.8422	0.8437	
Hispanic	1.3673***	1.3671***		1.2470***	1.2454***	
Citizen	0.4511***	0.4558***		0.6279***	0.6317***	
Less than high school	2.5018***	2.4975***		1.6607***	1.6556***	
Some college	0.8264*	0.8319*		0.8767***	0.8808***	
Two year college, trade	0.6559**	0.6612**		0.7963**	0.7999**	
Two year college, academic	0.6937**	0.6949**		0.8382**	0.8411**	
Bachelor's	0.4790***	0.4780***		0.7364***	0.7379***	
Master's	0.2654***	0.2637***		0.6496***	0.6497***	
Professional degree	0.4292*	0.3997*		0.6213***	0.5999***	
PhD	0.4903*	0.4632*		0.5900***	0.5702***	
In school	1.6459***	1.6472***		1.1814	1.1777	
Part-time	6.5533***	6.3516***		1.4599***	1.4333***	
Public employee	0.3181***	0.3190***		0.3591***	0.3615***	

(continued)

206

Table 8.6b: Hierarchical multinomial logistic regression of secondary and intermediary labour market employment on part-time employment and labour-related variables, male wage and salary workers aged 24–60 (continued)

	Secondary labour market[a]		Intermediary labour market[a]	
	Model 5	Model 6	Model 7	Model 8
	Exp (b)	Exp (b)	Exp (b)	Exp (b)
Individual level variables				
Agriculture, forestry, fishing and hunting	0.8776	0.9030	1.1995	1.1844
Mining	0.1720***	0.1770***	0.5416***	0.5484***
Construction	0.8648	0.8293	1.0688	1.0476
Manufacturing	0.2881***	0.3098***	0.5489***	0.5632***
Wholesale and retail trade	0.7168*	0.7239*	0.7329***	0.7321***
Transportation and utilities	0.3292***	0.3346***	0.5555***	0.5552***
Information	0.6388	0.6344	0.6005***	0.6013***
Financial	0.3650***	0.4037***	0.6329***	0.6524***
Educational and health services	0.5831**	0.5810**	0.8073*	0.7978*
Leisure and hospitality	1.6602*	1.4224	1.2410	1.1395
Other services	1.3265	1.3496	1.2225	1.2246
Public administration	0.4145***	0.4385**	0.7229**	0.7352**
Occupational level variables				
Intercept	0.4970***	0.4955***	4.1407***	4.1880***
Percent female	1.0158***	1.0050*	1.0041***	0.9996
Percent part-time		1.0443***		1.0207***
Percent Bachelor's or Advanced	0.9758***	0.9820***	0.9950***	0.9974**
Occupational-level N	474	474	474	474
Individual-level N	34,787	34,787	34,787	34,787

Note: All percentages are weighted. [a] The reference group is the primary labour market. *p < .05; **p < .01; ***p < .000.

Source: ASEC 2015

pattern with one exception. In Model 6, the effect of the percentage of women declines after we add the measure of the percentage of part-time, but it continues to be statistically significant. Across all the models, these results suggest an explanation for why the percentage of women in an occupation has a negative effect on the quality of jobs, that is, the sex composition (percentage female) effect is largely due to the percentage of workers in part-time jobs. Hence, the well-known female status composition effect is actually an effect of part-time employment.

In Table 8.7, we use hierarchical logistic regression to assess the effect of part-time employment on the odds that a worker's family income is below the federal poverty threshold. The results show that part-time workers are more likely to be poor than workers who have full-time jobs, net of the other variables in the model. These models also control for the percentage of workers who are female, the percentage that are employed part-time and the percentage with a bachelor's or advanced degree in the worker's occupation. In the model for women, the effect of the percentage of women in an occupation is statistically significant, but the effect is very small and not in the expected direction: as the percentage of women in the worker's occupation increases, the odds that they are poor declines slightly. In the model for males, the effect of the percentage of women is not significant. In both the male and the female models, however, the odds of being poor increase as the percentage of part-time workers in their occupation increases.

Historically, union membership and collective bargaining coverage have increased the wages and benefits of workers. As the ASEC survey does not collect union information on all of its participants, we estimated three separate logistic regression models that include a variable for union membership or coverage using the reduced number of cases in the monthly labour survey (the results are not shown but are available upon request from the first author). These models examine the effect of part-time work on the odds of having poverty earnings, the odds of not having employer-provided health insurance and the odds of not having a pension, controlling for union membership or coverage and other relevant labour market variables. We estimate each of the outcomes for each gender, controlling for all of the variables that are included in the hierarchical models in Tables 8.6a and 8.6b. However, instead of allowing the intercept to vary randomly for each occupation, we use fixed-effect dummies to measure the effect of occupation status (major occupational groups). Consequently, these models omit the three occupational-level variables used in the three hierarchical models.

Table 8.7: Hierarchical logistic regression of poverty on part-time employment and labour-related variables, wage and salary workers aged 24–60

	Female	Male
Individual level variables	Exp (b)	Exp (b)
Age	0.9603***	0.9753***
Black	2.2973***	1.6761***
Native	2.5672***	1.8756**
Asian	0.8965	1.1056
Pacific	1.3045	1.7232
Mixed	1.6792**	1.0545
Hispanic	1.3508***	1.2644**
Citizen	0.9074	0.5149***
Less than high school	1.7268***	1.9153***
Some college	0.8117**	0.8042**
Two year college, trade	0.7409**	0.5965**
Two year college, academic	0.7160**	0.5646***
Bachelor's	0.4424***	0.5965***
Master's	0.3168***	0.4624***
Professional degree	0.6643	0.6831
PhD	0.3591	0.4300*
In school	0.9588	0.9433
Part-time	**2.2372***	**2.6425***
Public employee	0.9921	0.6995*
Agriculture, forestry, fishing and hunting	1.8249**	1.3366
Mining	0.1990	0.5607
Construction	0.5135**	0.9463
Manufacturing	0.7409*	0.7243*
Wholesale and retail trade	0.9419	0.9670
Transportation and utilities	0.5723*	0.5805***
Information	1.0217	1.1757
Financial	0.5367***	0.6322*
Educational and health services	0.8300	0.9162
Leisure and hospitality	1.0659	1.1069
Other services	1.1584	1.2396
Public administration	0.4917**	0.6864
Occupational level variables		
Intercept	0.0440***	0.0557***
Percent female	0.9953*	0.9995
Percent part-time	**1.0148***	**1.0189***
Percent Bachelor's or Advanced	0.9827***	0.9888***
Occupational-level N	431	474
Individual-level N	32,571	34,787

Note: *p < .05; **p < .01; ***p < .000.

Source: ASEC 2015

As expected, union membership or coverage reduces the odds of having a job with the bad job characteristics. In contrast, in five of the six models, part-time employment increases the likelihood that the job will have the bad job features. The only exception is the female model for not having employer-provided health insurance; the variable for part-time employment in this model is not significant.

Conclusions and implications

We have sought to explain why some part-time jobs in the US are good and why some are bad or mediocre. We relied on dual labour market theory to derive a measure of differences in the quality of part-time jobs with regard to wages and benefits. Our model of labour market dualism shows that the overwhelming majority of part-time jobs are located in the secondary and intermediary labour markets. Only a small share of part-time jobs, between 16% and 17%, are located in the primary segment.

Although the majority of workers aged 23 and younger are employed part-time, almost two thirds of part-time workers are between the ages of 24 and 60. About two thirds of part-time workers are women and more than a third of this group work part-time to balance the demands of work and family. In contrast, men are much more likely to seek part-time work for economic reasons, especially when work is slack and full-time jobs are unavailable. Although there is no evidence that the part-time workforce is increasing as a share of all workers, it constitutes a large part of the workforce. As we expected, we find that women with children and an employed spouse are more likely than other employees to work part-time, but our analysis shows that the majority of these part-time workers hold intermediary or secondary jobs, even if they are college graduates.

Our multivariate analysis reveals that part-time workers have an increased risk of living in poverty, even when we control for a host of labour-related factors. This finding is important because it suggests that part-time workers are not likely obtain protection from the economic consequences of part-time employment by sharing income with other family members. Our research suggests that the prevalence of part-time employment in specific occupations may account for a large part of the well-known negative effect of occupational sex segregation on female earnings. However, this does not diminish the claim that women's work is devalued. Rather, it illuminates the economic penalty that women incur when they forgo full-time employment to care for children and ageing parents.

Finally, the recent research on dualisation has called attention to the growing disparities of income and opportunities in societies with highly developed economies, divides that extend well beyond the workplace and that remain with us over the life course. By looking beyond our boundaries and borders to the outsiders beyond our gates and walls, we may discover that the divides are greater and deeper than we previously considered.

Notes

[1] Most part-time employees work between 16 and 30 hours per week (see Table 8A.1).

[2] In 1955, the rate of part-time employment among all workers in the US aged 16 and older was between 11% and 12%. Part-time employment tends to be counter-cyclical, increasing when the unemployment rate is high and declining when it is low (see Figure 8.1; see also Tilly, 1996; Bureau of Labor Statistics, 2018).

[3] The CPS data used in our analyses were obtained from the National Bureau of Economic Research website (see: www.nber.org/cps/).

[4] Workers employed part-time for economic and non-economic reasons are sometimes called 'involuntary' and 'voluntary' part-time workers, respectively. However, these labels are somewhat misleading. Persons who work part-time 'voluntarily' may not necessarily want these jobs: while such workers may 'choose' their jobs, the range of choices available to them may be greatly restricted and depend on what they perceive (or do not perceive) as their other options. For example, some women who are classified as working part-time 'voluntarily' might well prefer full-time work if they could obtain adequate and affordable childcare (Cassirer, 2003). Moreover, an unknown number of 'voluntary' part-time workers have fewer hours than they prefer because disability or inadequate transportation prevents them from working full-time (Kalleberg, 1995).

[5] In addition to our measures of whether people work part-time for economic and non-economic reasons, our study also includes part-time workers who usually work part-time but were not at work during the week of the survey.

[6] Women with post-secondary degrees and with small children are more likely to opt for part-time employment, but only if they have an employed spouse.

References

Acker, J. (1989) *Doing comparable worth: gender, class, and pay equity*, Philadelphia, PA: Temple University Press.

Baron, N. and Newman, A.E. (1989) 'Pay the man: effects of demographic composition on prescribed pay rates in the California civil service', in R.T. Michael, H.I. Hartmann and B. O'Farrell (eds) *Pay equity: empirical inquiries*, Washington, DC: National Academy Press, pp 107–30.

Baron, N. and Newman, A.E. (1990) 'For what it's worth: organizations, occupations, and the value of work done by women and nonwhites', *American Sociological Review*, 55: 155–75.

Beck, E.M., Horan, P.M. and Tolbert, C.M. (1978) 'Stratification in a dual economy: a sectoral model of earnings determination', *American Sociological Review*, 43: 704–20.

Beck, E.M., Horan, P.M. and Tolbert, C.M. (1980) 'Social stratification in industrial society: further evidence for a structural alternative (reply to Hauser)', *American Sociological Review*, 45: 712–08.

Becker, G.S. (1964) *Human capital*, New York, NY: National Bureau of Economic Research.

Bergman, B. (1974) 'Occupational segregation, wages, and profits when employers discriminate', *Eastern Economic Journal*, 1: 103–10.

Bergman, B. (1986) *The economic emergence of women*, New York, NY: Basic Books, Inc.

Blank, R.M. (1990) 'Are part-time jobs bad jobs?', in G. Burtless (ed) *A future of lousy jobs?* Washington, DC: Brookings Institution, pp 123–55.

Blossfeld, H. and Hakim, C. (1997) *Between equalisation and marginalisation: women working part-time in Europe and the United States of America*, Oxford: Oxford University Press.

Bluestone, B. (1970) 'Labor markets and the working poor', *Poverty and Human Resources*, 6: 15–35.

Bureau of Labor Statistics (2018) 'Table 8A'. Available at: www.bls. gov/cps/cpsatabs.htm (accessed 7 February 2018).

Callaghan, P.S. and Hartmann, H. (1991) *Contingent work: a chart book on part-time and temporary employment*, Washington, DC: Economic Policy Institute.

Cassirer, N. (2003) 'Work arrangements among women in the United States', in S. Houseman and E. Osawa (eds) *Nonstandard work in developed economies: causes and consequences*, Kalamazoo, MI: W.E. Upjohn Institute for Employment Research, pp 307–49.

Current Population Survey (2015) *Annual Social and Economic (ASEC) supplement*, machine-readable data file, conducted by the Bureau of the Census for the Bureau of Labor Statistics, Washington, DC: US Census Bureau.

De Rugy, V. (2013) 'Are we becoming a part-time nation?', *National Review*, 5 August. Available at: www.nationalreview.com/corner/355160 (accessed 19 February 2018).

Doeringer, P.B. and Piore, M.J. (1971) *Internal labor markets and manpower analysis*, Lexington, MA: D.C. Heath and Company.

Emmenegger, P., Häuserman, S., Palier, B. and Seeleib-Kaiser, M. (2012) 'How we grow unequal', in P. Emmenegger, S. Häuserman, B. Palier and M. Seeleib-Kaiser (eds) *The age of dualization: the changing face of inequality in deindustrializing societies*, Oxford: Oxford University Press, pp 3–26.

England, P. (1992) *Comparable worth: theories and evidence*, New York: Routledge.

England, P., Hermsen, J.M. and Cotter, D.A. (2000) 'The devaluation of women's work: comment on Tam', *American Journal of Sociology*, 104: 1741–60.

Feldman, D.C. (1990) 'Reconceptualizing the nature and consequences of part-time work', *The Academic of Management Review*, 15: 103–12.

Fox News (2013) 'Part-time nation: ObamaCare forcing cuts to worker hours', 21 August. Available at: http://video.foxnews.com/v/2639587244001/?#sp=show-clips (accessed 19 February 2018).

Glass, J. and Estes, S.B. (1997) 'The family responsive workplace', *Annual Review of Sociology*, 23: 289–313.

Guardian (2016) 'Part-time nation: the "gig economy" leaves some working Americans financially vulnerable', Guardian Workplace Benefits StudySM: Fourth Annual, Guardian Life Insurance Company of America. Available at: www.guardiananytime.com/gafd/wps/wcm/connect/e03bbe15-f54e-40ca-85c0-91220ff4224f/2017-part-time-employee-benefits-study.pdf?MOD=AJPERES&CVID=lPW68Pt (accessed 19 February 2018).

Häuserman, S. and Schwander, H. (2012) 'Varieties of dualization: labor market segmentation and insider–outsider divides across regimes', in P. Emmenegger, S. Häuserman, B. Palier and M. Seeleib-Kaiser (eds) *The age of dualization: the changing face of inequality in deindustrializing societies*, Oxford: Oxford University Press, pp 27–51.

Houseman, S.N. (2001) 'Why employers use flexible staffing arrangements: evidence from an establishment survey', *Industrial and Labor Relations Review*, 55: 149–50.

Hudson, K. (2007) 'The new labor market segmentation: labor market dualism in the new economy', *Social Science Research*, 27: 286–312.

Kahne, H. (1992) 'Part-time work: a hope and a peril', in B.D. Wahrme, K.L.P. Lundy and L.A. Lundy (eds) *Working part-time: risks and opportunities*, New York: Praeger, pp 295–309.

Kalleberg, A.L. (1995) 'Part-time work and workers in the United States: correlates and policy issues', *Washington and Lee Law Review*, 52: 771–98.

Kalleberg, A.L. (2000) 'Nonstandard employment relations: part-time, temporary, and contract work', *Annual Review of Sociology*, 26: 341–65.

Kalleberg, A.L. and Sørensen, A.B. (1979) 'Sociology of labor markets', *Annual Review of Sociology*, 5: 351–79.

Kalleberg, A.L., Wallace, M. and Althauser R.P. (1981) 'Economic segmentation, worker power, and income inequality', *American Journal of Sociology*, 87(3): 651–83.

Kalleberg, A.L., Reskin, B.F. and Hudson, K. (2000) 'Bad jobs in America: nonstandard employment relations and job quality in the United States', *American Sociological Review*, 65: 256–78.

Kalleberg, A.L., Reynolds, J. and Marsden, P.V. (2003) 'Externalizing employment: flexible staffing arrangements in U.S. organizations', *Social Science Research*, 32(4): 525–52.

Kaufman, R.L., Hodson, R. and Fligstein, N.D. (1981) 'Defrocking dualism: a new approach to defining industrial sectors', *Social Science Research*, 10: 1–31.

Long, J.S. (1997) *Regression models for categorical and limited dependent variables*, Thousand Oaks, CA: Sage Publications.

Mincer, J. (1974) *Schooling, experience, and earnings*, New York, NY: Columbia University Press.

Nardone, T. (1995) 'Part-time employment: reasons, demographics, and trends', *Journal of Labor Research*, 16: 275–92.

Negrey, C. (1993) *Gender, time, and reduced work*, Albany, NY: State University of New York Press.

OECD (Organisation for Economic Co-operation and Development) (2017) 'OECD employment outlook, 2017 statistical annex', OECD.

Oster, G. (1979) 'A factor test of the theory of the dual economy', *Review of Economics and Statistics*, 61: 33–9.

Osterman, P. (1975) 'An empirical study of labor market segmentation', *Industrial Labor Relations Review*, 28: 508–23.

Peck, J. (1996) *Work-place: the social regulation of labor markets*, New York, NY: Guilford Press.

Phillips, M.M. (1997) 'Part-time work issue is greatly overworked', *Wall Street Journal*, 11 August.

Raudenbush, S.W. and Bryk, A.S. (2002) *Hierarchical linear models*, Thousand Oaks, CA: Sage.

Reich, M., Gordon, D.M. and Edwards, R.C. (1973) 'Dual labor markets: a theory of labor market segmentation', *American Economic Review*, 63(2): 359–65.

Rosenberg, S. (1989) 'Labor market restructuring in Europe and the United States', in S. Rosenberg (ed) *The state and the labor market*, New York, NY: Plenum Press, pp 3–16.

Rosenfeld, J. (2014) *What unions no longer do*, Cambridge, MA: Harvard University Press.

Rosenfeld, R.A. (1997) 'Employment flexibility in the United States: changing and maintaining gender, class, and ethnic work relationships', paper presented at the Conference on Reconfiguring Class and Gender, Australian National University, Canberra, 1 August.

Sorensen, E. (1989a) 'Measuring the effect of occupational and race composition on earnings', in R.A. Michael, H. Hartmann and B. O'Farrell (eds) *Pay equity: empirical inquiries*, Washington, DC: National Academy Press, pp 49–69.

Sorensen, E. (1989b) 'The crowding hypothesis and comparable worth', *Journal of Human Resources*, 25: 55–89.

Stratton, L.S. (1996) 'Are "involuntary" part-time workers indeed involuntary?', *Industrial and Labor Relations Review*, 49: 522–36.

Tam, T. (1997) 'Sex segregation and occupational gender inequality in the United States: devaluation or specialized training?', *American Journal of Sociology*, 102: 1652–92

Tilly, C. (1996) *Half a job: bad and good part-time jobs in a changing labor market*, Philadelphia, PA: Temple University Press.

Tomaskovic-Devey, D. (1993) *Gender and racial inequality at work: the sources and consequences of job segregation*, Ithaca, NY: ILR Press.

Turner, G. (2013) 'Its fact, not anecdote, that Obama-Care is turning us into a part time nation', *Forbes*, 27 August. Available at: www.forbes.com/sites/gracemarieturner/2013/08/27/its-fact-not-anecdote-that-obamacare-is-turning-us-into-a-part-time-nation/#5e24cbfd5944 (accessed 19 February 2018).

Wickham, J. (1997) 'Part-time work in Ireland and Europe: who wants what where?', *Work, Employment, and Society*, 11: 133–51.

Appendix

Table 8A.1: Distribution of part-time hours for part-time workers

	%
1 to 5 hours	2.6
6 to 10 hours	6.2
11 to 15 hours	8.3
16 to 20 hours	26.0
21 to 25 hours	19.1
26 to 30 hours	26.0
31 to 34 hours	11.9
Total	100
Unweighted N	6,833

Source: ASEC 2015

Table 8A.2: Age distribution of wage and salary part-time workers

Age group	Female	Male	Both sexes
16 through 19	10.4%	8.0%	9.0%
20 through 23	16.3%	12.3%	13.8%
24 through 29	14.2%	12.6%	13.2%
30 through 34	7.7%	8.9%	8.4%
35 through 39	7.8%	8.6%	8.3%
40 through 44	6.2%	8.2%	7.4%
45 through 49	5.8%	8.9%	7.7%
50 through 54	6.6%	8.3%	7.6%
55 through 59	6.5%	8.7%	7.9%
60 and over	18.4%	15.6%	16.7%
Total	100%	100%	100%
Unweighted N	7,040	12,120	19,160
Mean age	39.3	40.6	40.1

Source: ASEC 2015

9

Dualisation or normalisation of part-time work in the Nordic countries: work insecurity and mobility over time

Jouko Nätti and Kristine Nergaard

Introduction

Research interest in part-time work has recently increased in pace given the greater attention paid towards the growth in atypical employment in many Western countries. There is concern for increased social inequality, which is ascribed to the growth in poor-quality and insecure jobs, and that the growing group of outsiders with atypical employment contracts is not composed of random individuals (Kalleberg, 2009; Emmenegger et al, 2012). Women, young people, immigrants and people with little formal education are over-represented in these types of jobs. Although the trend away from permanent full-time positions can be partly explained by structural changes in the labour market, political decisions (or lack thereof) are highlighted as essential in explaining greater inequality between labour market insiders and outsiders (Emmenegger et al, 2012).

Part-time work, in particular, short or marginal part-time work, represents a form of employment that has the potential to give rise to greater inequality in the labour market (Eichhorst and Marx, 2012; Rubery and Grimshaw, 2016). However, part-time work as such is not tantamount to a marginal attachment to the labour market. Many part-time employees, and especially women, are satisfied with their working hours, and there is major variation among different part-time positions. We can thus distinguish between 'good' and 'bad' part-time work (Kalleberg, 2000; see also Chapter 1, this volume).

The Nordic countries stood out at an early stage with their high rates of labour force participation by women. Many of these women took part-time positions, often in public sector occupations. In general, these employment relationships did not differ significantly from full-time positions in terms of formal rights: part-time work by women was normalised (Ellingsæter, 1989) and might be referred to as 'good part-time' as the term is used in this book (see Chapter 1). Although normalisation of part-time work in the Nordic countries is commonly associated with part-time work among women, it is part of a larger picture. The Nordic labour market and welfare state regimes are well regulated and characterised by the broad coverage of collective agreements, strong trade unions and a political objective of low levels of wage inequality, as well as high aspirations on gender equality (Dølvik, 2013; Nergaard, 2014). This has resulted in inclusive labour markets with minor differences in job quality and job security (Gallie, 2007; Paugam and Zhou, 2007; Thelen, 2014). The controversy of part-time work has traditionally been linked to part-time work as a challenge to economic gender equality (Ellingsæter and Jensen, 2019).

Nonetheless, 'bad part-time' is also on the agenda in the Nordic labour markets (Rasmussen et al, forthcoming). In an increasingly internationalised labour market and with more jobs in the lower end of the services sector, it is not given that the labour market institutions will act as a buffer against more insecure jobs and employer-driven flexibility. Against this backdrop, we will analyse the characteristics of part-time work in two Nordic countries: Finland and Norway. Both countries have had high rates of female labour market participation for years, but while Finnish women entered full-time positions, many Norwegian women entered so-called 'normalised part-time work'. In terms of development towards more 'bad' part-time work, these two countries constitute a highly interesting comparison.

In this chapter, we adopt a longitudinal perspective and explore the patterns of part-time work in the two countries and also examine whether part-timers become more exposed to marginal jobs over time or if they enjoy mobility from part-time jobs to better, more secure, labour market positions. First, we ask whether part-time work is more closely associated with income and job insecurity than previously, that is, whether greater inequalities emerge over time between insiders and outsiders or between standard and non-standard work. The Nordic labour markets remain characterised by strong collective institutions and include social support schemes that will shield workers from having to accept the worst jobs (Barth and Moene, 2016; Broughton et al, 2016). At the same time, these countries will also find it more difficult to preserve their small differences in job quality between insiders and outsiders in the labour market at a time of decreasing unionisation rates and a more differentiated workforce (Andersen et al, 2014). We will therefore investigate whether part-time jobs are becoming more insecure over time, and whether the differences between part-time and full-time jobs are tending to increase.

Second, we are interested in mobility from part-time jobs to other positions in the labour market. One characteristic of strongly segmented labour markets is that some groups end up being permanently excluded (as outsiders). Hence, if we observe an increased risk of exclusion from the labour force among part-timers, this will point towards part-time positions being a risk for marginalisation. If, on the other hand, a part-time job functions as a bridge to a secure working life, we can expect transitions to full-time positions, potentially combined with stability in part-time work among prime-age women.

We cannot be entirely certain about what to expect with regard to the differences between Finland and Norway when it comes to the development of new types of part-time jobs. Finland has stronger collective institutions than Norway, that is, higher union density rates and collective agreement coverage, but it has also experienced periods of high unemployment, which may have forced some employees into jobs of a poorer quality than they would otherwise have accepted. The Norwegian tradition of normalised part-time work may also have an effect with regard to whether and how employers will consider part-time work as a strategy to enhance flexibility, in the sense of offering part-time jobs to persons who would prefer full-time positions. As a backdrop to these analyses, we will first describe and discuss the patterns of part-time work in Finland and Norway in terms of continuity and change.

Data, definitions and methods

European Union Labour Force Survey

The analyses apply data from the European Union Labour Force Survey (EU-LFS), from the years 1996 to 2016. Since the original numbers of respondents vary considerably between the countries, and in order to obtain more balanced data, we randomly selected similar annual samples from each country (Finland $N = 236,834$; Norway $N = 237,268$). The analysis includes respondents aged 15–64 in employment who participated directly in the survey (Finland $N = 159,897$; Norway $N = 210,979$).

Part-time work is here defined as less than 34 hours per week. Part-time work is assessed from questions on the number of hours per week that respondents usually work in their main job.[1] We focus on two *measures of insecure work*: insecurity that is related to an inadequate income level; and insecurity that is associated with the specific job (Berglund et al, 2014; Rasmussen et al, forthcoming).

Income insecurity is defined as being in a position where the level of income is perceived by the worker/employee to be inadequate and where he/she is dissatisfied with the number of hours worked in the present job. To measure the prevalence of income insecurity, we used three items where the respondent was asked to consider if he/she:

- wishes to work more hours than the present job allows (item 1);
- is seeking an additional job to add more hours to those worked in the present job (item 2); and
- is seeking a job with more hours worked than in the present job (item 3).

In the EU-LFS, items 2 and 3 are alternatives, of which the respondent can select only one. All three (partly overlapping) items express dissatisfaction with the number of hours worked in the present job.[2]

Job insecurity is related, in this context, both to respondents' degree of uncertainty in keeping their job and to their job stability. It is measured by two items:

- Searching for a new job because of risk or certainty of loss or termination of present job (item 4).
- Main activity one year earlier: unemployed (item 5).

If the respondent confirms that he/she is looking for a new job, then he/she is classified as job-insecure (item 4) (1.1% in 2016). Once again, item 4 and earlier items 2 and 3 are alternatives, of which the respondent can select only one. Item 5 relates to an insecure work history. Here, respondents are asked what their main activity was one year earlier, and if they state that they were unemployed, then they are classified as job-insecure (item 5) (2.0% in 2016).

The *combined work insecurity* indicator includes five insecurity measures, although we should hasten to add that the respondent can select only three items, as explained earlier. Thus, the scale is 0–3 (mean = 0.12; std. = 0.37). To illustrate the results better, we use a dummy of work insecurity, which is defined as answering 'yes' to one or more of the five questions (10.4%). Insecurity analysis will focus on the years 2006–16 because there were major changes to the questions before 2006 in Norway. In addition, this analysis will only focus on those respondents who answered all five items to increase the reliability of the results (Finland $N = 74,088$; Norway $N = 126,086$).

Background and control variables are gender (women, men), age (15–29, 30–44, 45–54, 55–64), education (primary, secondary, tertiary), nationality, professional status and contract type, occupation, and economic sector.

Nationality (national citizens, non-national citizens) is defined in terms of citizenship, which corresponds to the country issuing the passport. The challenge in labour force surveys has been that non-nationals have previously been under-represented.

We combined professional status (self-employed/employee) and contract type, which is based on respondents' perception of whether they have a permanent job or work contract of unlimited duration, or a temporary job or employment contract of limited duration. The combined variable has three groups: self-employed; employees with a permanent contract; and employees with a temporary contract.

In common with many other dualisation studies, we distinguish between occupations with high general skills, low general skills and specific skills (Fleckenstein et al, 2011; Wiss, 2017; Chung, 2018). High-general-skill occupations (managers, professionals, technicians and associate professionals) are considered as insiders, whereas low-general-skill (clerical support, service workers and elementary occupations) and specific skill occupations (craft workers, machine operators and assemblers) are treated as outsiders. Occupation is based on the International Standard Classification of Occupations (ISCO).

Economic sector is based on the Statistical Classification of Economic Activities in the European Community (NACE). For the analysis, we distinguished nine sectors. We also make a distinction between short/marginal part-time (1–19 hours per week) and long part-time (20–33 hours per week). In addition, we distinguish between voluntary part-time, that is, part-time workers who are satisfied with their working time, and involuntary part-time, meaning part-time workers who wish to work more hours.

Statistical methods

First, we map the development of part-time employment from 1996 to 2016 by country (see Figure 9.1). The figures are based on mean comparisons and are presented in order to visualise where and what kind of changes have happened over time. Second, the extent of part-time employment by background factors is presented by cross-tabulations (see Table 9.1). Third, we investigate the extent to which

Figure 9.1: Part-time work (1–33 hours/week) in Finland and Norway, 1996–2016, by gender and percentage of employed population (15–64 years old)

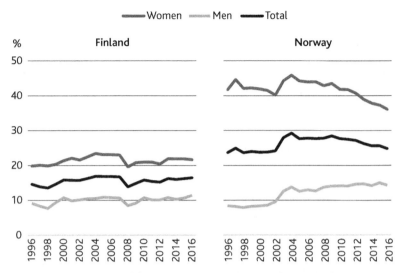

Notes: For Norway, 15 year olds are only included in the survey from 2006. The increase in Norway between 2002 and 2004 is partly due to changes in the EU-LFS data set, and calculations based on national EU-LFS data show that the change in part-time rates is more linear.

Table 9.1: Prevalence of part-time work, by background characteristics, in 1996–98 and 2014–16 in Finland and Norway (all employed, 15–64 years old)

	Finland			Norway		
	1996–98	2014–16	Change	1996–98	2014–16	Change
Total	14	17	+3	24	24	0
Gender						
Women	20	23	+3	42	35	−7
Men	9	12	+3	8	13	+5
Age groups						
15–29	29	34	+5	25	38	+13
30–49	11	13	+2	23	18	−5
50–64	14	16	+2	25	23	−2
Level of education						
Primary	18	27	+9	30	33	+3
Upper	14	19	+5	25	26	+1
Tertiary	11	14	+3	19	18	−1
Nationality						
National	14	18	+4	24	24	0
Non-national	27	21	−6	22	22	0

(continued)

Table 9.1: Prevalence of part-time work by background characteristics in 1996–98 and 2014–16 in Finland and Norway (all employed, 15–64 years old) (continued)

	Finland			Norway		
	1996–98	2014–16	Change	1996–98	2014–16	Change
Economic sector						
Agriculture	17	20	+3	21	21	0
Manufacturing, construction	5	6	+1	10	11	+1
Wholesale and retail trade; hotels and catering	23	28	+5	30	34	+4
Transport, storage and communications	11	14	+3	14	13	−1
Finance, real estate, business activities	16	17	+1	17	16	−1
Public administration	7	8	+1	14	10	−4
Education	29	29	0	29	26	−3
Human health and social work activities	15	18	+3	46	39	−7
Other services	25	35	+9	30	38	+8
Professional status and contract type						
Self-employed	15	22	+7	20	24	+4
Employee with a permanent contract	11	16	+5	23	22	−1
Employee with a temporary contract	32	30	−2	39	42	+3
Occupational skill level						
High general skills	12	14	+2	15	16	+1
Specific skills	7	10	+3	11	12	+1
Low skills	23	30	+7	45	49	+4
Weekly working hours						
1–19	5	6	+1	9	11	+2
20–33	10	12	+2	15	13	−2
Motives for part-time work						
Involuntary (could not find a full-time job)	5	4	−1	4	4	0
Voluntary (studies, health, family, other reasons)	7	9	+2	21	17	−4

part-time work has insecure elements. This is undertaken by analysing differences in the extent of insecurity between persons in part-time and full-time employment (see Table 9.2). In Tables 9.1 and 9.2, we use the combined 1996–98 and 2014–16 data to increase the reliability of the results because some of the subgroups cover a very small proportion of the employed.

Finnish and Norwegian Labour Force Panel data

The mobility of part-time work is analysed with the aid of the Finnish and Norwegian Labour Force Panel. In Finland, the monthly samples include respondents from five rotation groups and consist of approximately 12,000 persons. Each respondent is interviewed five times over a period of 15 months. In the Norwegian panel data, respondents are interviewed eight times over a period of 21 months. Transition tables are used in order to describe transitions and stability from part-time in T1 to different labour market situations in T2 (15 months later).

Part-time patterns in Finland and Norway: continuity or change?

Before discussing the prevalence of 'bad part-time', we will examine the development of part-time work. Important questions concern how part-time work among women developed in two countries with very different part-time traditions, and if we find an emergence over time of part-time positions in industries or occupational groups that are not associated with normalised, or 'good', part-time work.

Part-time employment (less than 34 hours per week) was more widespread in Norway than in Finland (see Figure 9.1) between 1996 and 2016, especially among women. However, the trends differ. Part-time work has increased among women in Finland, while it has decreased substantially in Norway from 2004 onwards. Over time, the part-time (or full-time) gap between Norwegian and Finnish women has decreased from 22 percentage points in the late 1990s to 12 percentage points today. Among men, the extent and trends of part-time work are more similar.

When examining the prevalence of part-time employment in population groups, we find both similarities and differences between the countries in two time periods (1996–98 and 2014–16) (see Table 9.1). In both countries, women, younger workers, less educated and low-skilled workers, and employees with temporary contacts are more likely to work on a part-time basis. Furthermore, part-time is most prevalent in the same economic sectors, such as wholesale and retail trade, hotels and catering, other services, and education, although part-time work in Norway is also common in social and health-care services.

The profile of part-time work varies to some extent between the countries: in Finland, part-time work is more common among people who are less privileged in the labour market (low-skilled, non-nationals), while in Norway, part-time work is also common among employees with a more stable labour market situation. One might also note the substantial difference between Finland and Norway in the social and health-care services sector. This large and female-dominated sector stands out as substantially different when it comes to the proportion of part-time workers, with a part-time gap between the two countries of 31 percentage points in the late 1990s and 21 percentage points today. In other sectors, the cross-country gap varies by 0 to 6–7 percentage points.

Although the proportion of part-time work as a percentage of total employment has remained relatively stable over time in both countries (minor increase in Finland; no change in Norway), there are interesting similarities and differences in some population groups. In both countries, part-time work has increased among the self-employed, men, younger workers (especially in Norway), the less educated and low skilled (especially in Finland), and in the same economic sectors, such as wholesale and retail trade, hotels and catering, and in the category 'other services' including personal services. This might indicate a growth in part-time work in groups that have a weak labour market position and might therefore experience job and income insecurity and precariousness.

At the same time, there are opposite trends in some population groups. Part-time work has decreased among Norwegian women, in the age group 30–49 years and in the public services, while no such changes can be observed in Finland. We also see country differences when looking at the duration of and motives for part-time work. The proportion of long part-time (20–33 hours) has decreased in Norway but increased in Finland. In a similar vein, voluntary part-time work has increased in Finland but decreased in Norway. One interpretation is that Norwegian policies to increase full-time jobs among women (and mothers) have worked (Ellingsæter and Jensen, 2019). Overall, it seems that the country profiles of part-timers have converged over time.

Are part-time jobs increasingly more insecure than full-time jobs?

A range of studies has shown that part-time work, and in particular, types of short part-time work, is closely related to income and job insecurity (Broughton et al, 2016; Rubery and Grimshaw, 2016). Dualisation scholars are now arguing that these types of differences between labour market insiders and outsiders have become more prevalent (Emmenegger et al, 2012; Rueda et al, 2015). So far, the insider–outsider debate has received limited attention within the context of the well-regulated Nordic regimes.

The first aim of this chapter is to examine whether part-time work is actually more closely linked to income and job insecurity than previously, and whether greater inequalities emerge between insiders and outsiders. We will therefore investigate this and whether the differences between part-time and full-time jobs are tending to increase.

In both countries, perceived work insecurity is higher among part-time than full-time workers (see Figure 9.2). However, there are clear differences between the countries. Work insecurity is more common in Finland, both among part-time and full-time workers. Furthermore, Finnish part-time workers are more exposed to work insecurity. This is most likely associated with the less privileged profile of Finnish part-timers.

While part-timers are clearly more exposed in terms of perceived job insecurity in both countries, the *difference* (insecurity gap) between full-timers and part-timers has remained fairly stable over the last 10 years. In Finland, insecurity has slightly increased, both among part-timers and full-timers, while it has remained at the same level among both part-timers and full-timers in Norway. Overall, changes over time in perceived insecurity are relatively minor. However, there seems to be slightly more variation over time in perceived insecurity among part-timers compared to full-timers, especially in Finland, which might indicate that the situation of part-timers is more influenced by changing labour markets than is that of full-timers.

Figure 9.2: Precariousness index among part-timers and full-timers in Finland and Norway, 2006–16

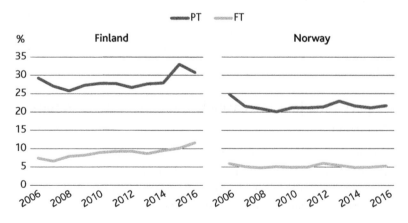

Next, we examine the differences in perceived insecurity between part-time and full-time workers in different population groups in two time periods (2006–08 and 2014–16). For which groups is part-time work a vulnerable position? Are there groups where the insecurity gap has increased over time, indicating a growth in 'bad' part-time jobs (see Table 9.2)? In line with the discussions in the international literature, we are aiming to discover in particular whether insecurity is increasing more among part-time employees with a weaker labour market position.

In both countries, insecurity differences are above the national average among the self-employed, non-nationals, low-skilled and in the wholesale/retail trade, hotels and catering occupations. These are groups where we would expect to find part-time employees with lower bargaining power vis-à-vis the employer, indicating that part-time is a higher risk position for some groups compared to others.

We also find differences between the countries. In Norway, insecurity differences between part-timers and full-timers are slightly larger among women than among men. The effect by gender is interesting since we would expect that part-time jobs in Norway, where part-time work is normalised, would in general be seen as good jobs. In Finland, we do not find a similar situation.[3] In addition, insecurity differences between part-timers and full-timers are larger in Finland – but not in Norway – among those with short working hours.

We also examine patterns in development over time and find noteworthy changes in some groups. In both countries, the insecurity difference has increased above the national averages among the self-employed. In Norway, the insecurity difference has grown among non-nationals while it has decreased in Finland. One explanation might be a higher inflow of migrants in Norway. In Finland, there is an increase in the insecurity difference among those with short (1–19) working hours and with tertiary education. This might indicate that part-time jobs involving short working hours are changing character, in line with the observation of marginal part-time as an increasing challenge in several countries (Broughton et al, 2016). In Norway, no such development is observed. The higher part-time rate in Norway means that employees in short/marginal part-time work represent a more diverse group, and measures to fight involuntary part-time (Ellingsæter and Jensen, 2019) might have been effective. However, as a whole, changes are relatively minor. These results do not indicate an increasing polarisation between part-timers and full-timers in either Finland or Norway.

When we combine motives for part-time work (voluntary versus involuntary) and work insecurity (low, medium, high), we obtain a

Table 9.2: Differences in the insecurity index between part-timers and full-timers, by background characteristics, in 2006–08 and 2014–16 in Finland and Norway (part-time and full-time employed, 15–64 years old)

	Finland			Norway		
	2006–08	2014–16	Change	2006–08	2014–16	Change
Total	20	20	0	17	17	0
Gender						
Women	21	21	0	19	18	−1
Men	19	21	+2	15	15	0
Age groups						
15–29	20	16	−4	18	18	0
30–49	23	24	+1	20	19	−1
50–64	14	15	+1	10	11	+1
Level of education						
Primary	21	19	−2	19	19	0
Secondary	23	21	−2	17	16	−1
Tertiary	14	19	+5	15	15	0
Nationality						
National	20	20	0	17	15	−2
Non-national	41	37	−4	26	34	+8
Economic sector						
Agriculture	16	13	−3	10	9	−1
Manufacturing, construction	12	16	+4	8	7	−1
Wholesale and retail trade; hotels and catering	24	28	+4	18	20	+2
Transport, storage and communications	14	22	+8	18	16	−2
Finance, real estate, business activities	20	20	0	14	20	+6
Public administration	10	14	+4	12	6	−6
Education	19	21	+2	20	15	−5
Human health and social work activities	20	13	−7	20	17	−3
Other services	30	25	−5	18	18	0
Professional status and contract type						
Self-employed	18	25	+7	14	21	+7
Employee with a permanent contract	16	17	+1	15	15	0
Employee with a temporary contract	22	17	−5	24	21	−3

(continued)

Table 9.2: Differences in the insecurity index between part-timers and full-timers, by background characteristics, in 2006–08 and 2014–16 in Finland and Norway (part-time and full-time employed, 15–64 years old) (continued)

	Finland			Norway		
	2006–08	2014–16	Change	2006–08	2014–16	Change
Occupational skill level						
High general skills	17	17	0	12	14	+2
Specific skills	16	15	−1	8	9	+1
Low skills	23	23	−2	20	19	−1
Weekly working hours						
1–19	22	26	+4	19	17	−2
20–33	20	17	−3	16	16	0
Motives for part-time work						
Involuntary (could not find a full-time job)	55	57	+2	66	63	−3
Voluntary (studies, health, family, other reasons)	8	6	−2	9	8	−1

more or less similar typology of part-time work as that proposed in the introductory chapter to this volume. As can be seen in Table 9.2, involuntary part-time work and high work insecurity are strongly correlated, which is partly explained by the fact that both include similar elements of underemployment. By cross-tabulating motivation and insecurity, we obtain six types of part-time work (see Table 9.3).

On the basis of this kind of typology, most part-timers belong to the group of 'equalised' workers (58% in Finland; 70% in Norway): they work on a voluntary basis without work insecurity. Another 9–10% are 'semi-secured': they work on a voluntary basis, with low insecurity. On the other hand, 30% in Finland and 19% in Norway are in a

Table 9.3: Typology of part-time work in 2006–08 and 2014–16 in Finland and Norway (part-time and full-time employed, 15–64 years old) (%)

	Finland			Norway		
	2006–08	2014–16	Change	2006–08	2014–16	Change
Equalised	60	58	−2	71	70	−1
Semi-secured	10	10	0	10	9	−1
Transitional	1	2	+1	1	2	+1
Underemployed	10	10	0	5	6	+1
Precarious	12	13	+1	10	10	0
Marginalised	6	7	+1	3	3	0

more problematic situation: they work on an involuntary basis either without insecurity ('underemployed') or with insecurity ('precarious' or 'marginalised'). Again, changes over time are minor. Thus, the majority of part-time work can be regarded as 'good' part-time work in the sense of voluntariness and low insecurity.

Are part-time jobs stepping stones into full-time work or dead-end jobs leading to unemployment?

As illustrated by several of the chapters in this book (see, eg, Chapters 3, 8 and 10), in many cases, a part-time job will leave the worker more exposed to precariousness. For this reason, the opportunity to move out of a part-time job is an important aspect of job quality (Fagan et al, 2014). The second aim of this chapter is to examine mobility in part-time work and especially transitions from part-time to full-time work or to unemployment. Are mobility rates changing over time and, if so, do we see a decline in upward transfers? Or, do the strong labour market institutions in the Nordic countries (still) ensure a high rate of positive transfers?

In earlier studies, much focus was placed on the extent to which part-time employment can act as a stepping stone to full-time work in a labour market career (Nätti, 1995; Bollé, 1997; O'Reilly and Bothfeld, 2002; Connolly and Gregory, 2010; see also Chapter 7). Francesconi and Gosling (2005) found that part-time employment is more likely to be a transitional process from non-employment into full employment for men than for women. In a similar vein, Månsson and Ottoson (2011) found that women have a lower probability of transition from involuntary part-time to full-time employment than men. Furthermore, Månsson and Ottosen (2011) argue that having short working time or a temporary contract results in a weaker position in the labour market than having a permanent part-time contract with relatively long working time. However, for some low-skilled workers, part-time work may provide a path to permanent and stable employment (Kauhanen, 2008).

According to the results, in *Finland*, half of part-timers remained in part-time work during the follow-up period (2014–16) (see Table 9.4). Every fourth part-timer moves to full-time work and the same proportion move to positions where they are not employed. Differences between the time periods are minor. In *Norway*, stability in part-time work is very high, especially since 2000: 70% of part-timers remained in part-time work during the follow-up period (2014–16) (see Table 9.4) whereas every fifth part-timer moved to full-time work. In other words, part-

Table 9.4: Transitions from part-time work (in T1) to different labour market statuses (in T2, 15 months later) in 2001–03, 2008–10 and 2014–16 among 15- to 64-year-old employees, Finland and Norway (%)

Part-time work in T1	Full-time	Part-time	Self-employed	Unemployed	Student	Retired, inability	Household work	Other	Total
Finland									
2001–03	23	48	2	7	10	4	2	4	100
2008–10	25	48	2	6	7	6	2	3	100
2014–16	25	51	2	4	6	6	2	4	100
Norway									
2001–03	21	66	1	2	4	3	1	1	100
2008–10	17	71	1	1	5	3	1	2	100
2014–16	18	70	1	2	5	3	0	1	100

Note: For Norway in 2001–03, ages ranged from 16–64 years.

Source: Finnish Labour Force Survey Panel and Norwegian Labour Force Survey Panel

time jobs are a much more stable labour market affiliation in Norway compared to Finland. The increase in full-time jobs among women in Norway (as observed in Figure 9.1) does not seem to take the form of higher rates of transfer from part-time to full-time jobs.

The higher part-time rates in Norway, with a tradition of normalised part-time work, mean that part-time is a more stable labour market affiliation than it is in Finland. Finnish part-timers face a higher risk of ending up outside the labour market but, at the same time, they also experience more mobility into full-time jobs. However, in neither of the countries do we find that part-time jobs have become more vulnerable over time, measured by the risk of transferring to unemployment or otherwise ending up outside the labour market.

In Tables 9A.1a and 9A.1b, we examine similar transitions in different population groups from two perspectives: the groups with *highest mobility* out of part-time jobs; and differences *within* population groups (gender, working-hour duration, age, level of education, occupation, economic sector, contract type). In both Finland and Norway, mobility from part-time to full-time work was above the average among younger employees, the more educated and employees with temporary contracts. In Norway, this also applies for men and for employees with long part-time hours. The implication is that part-time jobs more often function as a bridge into full-time jobs for groups who are new in the labour market (young people who are finishing their education, temporary employed) and groups that are less likely to be trapped in involuntary part-time jobs due to labour market resources (the highly educated).

In both countries, staying in part-time work was most common among women and older workers, as well as employees with permanent contracts. These groups are perhaps less likely to be trapped in involuntary part-time work due to personal choices related to their life phase. There will nevertheless be substantial variation among women when it comes to part-time employment. Kavli et al (see Chapter 4) analyse the Norwegian health-care sector and find that workers with low education and limited Norwegian-language skills are more exposed to involuntary part-time work.

Transitions to unemployment are of special interest when discussing part-time jobs as a potentially vulnerable labour market affiliation. In both countries, transitions from part-time jobs to unemployment were most common among employees with temporary contracts. Otherwise, we do not see any particular groups of part-time employees with notably higher unemployment risks. Since Finland has had higher unemployment rates compared to Norway, it is not surprising that transitions to unemployment are highest in Finland.

In Finland, gender differences are quite minor, although women stay in part-time work more often compared to men. The share of part-timers who end up in full-time work is the same for women and men. Gender differences are clearer in Norway. The ratio of Norwegian women who stay in part-time jobs is high, both compared to Norwegian men and to Finnish women, indicating the strong position that part-time jobs have among Norwegian women. In neither of the countries do our data indicate that women have a higher risk of moving from part-time jobs to unemployment compared to men. Actually, men working part-time have a slightly higher risk for unemployment in both countries.

Differences by education and between the occupational groups are relatively minor in both countries. We only find moderate differences between the economic sectors, indicating that it is difficult to identify sectors where part-time jobs are more of a risk factor compared to other sectors. One group that is of particular interest is employees in short part-time work. In neither Finland nor Norway are small jobs/marginal part-time jobs particularly associated with a substantial increased risk for moving into unemployment. However, in both countries, this group more often transfers into studies, which is not surprising as short part-time jobs can be combined with studies.

Discussion

In this chapter, we have examined part-time work from the perspective of labour market dualisation in two Nordic countries. We have explored whether there is also a trend towards more marginalised part-time work within the historically well-regulated labour markets of the Nordic countries. Furthermore, we have discussed whether there are differences between Norway, with a long tradition of normalised part-time jobs among women, and Finland, where full-time has been the normal working-time choice among women.

First, we asked whether part-time work is more closely associated with income and job insecurity than previously, that is, whether part-time jobs become more insecure over time, and whether the differences between part-time and full-time jobs tend to increase. In Finland, insecurity has slightly increased among both part-timers and full-timers, while in Norway, insecurity has remained at the same level over time in both cases. The insecurity differences between part-timers and full-timers have remained fairly stable in both countries. Thus, the results do not give support for polarisation in terms of increased work insecurity among part-time employees. Still, the results indicate that perceived work insecurity is higher among part-timers compared to full-time workers in both countries, and we also observe slightly more variation over time compared to full-timers.

At the same time, there are clear differences between the countries. Work insecurity is more common in Finland, both among part-time and full-time workers, compared to Norway. Furthermore, part-time jobs seem to be more insecure than full-time jobs, especially in Finland. This is probably associated with the less privileged profile of the Finnish part-timers compared to the Norwegian part-timers. Furthermore, Finland has also experienced periods of high unemployment, which may have forced some employees into jobs of a poorer quality than they would otherwise have accepted.

Second, we examined mobility from part-time jobs to other positions in the labour market. One characteristic of a labour market with major inequalities is that part-timers end up being permanently excluded (so-called outsiders). On the other hand, if a part-time job functions as a bridge to a more secure position in the labour market, we can expect transitions to full-time positions. The results indicate that part-time work is characterised by high stability: in Norway, two thirds of part-timers remained in part-time work during the follow-up period; in Finland, this was half of part-timers. Furthermore, transitions to full-time work were much more common than transitions to unemployment. Thus, part-time work is more often a bridge to full-time work than a trap leading to unemployment. Over time, there have been minor changes in the labour market mobility and insecurity of part-timers. Hence, our results do not show any increase in polarisation between part-timers and full-timers in terms of mobility into more insecure positions.

In both countries, mobility from part-time to full-time work was above the average among young workers, the more educated and employees with temporary contracts. Staying in part-time work was above the average among women and older workers. Transitions to unemployment were most common among employees with temporary contracts. When looking at mobility differences within population groups, the countries differ more. On the one hand, gender differences were clearer in Norway than in Finland; on the other hand, differences between age groups, educational levels and contract types were quite similar in the two countries.

All in all, we conclude that although part-time jobs are common in both Finland and Norway, we see few indicators of an increase in so-called 'bad part-time' over the last decade or so. Although part-time jobs are more insecure than full-time jobs, there are no indicators of these becoming more insecure or with fewer opportunities for mobility into full-time employment. Part-time work is more common in certain parts of the labour market, for example, in the service sectors and among young people. However, our analyses of the labour force surveys do not indicate that the nature of part-time work as such has changed into more 'bad part-time' and thereby contributed to greater differences between outsiders and insiders over time.

In this chapter, we have not examined the role of labour market institutions. However, it may seem that the Nordic labour market institutions, such as strong collective institutions and inclusive social support schemes, still act as a buffer that shields workers from having to accept the worst jobs – despite decreasing unionisation rates and a more differentiated workforce.

Notes

[1]   In Finland, 'usual hours worked' was defined as the modal value of the actual hours worked per week over a long reference period (four weeks to three months). Usual hours include contractual hours of work plus the overtime that the employee is expected to work regularly. In Norway, working hours per week are based on contracted (agreed) working hours per week in the main job; overtime is not included.

2   This is in accordance with time-related underemployment according to the International Labour Organisation (ILO) definition (16th International Conference of Labour Statisticians (ICLS), ILO, October 1998).

3   The gender difference disappears if we add background controls to the model.

References

Andersen, S.K., Dølvik, J.E. and Ibsen, C.L. (2014) 'Nordic labour market models in open markets', Report 132 ETUI, Brussels.

Barth, E. and Moene, K.O. (2016) 'The equality multiplier: how wage compression and welfare empowerment interact', *Journal of the European Economic Association*, 14(5): 1011–37.

Berglund, T., Furåker, B. and Vulkan, P. (2014) 'Is job insecurity compensated for by employment and income security?', *Economic and Industrial Democracy*, 35(1): 165–84.

Bollé, P. (1997) 'Part-time work: solution or trap?', *International Labour Review*, 136(4): 557–79.

Broughton, A. et al (2016) 'Precarious employment in Europe: patterns, trends and policy strategies', Directorate-General for Internal Policies, European Parliament.

Chung, H. (2018) 'Dualization and the access to occupational family-friendly working-time arrangements across Europe', *Social Policy & Administration*, 52: 491–507.

Connolly, S. and Gregory, M. (2010) 'Dual tracks: part-time work in life-cycle employment for British women', *Journal of Population Economics*, 23(3): 907–31.

Dølvik, J.E. (2013) 'Grunnpilarene i de nordiske modellene', Fafo-rapport 2013:13.

Eichhorst, W. and Marx, P. (2012) 'Whatever works: dualization and the service economy in Bismarckian welfare states', in P. Emmenegger, S. Häusermann, B. Palier and M. Seeleib-Kaiser (eds) *The age of dualization: the changing face of inequality in deindustrializing societies*, Oxford: Oxford University Press, pp 73–99.

Ellingsæter, A.L. (1989) *Normalisering av deltidsarbeidet. En analyse av endring i kvinners yrkesaktivitet og arbeidstid i 80-årene*, Oslo: Statistisk sentralbyrå (SØS/71).

Ellingsæter, A.L. and Jensen, R.S. (2019) 'Politicising women's part-time work in Norway: a longitudinal study of ideas', *Work, Employment and Society*. Available at https://doi.org/10.1177/0950017018821277

Emmenegger, P., Häusermann, S., Palier, B. and Seeleib-Kaiser, M. (2012) 'How we grow unequal', in P. Emmenegger, S. Häusermann, B. Palier and M. Seeleib-Kaiser (eds) *The age of dualization: the changing face of inequality in deindustrializing societies*, Oxford: Oxford University Press.

Fagan, C., Norman, H., Smith, M. and González Menéndez, M.C. (2014) *In search of good quality part-time employment*, Conditions of Work and Employment Series No. 43, Geneva: International Labour Office.

Fleckenstein, T., Saunders, A.M. and Seeleib-Kaiser, M. (2011) 'The dual transformation of social protection and human capital: comparing Britain and Germany', *Comparative Political Studies*, 12(44): 1622–50.

Francesconi, M. and Gosling, A. (2005) 'Career paths of part-time workers', University of Essex, Working Paper Series No. 19.

Gallie, D. (2007) *Employment regimes and the quality of work*, Oxford: Oxford University Press.

Kalleberg, A.L. (2000) 'Nonstandard employment relations: part-time, temporary and contract work', *Annual Review of Sociology*, 26: 341–65.

Kalleberg, A.L. (2009) 'Precarious work, insecure workers: employment relations in transition', *American Sociological Review*, 74: 1–22.

Kauhanen, M. (2008) 'Part-time work and involuntary part-time work in the private service sector in Finland', *Economic and Industrial Democracy*, 29(2): 217–48.

Månsson, J. and Ottoson, J. (2011) 'Transitions from part-time unemployment: is part-time work a dead end or a stepping stone to the labour market?', *Economic and Industrial Democracy*, 32(4): 569–89.

Nätti, J. (1995) 'Part-time work in the Nordic countries: a trap for women?', *Labour. Review of Labour Economics and Industrial Relations*, 2(2): 343–57.

Nergaard, K (2014) 'Social democratic capitalism', in A. Wilkinson, G. Wood and R. Deeg (eds) *The Oxford handbook of employment relations*, Oxford: Oxford University Press.

O'Reilly, J. and Bothfeld, S. (2002) 'What happens after working part time? Integration, maintenance or exclusionary transitions in Britain and Western Germany', *Cambridge Journal of Economics*, 26(4): 409–39.

Paugam, S. and Zhou, Y. (2007) 'Job insecurity' in D. Gallie (ed) *Employment regimes and the quality of work*, Oxford: Oxford University Press, pp 179–204.

Rasmussen, S., Nätti, J., Larsen, T.P., Ilsøe, A. and Garde, A.H. (forthcoming) 'Non-standard employment in the Nordics – towards precarious work?', *Nordic Working Life Studies*.

Rubery, J. and Grimshaw, D. (2016) 'Precarious work and the commodification of the employment relationship: the case of zero hours in the UK and mini jobs in Germany', in G. Bäcker, S. Lehndorff and C. Weinkopf (eds) *Den Arbeitsmarkt verstehen, um ihn zu gestalten: Festschrift für Gerhard Bosch*, Wiesbaden: Springer, pp 241–54.

Rueda, D., Wibbels, E. and Altamirano, M. (2015) 'The origins of dualism', in H. Kriesi, H. Kitschelt, P. Beramendi and S. Häusermann (eds) *The politics of advanced capitalism*, Cambridge: Cambridge University Press.

Thelen, K. (2014) *Varieties of liberalization and the new politics of social solidarity*, New York, NY: Cambridge University Press.

Wiss, T. (2017) 'Paths towards family-friendly working time arrangements: comparing workplaces in different countries and industries', *Social Policy & Administration*, 51(7): 1406–30.

Appendix

See Tables 9A.1a and 9A.1b overleaf.

Table 9A.1a: Transitions from part-time work (in T1) into different labour market states (in T2) during 2001–16, by background factors, in Finland (%)

Part-time work in T1	Full-time	Part-time	Self-employed	Unemployed	Student	Retired, inability	Household work	Other
Total	26	46	2	6	8	7	2	3
Gender								
Women	26	49	2	5	7	6	3	2
Men	26	41	4	6	10	7	0	5
Working time (hours)								
1–19	24	46	3	5	10	7	2	3
20–34	27	48	2	6	6	6	2	3
Age								
15–29	31	37	2	6	15	2	3	4
30–49	33	47	3	7	3	3	3	2
50–64	13	59	3	4	1	17	0	3
Level of education								
Primary	20	45	2	7	13	7	1	5
Secondary	29	46	2	6	8	6	2	2
Tertiary	29	50	3	4	2	8	3	1

(continued)

Table 9A.1a: Transitions from part-time work (in T1) into different labour market states (in T2) during 2001–16, by background factors, in Finland (%) (continued)

Part-time work in T1	Full-time	Part-time	Self-employed	Unemployed	Student	Retired, inability	Household work	Other
Occupation								
High general skills	28	46	4	5	5	7	3	2
Specific skills	25	40	4	6	8	11	1	5
Low skills	26	46	2	6	10	6	2	3
Economic sector								
Agriculture	21	38	8	5	14	8	1	5
Manufacturing, construction	23	46	3	4	7	11	1	4
Wholesale and retail trade; hotels and catering	28	48	2	5	8	4	2	2
Transport, storage and communications, finance, real estate, renting and business activities	27	45	3	5	8	6	2	3
Public administration, education, human health and social work activities	27	48	2	5	5	8	2	3
Other services	23	41	3	10	13	6	1	4
Contract type								
Permanent	25	53	2	3	5	8	2	2
Temporary	30	30	3	11	14	4	2	5

Source: Finnish Labour Force Survey Panel

Table 9A.1b: Transitions from part-time work (in T1) into different labour market states (in T2) during 2001–16 by background factors, in Norway, employees 15–64 years (%)

	Full-time	Part-time	Self-employed	Unemployed	Student	Retired, disability	Household work	Other
Total	19	69	1	2	5	3	1	1
Gender								
Women	17	73	0	1	4	3	1	1
Men	28	52	2	3	9	4	0	2
Working time								
1–19 hours	14	68	1	2	8	4	1	1
20+ hours	22	70	1	1	2	2	1	1
Age								
15–29	23	73	1	1	1	2	1	1
30–49	21	80	1	1	0	7	1	1
50–64	10	69	1	2	5	3	1	1
Level of education								
Primary	17	67	1	2	8	3	1	2
Secondary	18	71	1	2	4	3	1	1
Tertiary	24	68	1	1	2	2	1	1

(continued)

Table 9A.1b: Transitions from part-time work (in T1) into different labour market states (in T2) during 2001–16 by background factors, in Norway, employees 15–64 years (%) (continued)

	Full-time	Part-time	Self-employed	Unemployed	Student	Retired, disability	Household work	Other
Occupation								
High general skills	23	70	1	1	2	2	1	1
Specific skills	27	57	2	2	5	6	1	2
Low skills	16	70	0	2	6	3	1	1
Economic sector								
Agriculture	24	53	4	1	11	3	1	2
Manufacturing, construction	21	65	1	2	5	4	1	1
Wholesale and retail trade; hotels and catering	19	66	1	3	8	2	1	1
Transport, storage and communications, finance, real estate, renting and business activities	23	63	1	3	5	3	1	2
Public administration, education, human health and social work activities	18	74	0	1	2	3	1	1
Other services	16	66	2	2	9	3	1	2
Contract type								
Permanent	17	73	1	1	3	3	1	1
Temporary	24	54	1	4	10	3	1	3

Source: Finnish Labour Force Survey Panel

PART THREE
Work–life balance, gender and part-time work

10

The interplay of welfare state policies with supply- and demand-side factors in the production of marginalised part-time employment among women in Germany

Birgit Pfau-Effinger and Thordis Reimer

Introduction

The primary focus of this chapter is a specific form of part-time work in Germany, the so-called 'Minijob', which entails specific features and risks. This empirical study examines how demand- and supply-side factors interact with welfare state institutions and politics in the production of the marginal employment of women in part-time jobs.

A common argument in the debate regarding the segmentation of labour markets and related social inequality is that the development of atypical employment, including part-time employment, is embedded in firms' strategies to establish a 'secondary segment' of marginalised workers in low-skilled jobs. According to this perspective, most firms combine two employment types: (1) a 'primary segment' of core workers with relatively high professional or firm-specific skills who receive greater job protection rights and social security benefits; and (2) a 'secondary segment' that meets firms' need for flexibility with temporary employment or part-time contracts, in which both job protection rights and social security earnings are significantly less than those in the primary segment. Thus, work in the secondary segment is connected with higher social and economic risks than is work in the core segment (Doeringer and Piore, 1971; Sengenberger 1981). Analysts suggest that specific groups of workers, particularly those who are less integrated in the labour force, are prepared to accept positions in the secondary segment. Such arguments particularly associate this group with lower-skilled workers and women, who are assumed to also have an 'alternative role' outside the labour force as housewives and mothers (Projektgruppe Arbeitsmarktpolitik and Offe, 1977; Sengenberger, 1981).

As a consequence of 21st-century economic reforms, many welfare states have taken specific measures that have strengthened the division between core workers in the primary employment segment and marginal workers in the secondary employment segment in order to support firms' segmented employment strategies. These developments contributed to a 'dualisation' of the employment system by extending the protection of professional core workers and, at the same time, extending the labour market risks related to marginal jobs (Palier and Thelen, 2010), such as the deregulation of labour law, collective agreements and social rights. These developments have resulted in an increase in the secondary segment of the labour market and a growing proportion of workers who face the social and economic risks attendant to marginal work.

In this discourse, many authors generally treat part-time employment as a specific type of marginalised employment. Others have argued that part-time employment cannot be characterised as marginal per se (Pfau-Effinger, 1998; Chou et al, 2017), particularly in case of such work in the primary segment of employment. Here, part-time contracts often serve as a measure of work–family reconciliation and, in this sense, primarily serve employees' interests. However, some forms of secondary sector work are seen as particularly precarious as some elements of job protection and social security benefits that are usually connected with regular employment may not apply in these cases. In Germany, a specific form of marginal part-time employment called the 'Minijob' was introduced in 2001 as part of the so-called 'Agenda 2010', a series of path-breaking reforms of the labour market and unemployment policies implemented by the Red–Green government in the early 2000s, which aimed at deregulating substantial parts of labour law and social security rights.

Until now, there has been limited research that analyses how demand-side and supply-side factors interact in their production of a marginalised group of female workers. We argue that it is only possible to understand this issue by analysing the deregulated nature of the political framework of Minijobs, as well as interactions between the labour market behaviour of workers on the supply side and the strategies of firms regarding the organisation of jobs and the recruitment of workers on the demand side. This empirical study examines how politics has contributed to the creation of a marginalised form of part-time employment at the institutional level, and examines which factors at the supply side and demand side characterise the marginal employment of women in this specific type of part-time jobs. We examine workplace characteristics such as firm size and public versus private sector participation on the demand side, while on the supply side, we investigate the role of factors such as women's individual and household characteristics.

'Minijobs': a politically constructed form of marginal employment for women

In 2001, Germany's Red–Green government reintroduced already-existing marginal part-time employment legislation (*Geringfügige Beschäftigung*) under a new name ('Minijobs') and characterised it as an innovative instrument of labour market policy. This action was part of the government's 'Agenda 2010' strategy, which, among other things, extended the low-wage employment sector on the basis of the deregulation of employment protections.

The institutional regulations related to Minijobs differ substantially from those attached to regular part-time employment, such that working in Minijobs confers both short- and long-term social and economic risks. Short-term consequences include the lower income of such jobs, which pay a maximum of €450, a rate that is clearly below the poverty level. The average gross hourly wage of €10.32 for Minijobs is substantially lower than the wages associated with regular part-time and full-time employment, and for 12.5% of such workers, Minijob wages are actually set below the German minimum hourly wage of €8.50 (RWI, 2016).

In contrast to formal employed workers, Minijobbers are not eligible for health insurance or unemployment benefits. Moreover, normal employment protection legislation does not apply to Minijobs; hence, workers have limited recourse in case of dismissal (Absenger and Priebe, 2016). Over the long term, Minijob workers are only eligible to collect very low levels of pension funds, thus substantially increasing their risk of poverty in old age. The recruitment of Minijobbers therefore offers firms the possibility of establishing a segment of marginal work with flexible jobs and low wage costs that is based on substantially lower tax and social security obligations than those accompanying regular employment contracts. For employees, working in a Minijob offers the option of expanding household income by supplementing the wages earned by a full-time working husband, without compromising women's ability to provide childcare or care for older relatives.

The introduction of marginal employment under the name of 'Minijobs' was part of a programme of the Red–Green government that had the explicit aim of establishing a new low-wage sector, mainly in the field of social services. For this purpose, the government established an expert committee that included several economists and one prominent sociologist (Beck, 1997; Commission for Future Questions of Bavaria and Saxony, 1997). The committee developed a proposal for a low-wage sector that was strongly based on the idea of extending the sector of voluntary work (now called 'citizens' work') and 'marginal part-time work' in the field of social services. The 'Hartz' reforms (named after the head of the committee, Peter Hartz) of Agenda 2010 were, in part, based on the recommendations of this committee.

How could such a precarious form of employment have been introduced by a government dominated by the progressive, centre-left Social Democratic Party? One factor facilitating the establishment of Minijobs is that the reform of the German labour market policy was accompanied by a political top-down discourse that was largely based on neoliberal cultural values. The deregulation of labour law was legitimised with a neoliberal narrative that advocated deregulation as a necessary instrument to combat unemployment by creating new jobs (Knuth, 2014).

A second reason is that even as the government pretended that the Minijob was an innovative instrument of labour market policy, this system had, in fact, existed since the 1960s and was already well established in the institutional and cultural structures surrounding the employment system. Marginal part-time employment was originally introduced in 1961 by the German government under the label 'Geringfügige Beschäftigung', which means 'low-level employment' or 'marginal employment', and the associated institutional regulations were approximately the same as those applied in the case of Minijobs. 'Geringfügige Beschäftigung' comprised part-time work with relatively short working hours and was restricted to a certain wage threshold per month in order to exempt them from income tax, which was then set at 300 Deutschmarks and is now limited to €450. The system was established with the explicit aim of offering the option for women in relatively low-income households led by male breadwinners to act as additional earners by taking on a relatively small number of weekly working hours (Brinkmann and Kohler, 1981).

A third factor facilitating the introduction of Minijobs in the early 2000s was that the relevant actors used the common cultural beliefs that were already linked with the previous form of marginal employment ('Geringfügige Beschäftigung'). This is evident in the publications of Ulrich Beck (1997) and the report of the expert committee

(Commission for Future Questions of Bavaria and Saxony, 1999), which defined women as additional workers in the male–breadwinner couple, with innate skills and motivations, who are inclined towards altruistic care work and do not expect to receive regular wages in terms of 'normal' wages (Effinger and Pfau-Effinger, 1999).

Altogether, the introduction of marginal and deregulated part-time employment containing high economic and social risks for workers was an active political measure by the Red–Green government to trigger the extension of the secondary segment of employment for firms. On the demand side, the introduction of the Minijob system motivated firms to employ particularly vulnerable groups of women in highly precarious forms of employment, whereas on the supply side, this development motivated such women to act on the basis of traditional employment patterns in the context of the male-breadwinner-headed family. Hence, the Minijob legislation can be seen as a strategic element of dualisation in the employment system of the German welfare state that particularly creates economic risks for women and contributes to the persistence of traditional patterns of gender inequality.

It should be mentioned that Minijobs differ significantly from regular part-time employment in Germany. Regular part-time jobs traditionally comprise working hours below the level of full-time employment and above that of marginal part-time employment. Labour law does not distinguish between regular part-time employment and standard employment with regard to rights related to the employment contract and eligibility for social security benefits (Brinkmann and Kohler, 1981). Many firms prefer to offer regular part-time jobs on the basis of 50% of the usual weekly hours as this provides them with the option of combining two half-time jobs to fill one full-time position. However, as many women work part-time in order to be able to spend time with their children in the afternoon, women's work in a 50% part-time job is usually confined to the first half of the working day (Jaehrling, 2017).

The development of Minijobs in Germany

From 2000 to 2017, the number of employed people in Germany increased from 29,862,000 to 33,269,000 (Federal Statistical Office Germany, 2017); this growth was exclusively based on the increase in part-time work and other forms of atypical employment. The number of full-time permanent jobs in dependent employment decreased during this period from 22,130,000 to 22,017,000, whereas the number of people working part-time increased from 7,732,000 to 11,252,000 (Federal Statistical Office Germany, 2017). In 2000, shortly before the Minijob system was introduced, the proportion of people working in the previous version of marginal part-time employment (*Geringfügige Beschäftigung*) in relation to all employed people (without the self-employed) was 5.9% (Federal Statistical Office Germany, 2017). After the introduction of the Minijob legislation, the proportion of people working in marginal part-time employment increased to 8.1% in 2010 and then decreased again to 6.5% by 2016 (Federal Statistical Office Germany, 2017). In 2000, the proportion of women working in marginal part-time employment among all employed women was 11.1%. It increased to 13.1% by 2010 and decreased to 10.3% by 2016, while in the same year, only 3.0% of all employed men had a Minijob (Federal Statistical Office Germany, 2017). The main sectors employing workers in Minijobs include the food industry, hotels and restaurants, retail trade, and other personal services, and the proportion of workers in Minijobs is relatively high in relation to all workers in these sectors. In hotels and restaurants, for example, every third worker works in a Minijob (Hohendanner and Stegmaier, 2012). It has been shown that Minijobs are an 'end station' rather than a 'stepping stone' (see Chapter 1) into full-time standard employment (Lietzmann et al, 2016). The Hartz reforms of German labour market policies strongly contributed to the growth of Minijobs for women in the early 2000s. A main reason is that these reforms created immense pressure to take up jobs among those who were unemployed and received 'Unemployment Benefit 2' longer than one year as such benefits under Hartz IV are below the relative poverty level and are means-tested at the household level. These people are expected to accept any job offer, with nearly no restrictions with regard to working time, pay, occupation and skill levels (Knuth, 2014; Jaehrling, 2017). Another reason is that the increase in the share of women working in Minijobs just prolonged a trend that already existed as the proportion of women working in marginal part-time work had already increased before the introduction of Minijobs (from 4.1% in 1991, to 4.8% in 1995, to 11.1% in 2000) (Federal Statistical Office Germany, 2017); therefore, it was connected to the increase in women's employment rates (eg Jaehrling, 2017).

Literature overview and analytical framework

Women's employment behaviour is a much-debated issue in comparative social sciences. A broad range of studies explains women's employment behaviour with supply-side factors, such as individual or household characteristics. For example, rational choice theory posits that women's labour market integration varies in relation to their family status, and that their employment decisions aim at utility maximisation. This argument was mainly developed in the context of the 'New Home Economics' framework developed by Gary Becker (1981), who proposed the existence of 'intrinsic differences between the sexes', whereby women are 'biologically committed to the care of children' (Becker, 1981: 37–40). However, feminist theorists stress that the gender division of labour is a result of power relations rather than being biologically rooted, and they charge that rational choice theory neglects the differences in interests between individual women and men by treating the private household as a monolithic block in which both genders pursue the common aim of household efficiency (Katz, 1997). Moreover, feminists argue that rational choice approaches cannot explain why women with similar characteristics and living situations act differently in their employment behaviour (McRae, 2003).

Thus, although the New Household Economics framework assumes the presence of a stable gender division in private households, other approaches treat women's employment decision-making as individual utility-maximising behaviour that varies according to specific factors, including the availability and amount of a husband's/partner's income, the number of children in the household and women's educational level. Research has demonstrated substantial cross-country variations in the relationship between women's labour supply and their partners' income (eg Matysiak and Steinmetz, 2008). Studies have indicated that women with more children are more likely to reduce their working time or even drop out of the labour market entirely (eg Baumgartner, 2003), and that a lack of public day care for children may impact this decision (Kangas and Rostgaard, 2007).

The 'gender arrangement' approach of Pfau-Effinger questions the assumptions underlying both rational choice approaches and individual utility-maximising behaviour to explain women's employment behaviour. This framework argues that women's employment behaviour is based on the orientation of the cultural family ideals prevailing in their society and on the degree to which the realisation of their personal family/cultural orientation is supported by welfare state policies, as well as with the context of firms' strategies and their negotiation power vis-à-vis the firm (Pfau-Effinger, 1993, 1998). This theoretical approach has been supported by empirical studies demonstrating that women's family/cultural orientation towards employment and childcare influences their participation in the labour market, whereby women with a more family-centred cultural orientation work fewer hours than women with a more career-centred orientation (Jensen et al, 2017).

In forming hypotheses for this study, we assumed a particularly high likelihood that women in specific groups, such as older women and women with children under school age, would accept jobs with shorter working hours and working conditions connected to higher social and economic hazards. It is common for women in such groups to seek part-time jobs as many women in these stages of their life course tend to be more culturally oriented towards a combination of part-time work and caring for their families and children. We also assumed that these groups of women are more likely to work in Minijobs instead of part-time or full-time jobs with full job security because they are particularly vulnerable due to having relatively low negotiation power vis-à-vis their employers. Third, we assumed a higher likelihood of firms using Minijobs to employ workers who have lower negotiation power and a higher need for flexibility.

Therefore, on the supply side, the relevant factors for women's work in Minijobs are hypothesised as including individual characteristics such as education level and age, along with the household characteristics of having children and living with a partner (with whom the woman is married) in the household. On the demand side, we emphasised the role of firm characteristics such as firm size and whether the firm is established in the public sector or in the private sector. In the following, we introduce our main hypotheses concerning the question of why German women work in Minijobs.

Demand-side factors

It is particularly easy for firms to utilise the strategy of 'hire and fire' for Minijob workers because such workers have limited legal protections against dismissal. Moreover, smaller firms can use Minijobs as a means of increasing their workforce, particularly during peak work hours and days (Jaehrling, 2017). In addition, the legal obligation to establish shop stewards does not apply to small firms, meaning that they therefore have lower levels of unionisation, which, in turn, results in a relatively low chance that a union will combat the establishment of Minijobs:

> **Hypothesis 1**: women working in small firms are more likely to work in Minijobs than women working in larger firms.

We also thought that firms in the public sector would be less likely to use Minijobs because working conditions are more strongly based on political decisions than they are in the private sector, and in many countries, the public sector is perceived as advocating favourable working conditions. However, this role has significantly eroded over the past decade in many European societies (Martin and Thelen, 2007). Nevertheless, public sector unions are more powerful and successful than unions in the private sector and are thus better equipped to successfully combat the use of Minijobs by employers (Hirsch et al, 2010):

> **Hypothesis 2**: women working in the public sector are less likely to work in Minijobs than women working in the private sector.

Supply-side factors

As discussed earlier, Minijobs represent a particularly precarious form of employment, whereby labour laws provide workers with limited protection. Therefore, it is plausible to assume that particularly vulnerable groups of women will work in Minijobs, namely, women who have difficulties in finding other types of jobs in the labour market. As such, we mainly expect women with lower levels of education to work in Minijobs. Women's employment behaviour varies significantly between low-skilled and high-skilled workers, and more highly educated women tend to work more hours than do women with little or no education (Jensen et al, 2017):

> **Hypothesis 3**: women with lower educational levels are more likely to work in Minijobs than are highly educated women.

Women's employment in Minijobs may differ among age groups. There are two reasons for the plausibility of assuming that women of a later working age have a higher likelihood of working in Minijobs. First, women of the older generation are more likely than younger women to be oriented towards the traditional cultural ideal of the 'male breadwinner/female care' model (Pfau-Effinger and Euler, 2014). Therefore, a relatively large proportion of older women in Germany prefer to work part-time instead of full-time in order to be able to perform household work for their husbands or provide care for grandchildren (Brandt and Hank, 2014). Second, women of a later working age are particularly vulnerable in the labour market. Older women who have been unemployed or are returning to employment after a long family break are disadvantaged in the recruitment process when compared with younger women as many employers may consider their general skills to be outdated. Therefore, it is plausible to assume that older women find themselves in situations where they do not have an option other than to pursue precarious employment in the form of a Minijob more often than do younger women (Knuth and Kalina, 2002). As such, it can be assumed that many older women will obtain a Minijob if they want to work part-time:

> **Hypothesis 4**: older women are more likely to work in a Minijob than are younger women.

Empirical studies have shown that part-time work is common among women who aim to reconcile employment and childcare demands. This situation particularly relates to countries in which the main cultural family ideal for the work–family relationship is defined by the 'male breadwinner/female part-time care' model. This cultural family model is based on the assumption that mothers ideally provide care for children under age three at home by themselves, and that mothers of children under school age and in primary school (ages 6–10) should work part-time at most as their children should receive maternal care at home in the afternoon (Pfau-Effinger, 2012). In these countries, employed women with children under school age typically work part-time (Chou et al, 2017). The 'male breadwinner/female part-time care' family model is culturally dominant in Germany, particularly in West Germany (Pfau-Effinger and Smidt, 2011). In principle, it is possible for German women to return to a full-time job after the parental leave period because the German welfare state has offered comprehensive social rights and infrastructure to support full-time public day care for all children under school age (Section 24 of Social Code VIII, SGB VIII, last changes from 30 October 2017). However, many Germans, particularly in West Germany, believe that women with children under school age should ideally stay at home or work shorter hours; hence, part-time employment is the common form of employment among women with young children (Pfau-Effinger, 2012). Thus, it is plausible to assume that the orientation towards the cultural family model of the 'male breadwinner/female part-time carer' is another major reason as to why women in Germany work in Minijobs:

Hypothesis 5: women with young children are more likely to work in Minijobs.

Since the income derived from Minijobs is below the poverty level, women cannot rely exclusively on such work, and therefore depend on other sources of household income. In the cultural context of Germany, income transfer within the family based on the male-breadwinner arrangement is a common resource for women in couples (Frericks et al, 2016). We therefore assume that women are more likely to work in Minijobs when they live with a partner in their household:

Hypothesis 6: women with a (married) partner in the household are more likely to work in Minijobs.

Method

Our statistical analyses were conducted using German Socio-Economic Panel (SOEP) data from wave 2014, with information regarding women's employment in 2013. The SOEP is a representative longitudinal study of private households that samples nearly 11,000 households and 30,000 people every year. The data provide information on household composition, individual socio-economic characteristics and employment characteristics, and the sample includes employed women aged between 15 and 64 ($N = 9,030$). We employed binomial logistic regression to analyse the likelihood of women in Germany to work in Minijobs. Binomial logistic regression is used to obtain odds ratios of an event in the presence of more than one explanatory variable, and this method enabled the analysis of the association of a set of supply- and demand-side variables in a manner that avoided confounding effects (Sperandei, 2014). For this study, the dependent variable was coded as 1 for women working (exclusively) in Minijobs ($N = 1,316$) and 0 for women with standard employment ($N = 7,714$), indicating a quite similar proportion of women working in Minijobs in the sample as that seen in German population statistics. The model included variables of supply-side factors (individual characteristics of age and education; household characteristics of the presence/absence of children in the household and partner/marital status) and demand-side factors (workplace characteristics of civil service and firm size). Table 10.1 provides an overview of the variables included in the model.

Table 10.1: Variable overview

Dichotomous variables	N	%
Minijob (working exclusively in a Minijob)	1,316	14.6
Age 16–31	1,736	19.2
Age 32–48	4,578	50.7
Age 49–65	2,716	30.1
High education (university degree)	2,233	24.7
Medium education (at least three years of training; no university degree)	4,862	53.8
Low education (less than three years of training)	1,935	21.4
Married (or living with a partner in the same household)	4,971	55.0
No children in household	3,968	43.9
Youngest child in household 0–1	122	1.4
Youngest child in household 2–7	2,087	23.1
Youngest child in household 8–12	1,276	14.1
Youngest child in household 13–18	1,577	17.5
Civil service (working at public employer)	2,424	26.8
Large firm (firm with at least 200 employees)	3,448	38.2
Medium-sized firm (firm with 20 to 199 employees)	2,379	26.3
Small firm (firm with 1 to 19 employees)	2,581	28.6

Source: Authors' calculations from SOEP, wave 2014

Results

Some descriptive numbers for the demand side and the supply side are provided before presenting the results of the regression analysis (see Table 10.2). With regard to the demand side, results indicate that the proportion of women working in Minijobs is highest in small firms and lowest in big firms. This indicates support for Hypothesis 1. The percentage of women working in Minijobs was significantly higher in the private sector (19.5%) than it was in the public sector (7.1%), thus providing support for Hypothesis 2 in demonstrating that women in the private sector are more at risk of working in a Minijob than are women working in the public sector.

With regard to the supply side, the percentage of women working in Minijobs according to their age, their youngest children's age and their marital status is presented in the following. Women younger than 32 were most likely to work in Minijobs, followed by women older than 48. Women with no children in the household were least likely to work in Minijobs, whereas women with children below the age of two were most likely to work in Minijobs. Among the group of married women who live together with their partner in the same household are more women working (exclusively) in Minijobs. This

Table 10.2: Women in Minijobs according to demand- and supply-side factors

		%
Company size	1–19	72.0
	20–199	18.1
	>= 200	12.4
Sector	Public	4.9
	Private	15.5
Age	16–31	14.7
	32–48	11.1
	49–65	13.0
Age of youngest child	No children	10.3
	0–1	29.2
	2–7	16.0
	8–12	15.1
	13–18	18.6
Marital status	Married	16.5
	Not married	8.7

Note: Weighted data.

Source: Authors' calculations from SOEP, wave 2014

indicates that Minijobs are still secondary wage-earner strategies in traditionally gendered couples.

Considering the reasons behind why women work in Minijobs, Table 10.3 presents the results of a binomial logistic regression[1] that modelled women's risk of working in a Minijob as a set of supply- and demand-side factors.

The results show both supply-side and demand-side factors to be significant in measuring women's risks of working in Minijobs, indicating that both are at least to some extent suited to explain why women in Germany work in Minijobs.

With regard to demand-side factors in this model, the odds for women of working in a Minijob are about approximately 200% higher (odds ratio 2.972) for women working in very small firms (1–19 employees) than for women working in bigger firms (20 employees and more), supporting Hypothesis 1. The odds ratio of working in a Minijob for women in the public sector compared to women in the private sector is 0.474. Thus, the risk of working in Minijobs is significantly lower for women employed in the public sector, which supports Hypothesis 2. Altogether, these results reveal that women's risk of working in Minijobs is significantly influenced by demand-side factors.

With regard to supply-side factors, having low education, being younger than 32, living with children below age two and being

Table 10.3: Binomial logistic regression: employed women's risks of working in Minijobs

Term	Odds ratio	SE
Constant term	0.081***	0.105
Private sector (= ref) with OR = 1.000		
Public sector	0.474***	0.094
Firm with less than 20 employees	2.972***	0.074
Firm with 20 to 199 employees	1.301***	0.086
Firm with more than 200 employees (ref) with OR = 1.000		
Age 16–31	1.878***	0.089
Age 32–48 (= ref) with OR=1.000		
Age 49–65	1.282***	0.089
High education	0.413***	0.102
No high education (= ref) with OR = 1.000		
Low education	1.828***	0.070
More than low education (= ref) with OR = 1.000		
Married	2.083***	0.073
Not married (= ref) with OR = 1.000		
No children in household	0.581***	0.092
Children (youngest) in household 0–1	1.809**	0.231
Children in household 2–7	1.017	0.098
Children in household 8–12	0.949	0.108
Children in household 12–17 (= ref) with OR = 1.000		

Note: *** $p < .01$; ** $p < .05$; * $p < .10$.

Source: Authors' calculations from SOEP, wave 2014

married comprise the highest risks for German women of working in a Minijob. The odds of working in a Minijob for lower-educated women are about 80% higher (odds ratio 1.828) than for women with more education. In contrast, the odds ratio of working in Minijobs for women with a university degree compared to women with no university degree is lower (odds ratio 0.413). These results provide support for Hypothesis 3. Women aged 16–31 have a nearly 90% higher risk (odds ratio 1.878) of working in Minijobs than women aged 32–48. At the same time, older women above 48 have a 30% higher risk (odds ratio 1.282) than middle-aged women of working in Minijobs. These results indicate support for Hypothesis 4; however, they also suggest that younger women are exposed to the highest risk of working in Minijobs. With regard to living with children, the risk of working in a Minijob is unevenly distributed among women according to whether they have children in the household, and if so, according to the age of their youngest child. The odds ratio of women with no children in the household of working in a Minijob compared to women with children aged 13–18 is 0.581. What is more, women with children below the age of two have an (additional) 80% higher risk of working in a Minijob (odds ratio 1.809) than women with children aged 13–18. In contrast, there is no significant difference in risks between women with their youngest children aged 2–12 and those aged 13–18. These results indicate a significant higher risk of working in Minijobs for women with children in the household, particularly when they are less than two years old. Hypothesis 5 is therefore supported, particularly for women with children below age two. The odds for married women of working in a Minijob compared to unmarried women increase by about 100% (odds ratio 2.083), thus supporting Hypothesis 6.

These results demonstrate that specific groups of employed women in Germany are more likely to be exposed to the financial and social risks that accompany being employed in the marginal employment of a Minijob. This is particularly true for women who live together with their husband and their children in the household (in particular, when there are children under the age of two years), who are educated at a low level, and who work in small, non-public firms.

Discussion and conclusion

This chapter examined how politics has contributed to the creation of the Minijob as a marginalised form of part-time employment at the institutional level. It shows how the Minijob, which was reintroduced in the early 2000s by the German welfare state, provides firms with the option of extending employment in the secondary segment, which is connected to particularly high social and economic hazards for employees. These risks include low hourly wages and a high poverty risk due to the monthly earnings limit of €450. In addition, Minijobbers face a high risk of unemployment because the normal job-security regulations do not apply to this form of marginal employment and they have a higher risk of poverty in old age due to marginal pension entitlements.

The German government re-established this form of employment with its 'activation' programme ('Hartz') in the context of the Agenda 2010 labour market reforms of the early 2000s. The introduction of Minijobs can be seen as part of a general 'dualisation' of the German labour market, particularly aimed at supporting firms by providing them with more flexibility in creating economical jobs in the secondary segment of the labour market, with reduced working time, cheaper wages and limited protection against dismissal (Palier and Thelen, 2010). It was shown that the Minijob is not a new concept in the German labour market policy; rather, it employed an already-existing instrument to enable married women to act as secondary earners in male-breadwinner households.

On the basis of an empirical study, the supply-side and demand-side factors that characterise the marginal employment of women in this specific type of part-time employment were analysed. We assumed that the likelihood of women accepting a job with relatively short working hours and working conditions comprising high social and economic risks would be particularly high for specific groups, including older women and women with children under school age. We predicted that it would be more common for women in these groups to pursue part-time employment because many women in these stages of their life course are more culturally oriented towards the combination of part-time work and caring for their families and children. We also assumed that among these groups, those who are particularly vulnerable – such as women with lower education – would have a higher likelihood of working in a Minijob than working in a part-time or full-time job with full job security as these women have lower negotiation power vis-à-vis employers. Therefore, on the supply side, the relevant factors for women's work in Minijobs were hypothesised as the role of individual characteristics, such as age and the level of education, as well as household characteristics, such as having children and living with a partner in the household. On the demand side, we assumed a higher likelihood of using Minijobs among firms that have a greater need for various forms of flexibility and among firms that can more easily utilise the strategy of 'hire and fire' for workers since workers here are less protected than in others. We identified relevant factors like firm size and participation in the public sector or the private sector as being relevant to the likelihood of employing Minijobbers.

With regard to the supply-side factors, the results of our analyses revealed that women with lower levels of education, married or partnered women, and women with children under age two are more prone to working in a Minijob. Taken together, this indicates a supply-side perspective that identifies less-educated, married women with young children as having the highest risk of working in Minijobs. These risks may become smaller or increase when demand-side factors are considered as women's likelihood of working in a Minijob is greater in small- or medium-sized firms and in the private sector. Taking together both supply- and demand-side factors, lower-educated, married women who work in small firms in the private sector and have young children are at the highest risk of working in the marginal employment form of 'Minijobs'.

The introduction of the Minijob by the German government is a good example of a welfare state dualisation strategy that actively supports firms in extending a secondary segment of marginal employment (Palier and Thelen, 2010). On the basis of the limited working hours, low wages and high social risks related to Minijobs, these policies have also contributed towards reinforcing traditional structures of gender inequality. It was possible for the Red–Green government to legitimise the reintroduction of this type of marginal employment because it linked the discourse related to Minijobs with traditional cultural ideals emphasising the male-breadwinner-led family and women's responsibility for housework and childcare, which have remained dominant, at least in the context of West Germany (Pfau-Effinger and Euler, 2014). This type of labour market policy is therefore problematic from a gender-equality perspective since women are more likely to work in Minijobs than men, resulting in the higher vulnerability of women regarding social and financial hazards.

It should also be considered that in industrial societies like Germany, in which the cultural family model of the male-breadwinner marriage played a strong role in the 20th century, this cultural family model is increasingly losing its cultural and actual relevance (Pfau-Effinger, 2012). This leaves women in a particularly precarious and insecure position if they are exposed to Minijobs and other work contracts that are inferior to the standard employment relationship (Mückenberger, 1985) of the labour market insiders (eg Emmenegger et al, 2012).

We recommend that future research include more direct and in-depth analyses of the motives of women working in marginal part-time employment, particularly those who have less education, have a partner/are married and are living with young children. It remains an open question as to whether a Minijob represents these women's only opportunity for employment because their skills do not match the recruiting criteria of firms for regular full-time or part-time employment, or whether they choose to work in Minijobs because the limited working hours better align with their current life situation.

Note

[1] The model is significant as a whole ($p = 0.000$), as are all the included variables. The effect size of the model was estimated with Nagelkerkes R^2 (0.176). According to Cohen (1992), this is an effect size of 0.46 and can be interpreted as a strong effect.

References

Absenger, N. and Priebe, L. (2016) 'The Firm Constitution Law 2016 – gaps in workers' participation and reform need', *WSI-Mitteilungen*, 69(3): 192–200.

Baumgartner, A.D. (2003) *Women in medium employment age*, IDA ForAlt, Bern: Bundesamt für Sozialversicherung.

Beck, U. (1997) 'The soul of democracy. How we can finance voluntary work instead of unemployment', *Die Zeit*, 49: 7–8.

Becker, G.S. (1981) *A treatise on the family*, Cambridge, MA: Harvard University Press.

Brandt, M. and Hank, K. (2014) 'Scars that will not disappear: long-term associations between early and later life unemployment under different welfare regimes', *Journal of Social Policy*, 43(4): 727–43.

Brinkmann, D. and Kohler, H.C. (1981) 'Am Rande der Erwerbsbeteiligung: Frauen mit geringfügiger, gelegentlicher oder befristeter Arbeit' ['At the margin of employment: women with marginal, casual or fixed-term employment'], in W. Klauder and G. Kuehlewind (eds) *Probleme der Messung und Vorausschätzung des Frauenerwerbspotentials* [*Measurement problems and forecast of purchase potential*], Nuremberg: IAB.

Chou, Y.-C., Pfau-Effinger, B., Kröger, T. and Ranci, C. (2017) 'Impact of care responsibilities on women's employment: a comparison between European and East Asian welfare states', *European Societies*, 19(1): 157–77.

Cohen, J. (1992) 'A power primer', *Psychological Bulletin*, 122(1): 155–9.

Commission for Future Questions of Bavaria and Saxony (1997) 'Employment and unemployment in Germany – development, causes and instrument', Bonn.

Doeringer, P.B. and Piore, M. (1971) *Internal labor markets and manpower analysis*, Lexington, MA: Heath Lexington.

Effinger, H. and Pfau-Effinger, B. (1999) 'Freiwilliges Engagement im Sozialwesen – Ausweg aus der Krise der Erwerbsgesellschaft und des Wohlfahrtsstaates?' ['Voluntary work in social services – solution for the labour market crisis?'], in E. Kistler, H.-H. Noll and E. Priller (eds) *Messkonzepte der Kräfte zivilgesellschaftlichen Zusammenhalts*, Berlin: Sigma, pp 307–24.

Emmenegger, P., Häusermann, S., Palier, B. and Seeleib-Kaiser, M. (eds) (2012) *The age of dualization: The changing face of inequality in deindustrializing societies*, New York: Oxford University Press.

Federal Statistical Office Germany (2017) 'Atypische Beschäftigung' ['Atypical employment']. Available at: www.destatis.de/DE/ZahlenFakten/GesamtwirtschaftUmwelt/Arbeitsmarkt/Erwerbstaetigkeit/TabellenArbeitskraefteerhebung/AtypKernerwerb ErwerbsformZR.html (accessed 6 May 2018).

Frericks, P., Höppner, J. and Och, R. (2016) 'Institutional individualisation? The family in European social security institutions', *Journal of Social Policy*, 45(4): 747–64.

Hirsch, B., Schank, T. and Schnabel, C. (2010) 'Works councils and separations: voice, monopoly, and insurance effects', *Industrial Relations: A Journal of Economy and Society*, 49(4): 566–92.

Hohendanner, C. and Stegmaier, J. (2012) *Geringfügige Beschäftigung in deutschen Betrieben. Umstrittene Minijobs* [*Marginal employment in German firms: Contested Minijobs*], Institut für Arbeitsmarkt- und Berufsforschung (IAB), IAB-Kurzbericht 24/12, Nuernberg: IAB.

Jaehrling, K. (2017) 'The atypical and gendered "employment miracle" in Germany: a result of employment protection reforms or long-term structural changes?', in A. Piasna and M. Myant (eds) *Myths of employment deregulation: how it neither creates jobs nor reduces labour market segmentation*, Brussels: ETUI, pp 165–84.

Jensen, P.H., Och, R., Pfau-Effinger, B. and Møberg, R.J. (2017) 'Explaining differences in women's working time in European cities', *European Societies*, 19(2): 138–56.

Kangas, O. and Rostgaard, T. (2007) 'Preferences or context: opinions of childcare', *Journal of European Social Policy*, 17(3): 240–56.

Katz, E. (1997) 'The intra-household economics of voice and exit', *Feminist Economics*, 3: 25–46.

Knuth, M. (2014) *Labour market reforms and the 'jobs miracle' in Germany*, Brussels: European Economic and Social Committee.

Knuth, M. and Kalina, T. (2002) 'Early exit from the labour force between exclusion and privilege: unemployment as a transition from employment to retirement in West Germany', *European Societies*, 4(4): 393–418.

Lietzmann, T., Schmelzer, P. and Wiemers, J. (2016) *Does marginal employment promote regular employment for unemployed welfare benefit recipients in Germany?*, IAB-Discussion Paper 18/2016, Nürnberg: Institut für Arbeitsmarkt- und Berufsforschung.

Martin, C.J. and Thelen, K. (2007) 'The state and coordinated capitalism: contributions of the public sector to social solidarity in post-industrial societies', *World Politics*, 60: 1–36.

Matysiak, A. and Steinmetz, S. (2008) 'Finding their way? Female employment patterns in West Germany, East Germany, and Poland', *European Sociological Review*, 24(3): 331–45.

McRae, S. (2003) 'Choice and constraints in mothers' employment careers: McRae replies to Hakim', *The British Journal of Sociology*, 54: 585–92.

Mückenberger, U. (1985) 'Die Krise des Normalarbeitsverhältnisses', *Zeitschrift für Sozialreform*, 31(7): 415–35.

Palier, B. and Thelen, K. (2010) 'Institutionalizing dualism: complementarities and change in France and Germany', *Politics & Society*, 38(1): 119–48.

Pfau-Effinger, B. (1993) 'Modernisation, culture and part-time employment: the example of Finland and Germany', *Work, Employment and Society*, 7(3): 383–410.

Pfau-Effinger, B. (1998) 'Culture or structure as explanations for differences in part-time work in Germany, Finland and the Netherlands?', in C. Fagan and J. O'Reilly (eds) *Part-time prospects: an international comparison of part-time work in Europe, North America and the Pacific Rim*, London: Routledge, pp 177–98.

Pfau-Effinger, B. (2012) 'Women's employment in institutional and cultural context', *International Journal of Sociology and Social Policy*, 32(3): 530–43.

Pfau-Effinger, B. and Euler, T. (2014) 'Wandel der Einstellungen zu Kinderbetreuung und Elternschaft in Europa – Persistenz kultureller Differenzen' ['Change in the attitudes towards childcare and parenthood – persistence of cultural differences'], *Soziale Welt*, 20(1): 175–93.

Pfau-Effinger, B. and Smidt, M. (2011) 'Differences in women's employment patterns and family policies: Eastern and Western Germany', *Community, Work & Family*, 14(2): 217–32.

Projektgruppe Arbeitsmarktpolitik and Offe, C. (1977) *Opfer des Arbeitsmarktes* [*Victim of the labour market*], Neuwied/Darmstadt: Luchterhand.

RWI (Rheinisch Westfälisches Institut fuer Wirtschaftsforschung) (2016) 'Nachfolgestudie zur Analyse der geringfügigen Beschäftigungsverhältnisse (Minijobs) sowie den Auswirkungen des gesetzlichen Mindestlohns' ['Follow-up study of marginal employment (Minijobs) and the consequences of a legal minimum wage'], Gutachten im Auftrag des Ministeriums für Arbeit, Integration und Soziales des Landes Nordrhein-Westfalen, November 2016: RWI.

Sengenberger, W. (1981) 'Labour market segmentation and the business cycle', in F. Wilkinson (eds) *The dynamics of labour market segmentation*, London: Academic Press, pp 255–6.

Sperandei, S. (2014) 'Understanding logistic regression analysis', *Biochem Med*, 24(1): 12–18.

11

Part-time strategies of women and men of childbearing age in the Netherlands and Australia

Mara A. Yerkes and Belinda Hewitt

Introduction

Scholars have argued that labour markets are segmented into primary and secondary markets, with insiders working in well-protected and well-paid jobs in the primary segment and outsiders working in more precarious, poorly paid jobs in the secondary segment (eg Dickens and Lang, 1993). More recently, this argument has been revisited because the prevalence of precarious employment continues to grow (Emmenegger et al, 2012b; Palier and Thelen, 2010; Prosser, 2016). Dualisation scholars contend that labour market outsiders are particularly affected by processes of globalisation, post-industrialisation and labour market liberalisation. Part-time work is often seen as an indicator of participation in a secondary labour market, yet this assumption may not always hold.

In the Netherlands, the 'part-time work champion' of the industrialised world (Visser, 2002; Yerkes, 2009), nearly two thirds of women and one fifth of men work part-time (OECD, 2017). Part-time work is highly regulated, and workers enjoy the same pro rata rights as full-time workers (Yerkes and Visser, 2006). On the one hand, dualisation might be absent as such high levels of protection are uncommon in other countries with high rates of part-time work. Australia also has relatively high levels of part-time employment, with 38.4% of women and 15.1% of men working part-time (OECD, 2017). However, in contrast to the Netherlands, part-time work conditions are less favourable, making dualisation more likely in Australia than the Netherlands. For example, Australian employees can often only reduce hours by changing jobs and shifting to lower-status employment sectors (Roeters and Craig, 2014). On the other hand, dualisation may be evident in both countries. Similar to Australia, women, and

265

mothers in particular, use part-time work as a strategy to combine work and care (Yerkes, 2009).

Even though similar part-time trends are visible, particularly in relation to gender and parenthood, the *conditions* under which part-time work strategies are used differ. Therefore, the part-time work strategies of women and men of childbearing age in Australia and the Netherlands are explored in this chapter. We start by focusing on the part-time work strategies of both men and women: how do women and men differ in their part-time employment patterns? We then unpack the variation in women's part-time employment strategies: which drivers and mechanisms explain these seemingly comparable part-time employment strategies across the two countries? We examine these questions cross-sectionally using European Social Survey (ESS) data (from 2014) for the Netherlands and Household Income and Labour Dynamics in Australia (HILDA) data (from 2014) for Australia. Placed in a comparative context, these analyses provide insight into varying policy and cultural contexts in relation to part-time employment strategies and possible dualisation effects in both countries.

The context of part-time work in the Netherlands and Australia

Part-time work is highly gendered in both countries. In Australia, 38.4% of women work less than 30 hours a week; in the Netherlands, this holds true for nearly 60% of women (OECD, 2017). While part-time work among men has increased slightly in both countries over the last two decades, men are much less likely to work part-time; in 2016, the figures were 15.1% for Australia and 18.7% in the Netherlands. While part-time work is a strategy used by women across all age groups in Australia and the Netherlands, men in the age range of 15–24 are much more likely to work part-time than men aged 25–54, for example. Part-time work is also slightly higher for men near retirement age.

There is some evidence that part-time work as a work–family strategy could be changing in the Netherlands. In the past 15 years, the Dutch government has encouraged women, and mothers in particular, to take part in paid employment and work longer hours. Significant childcare improvements have been made (Yerkes, 2014), although some aspects, such as flexibility, affordability and quality, remain problematic (Yerkes and Javornik, 2018). Leave options, such as well-paid, gender-egalitarian parental leave or paid paternity leave of more than a few days, remain limited (Yerkes and Den Dulk, 2015). It is not clear what mothers' and fathers' strategies for combining work and care are in this mixed work–family policy environment. For these reasons, it is necessary to reconsider the strategies of women and men of childbearing age working part-time in the Netherlands.

Australia provides an interesting comparison. With the exception of Switzerland, the Netherlands and Australia share the highest rate of part-time work in industrialised countries (OECD, 2017). In line with developments in the Netherlands, trend data from the Organisation for Economic Co-operation and Development (OECD) suggest that Australian women aged 25–54 are also increasingly working full-time (30 hours or more a week). There have also been minor increases in the percentage of men aged 25–54 working part-time, from 5.5% in 2001 to 7.7% in 2016. Their regulation of part-time work differs, but work–family policies in both countries are similarly gendered and in flux. Significant improvements have been made in childcare quality in Australia (Whiteford, 2015), for example, but issues around accessibility, availability, affordability and flexibility remain (Baxter and Hand, 2016; Yerkes and Javornik, 2018). Leave options, including paid parental leave (Martin et al, 2011) and paid leave for fathers and partners (Martin et al, 2014), have improved the work–family situation by providing most families with access to leave payments. Yet, gendered work–care patterns remain in place during the first 12 months of a child's life (Rose et al, 2015). Thus, similar to the Netherlands, considerable changes have taken place in the work–family policy landscape in recent years, but various obstacles remain, warranting a closer look at women's and men's strategies for combining work and care in these policy environments.

Dualisation in the Dutch and Australian contexts

One purpose of this edited volume is to determine the extent to which part-time work segregates labour markets into insiders and outsiders. While dualisation is defined by a differentiation in rights and entitlements or access to services between part-time and full-time workers (Emmenegger et al, 2012a), such differentiation may also take place between part-time workers. As a result, certain workers are more adversely affected by labour market and welfare state changes than others (Palier and Thelen, 2010; Emmenegger et al, 2012b). Dualisation can also lead to a narrowing of insider groups and a widening of outsider groups, whereby some people who were previously considered insiders become outsiders. It is also possible that labour market and welfare state changes or an absence of state intervention in some areas will produce new forms of institutional dualism (Palier and Thelen, 2010; Emmenegger et al, 2012a).

In this chapter, we are interested in bridging dualisation theory with work–family theory. Parents often rely on flexible working forms to reconcile the demands of paid employment and the care for (young) children (Den Dulk et al, 2005; Miani and Hoorens, 2014). Flexibility in start and end times, the ability to temporarily reduce one's hours, or working part-time are all forms of flexibility sought by parents. Despite the increased availability of flexible work policies to both mothers and fathers (Hegewisch, 2009; Hegewisch and Gornick, 2011), mothers overwhelmingly make greater use of flexible work forms (Miani and Hoorens, 2014). Part-time work, in particular, developed as a means for mothers to combine work and care (O'Reilly and Fagan, 1998; Yerkes, 2009), and remains a gendered phenomenon (Hegewisch and Gornick, 2011; Miani and Hoorens, 2014).

The negative effects of gendered patterns in part-time and other flexible work forms are well documented. Women face prospects of lower earnings (Bardasi and Gornick, 2008; Budig and Hodges, 2010), lower occupational status (Dex et al, 2008), reduced management opportunities and delayed career trajectories (Williams et al, 2013). Depending upon the length of time spent in part-time employment, women also face reduced entitlements to social protection arrangements (Dekker, 2007; Emmenegger et al, 2012a). Similarly, working conditions and job quality are found to be lower for part-time workers (Gallie et al, 2016).

Given the overwhelmingly negative consequences of part-time work, researchers continue to ask why mothers accept such working arrangements. Part-time workers may be more satisfied with employment than full-time workers because they can enjoy the positive aspects of employment without the added stress of full-time hours, particularly in combination with household or care responsibilities (Treas et al, 2011). Additionally, part-time work may be accepted because it fits parents', and in particular mothers', care preferences in some countries (eg Lewis et al, 2008). From this perspective, the gender difference in part-time work may be unequal yet equitable as mothers view these employment outcomes as fair (McDonald, 2013). Indeed, recent evidence from Australia suggests that mothers entering into flexible working arrangements upon returning to work after childbirth often do not see such arrangements as *unfair* (Yerkes et al, 2017), dependent upon their educational level and career prospects. In occupations where part-time work was largely expected following childbirth, Australian mothers rarely questioned the fairness of flexible working arrangements. In other words, in female-typed occupations, motherhood penalties are already built in and accepted (Yerkes et al, 2017: 487). The presence of such structural constraints suggests that one should be critical of viewing part-time work as gender equitable in this case (McDonald, 2013: 983).[1] In Australia, then, it appears that structural constraints create a dualised labour market in which significant gender differences, as well as occupational differences, exist.

Structural opportunities and constraints at the country and individual levels are equally important when understanding parents', and in particular mother's, employment patterns (cf Kangas and Rostgaard, 2007). Parents' employment decisions are shaped by what they view as possible in a given cultural and institutional context (Hobson, 2016), as well as by a complex interaction of individual, community-level and social factors (cf Hobson, 2014; Annink, 2017; Javornik and Kurowska, 2017; Yerkes and Javornik, 2018). Yet, it has proven empirically difficult to ascertain the extent to which the institutional context, that is, policy and legal frameworks, matter for part-time work and other flexible work forms. Scholarship in the field of gender and employment studies produces mixed empirical results on the extent to which institutional frameworks ameliorate the negative effects associated with part-time work. Treas and colleagues (2011) find that in countries with generous welfare states, where family living standards are less dependent on women's working hours, part-time work appears to allow women to benefit from the 'best of both worlds': employment and motherhood/homemaking. In contrast, the five-country study by Roeters and Craig (2014) concludes that the country of residence is not important for shaping the effects of part-time work. Given these mixed empirical results, the conclusion of Hegewisch (2009: ix) is possibly the most plausible: while statutory frameworks around part-time work and other flexible work forms matter, such frameworks are no 'magic bullet for changing gender specific flexible work patterns'.

In this chapter, we partially contribute to this debate by examining the extent to which these gender-unequal part-time work patterns reflect insider–outsider labour market effects (eg based on gender and occupational effects) by comparing a country with high protection of part-time workers (the Netherlands) with a country with minimal protection of part-time workers (Australia). While we cannot directly control for country-level differences in our two-country study, we do have two countries with different institutional contexts. In the Netherlands, the regulation of part-time work through anti-discrimination legislation and rights to adjust working hours means that part-time workers in the Netherlands have better employment conditions than workers in other countries (Yerkes and Visser, 2006; Bartoll et al, 2014). Given the higher protection afforded to part-time work and part-time workers, we should expect that the gender and occupational effects generally thought to occur in other countries will be lower (eg in the Netherlands) than in countries where part-time workers do not have similar protection under the law (eg in Australia).

Data and methodology

We rely on two different data sets for the analyses in this chapter. For the Netherlands, we use data from the seventh round of the ESS (ESS 2014/15) (for details, see: www.europeansocialsurvey.org). ESS data collection is cross-sectional, starting in 2001. Data are collected every two years using face-to-face interviews. Fieldwork for Round 7 was carried out in the Netherlands between September 2014 and January 2015, resulting in a total sample of 1,919 respondents aged 15 and over (response rate = 58.6%).

. The data for Australia come from wave 14 (2014) of the HILDA survey. HILDA is a longitudinal panel survey that has been running since 2001. Wave 1 comprised 7,682 households and 13,969 individuals. Households were selected using a multi-stage sampling approach, and a 66% response rate was achieved (Summerfield et al, 2016). Within households, data were collected from each person aged over 15 years using face-to-face interviews and self-completed questionnaires, and achieved a 92% response rate of household members (Watson and Wooden, 2002). Using the same approach, in 2011, a top-up sample of 2,153 households (63% response rate) and 4,009 individuals (93.7% response rate) was collected. HILDA is an evolving panel, and the sample includes any new household members resulting from changes in the composition of the original households.

For the current analyses, we included all respondents in HILDA wave 14 (n = 17,512) and ESS data for 2014 (n = 1,919), with the following restrictions. We restricted the analytic sample to men and women in paid employment for at least one hour per week (HILDA n = 10,946; ESS n = 1,778). To capture men and women at their prime working and child-rearing ages, we further limited the sample to those aged between 18 and 55 (HILDA n = 8,887; ESS n = 972). We excluded men and women who were self-employed or working in family businesses (HILDA n = 1,010; ESS n = 116), and those employed in the defence force (HILDA $n = 16$; ESS $n = 1$). In addition, we dropped cases where there were missing data on the dependent variable (HILDA $n = 22$; ESS $n = 0$) and key independent variables (HILDA $n = 12$; ESS $n = 49$). After these limitations and exclusions, the final analytic sample for HILDA comprised 7,769 respondents: 3,893 women and 3,876 men. For the ESS, the final analytic sample comprised 851 respondents: 472 women and 303 men. Descriptive information on both samples can be found in Table 11.1.

Measures

Dependent variables

We used two dependent variables: one for the analysis comparing men and women; and one for the analysis of women only. Due to the very low numbers of men working part-time, we used a simple dichotomous measure of working (1) full-time (35 hours+ [reference]) or (2) part-time (less than 35 hours per week). For women, we further expanded the measure for part-time hours to capture more refined groupings of part-time employment that better reflect women's work, including: (1) full-time (reference); (2) long part-time hours (20 to 34 hours per week); and (3) short part-time hours (1 to 19 hours per week).

Independent variables

We also include a range of measures capturing socio-demographic, employment and family characteristics. Part-time work strategies vary across the life course and educational levels. We include a categorical measure for age in all models (18–24 [reference], 25–34, 35–44, 45–55) and we use the International Standard Classification of Education (ISCED) to develop a measure of (1) low (indicating no secondary education), (2) medium (indicating completed secondary education) and (3) high education (indicating completed tertiary education). We also include a measure for household income, broken down into quintiles from the whole sample population (not the restricted analytic sample), ranging from (1) the bottom 20% (reference) to (5) the top 20% of income.[2] For the Netherlands, this measure is based on the household's total net income (of all household members) from all sources (eg wages, pensions, benefits). For Australia, this measure is based on total household disposable income (net after tax) for the financial year (July 2013 to June 2014) from all sources, including

Table 11.1: Dependent variables and key independent variables, descriptive statistics for the Netherlands (ESS 2014) and Australia (HILDA 2014)

	Netherlands		Australia	
	Women	Men	Women	Men
	%/Mean SD	%/Mean SD	%/Mean SD	%/Mean SD
Work hours				
FT	30	79	47	81
PT	70	21	53	19
Work hours (women only)				
FT	31		47	
PT long	50		29	
PT <20 hours	19		8	
Age categories:				
18–24	9	9	20	21
25–34	24	26	28	30
35–44	31	28	24	25
45–55	36	37	28	24
Relationship status:				
Not living with anyone (ref)	47	56	35	33
Cohabiting or married	53	44	65	67
Youngest child:				
No children <18 in household (ref)	40	64	60	63
Child<3	7	7	10	15
Child 3–4	7	5	5	5
Child 5 or older	46	34	25	17
ISCED:				
Low (ref)	21	22	13	15
Medium	45	43	50	58
High	34	35	37	27
Income (deciles):				
Lowest 20% (ref)	16	12	9	9
	12	13	17	17
	22	23	22	24
	28	25	27	26
Highest 20%	22	27	25	24
ISCO-88:				
Managers (ref)	7	12	10	15
Professionals	22	18	26	16
White collar	58	40	57	32
Blue collar	13	30	7	37
N	303	472	3,893	3,876

wages, business income, pensions and benefits. Family characteristics, such as marital status and the presence of pre-school children in the household, are crucial for understanding differences in part-time strategies (O'Reilly and Fagan, 1998). In our models, relationship status indicates (1) not in a live-in relationship (reference) and (2) cohabiting or married. We measure the age of the youngest child in the household, including (1) no children under 18 in the household (reference), (2) child under three years of age, (3) child between three and four years of age, and (4) child aged five or older, as an indicator for the presence of a pre-school child aged four or under in the household (1 = yes). Lastly, two key employment characteristics include occupation and contract type. Part-time work structures are also often built into particular occupations, creating 'mommy tracks' that penalise mothers through lower pay and poor career prospects (eg Kalleberg, 2000). This occupational effect is particularly prevalent among women, demonstrating the intersection between gender and class effects in employment (Korpi, 2010). Occupation was initially coded using the International Standard Classification of Occupations 88 (ISCO-88) two-digit coding, but due to small numbers in some groups, the occupations were collapsed to (1) managers (ISCO-88 10 to 13 [reference]), (2) professionals (ISCO-88 20 to 24), (3) white-collar workers (ISCO-88 30 to 59) and (4) blue-collar workers (ISCO-88 60 to 99).

Analytical strategy

Our analysis proceeded in two stages. In the first stage, we estimated a logistic regression model to examine the likelihood of working part-time versus full-time and to compare the characteristics of men and women who work part-time. We estimated one model including all covariates. In the second stage, we used a multinomial logistic regression to compare women who were working long part-time hours and women who were working short part-time hours with women who were working full-time. The models were estimated separately for the Netherlands and Australia. Following Mood (2010) and Connelly (Connelly et al, 2016), we present our results as average marginal means to ease their interpretation. Coefficients can thus be interpreted as a discrete change from the base level holding all other measures constant at their means. The use of average marginal means not only allows for a more straightforward interpretation of the results, but also allows us to make comparisons across samples and groups (Mood, 2010: 78).

Results

Men and women are not equally likely to work part-time in the Netherlands and what predicts part-time working differs for women and men (see Table 11. 2). The results indicate that age is negatively and significantly associated with working part-time. Men aged 35 and older in the Netherlands, and men and women aged 25 and older in both countries, are significantly less likely to work part-time than men and women aged 18–24. Men who are living with a partner in Australia are significantly less likely to work part-time than men who are not living with a partner. Relationship status is not significantly associated with working part-time for Australian women. In contrast, relationship status is not significantly associated with working part-time for men in the Netherlands, but married and cohabiting Dutch women are more likely to work part-time than women not married or cohabiting. Having a child in the household is significantly and positively associated with women working part-time, but not for men. This factor is significant in both countries and the magnitude of this association is larger when children are (very) young. Education is not significant for men or women in either country. Women with a secondary education in Australia are less likely to work part-time than women with less than a secondary education, but this effect just borders on significance. Income is strongly and negatively associated with part-time work in Australia. This contrasts with findings in the Netherlands, which show that households where Dutch women work part-time, holding all other measures constant at their means, are more likely to be in the lowest income quintile (lowest 20% of household incomes). Women in the highest quintile of income in the Netherlands are strongly and significantly less likely to work part-time than women from the lowest income quintile. This result could indicate that in higher-income households, men and women both work full-time. Occupation is significantly associated with working part-time for women in both countries. Compared to managers, women in all other occupation groups are significantly more likely to be working part-time. Men across all occupational groups in Australia are more likely to be working part-time in comparison to managers. In the Netherlands, this only holds true for white-collar workers.[3]

In Table 11.3, we present the results of comparing women in the Netherlands and Australia working long or short part-time hours versus full-time. When distinguishing between long and short part-time hours, there are some interesting similarities and differences for women compared to the first stage of analysis, where all part-time work

Table 11.2: Average marginal means of characteristics associated with part-time employment (reference full-time) for employed men and women in the Netherlands (ESS 2014) and Australia (HILDA 2014)

	Netherlands				Australia			
	Men		Women		Men		Women	
	Marginal mean[a]	SE	Marginal mean	SE	Marginal mean	SE	Marginal mean	SE
Age categories:								
18–24 (ref)	–		–		–		–	
25–34	-0.17†	.10	-0.17**	.06	-0.19***	.02	-0.25***	.02
35–44	-0.20†	.10	-0.23***	.06	-0.20***	.02	-0.21***	.02
45–55	-0.21*	.10	-0.16**	.06	-0.20***	.02	-0.16***	.02
Relationship status:								
Not living with anyone (ref)	–		–		–		–	
Cohabiting or married	-0.06	.05	0.10*	.05	-0.07***	.02	0.01	.02
Youngest child:								
No children <18 in household (ref)	–		–		–		–	
Child <3	-0.06	.08	0.28***	.07	-0.01	.02	0.36***	.02
Child 3–4	-0.09	.08	0.23**	.08	-0.03	.03	0.39***	.03
Child 5 or older	0.01	.07	0.21***	.05	-0.03	.02	0.24***	.02
ISCED:								
Low (ref)	–		–		–		–	
Medium	0.03	.05	0.04	.06	-0.01	.02	-0.05†	.02
High	0.04	.07	-0.03	.07	0.01	.02	-0.04	.03

(continued)

Table 11.2: Average marginal means of characteristics associated with part-time employment (reference full-time) for employed men and women in the Netherlands (ESS 2014) and Australia (HILDA 2014) (continued)

| | Netherlands | | | | Australia | | | |
| | Men | | Women | | Men | | Women | |
	Marginal mean[a]	SE	Marginal mean	SE	Marginal mean	SE	Marginal mean	SE
Income (deciles):								
Lowest 20% (ref)	–		–		–		–	
	−0.01	.09	−0.12†	.07	−0.10***	.02	−0.15***	.03
	−0.13	.08	−0.17**	.06	−0.10***	.02	−0.15***	.03
	−0.06	.08	−0.15†	.06	−0.14***	.02	−0.19***	.03
Highest 20%	−0.07	.09	−0.25***	.07	−0.12***	.02	−0.20***	.03
ISCO–88:								
Managers (ref)	–		–		–		–	
Professionals	0.07	.07	0.24*	.09	0.04**	.02	0.23***	.03
White collar	0.14*	.06	0.29**	.10	0.18***	.02	0.34***	.02
Blue collar	0.06	.07	0.26**	.12	0.05**	.02	0.35***	.04
N	303		472		3,876		3,893	

Notes: [a] Discrete change from the base level holding all other measures constant at their means.
† p < .10; * p < .05; ** p < .01; *** p < .001.

Table 11.3: Average marginal means of characteristics associated with long part-time hours and short part-time hours (reference full-time) for employed women in the Netherlands (ESS 2014) and Australia (HILDA 2014)

| | Netherlands | | | | Australia | | | |
| | Long part-time hours | | <20 part-time hours | | Long part-time hours | | <20 part-time hours | |
	Marginal mean	SE	Marginal mean	SE	Marginal mean	SE	Marginal mean	SE
Age categories:								
18–24	–		–		–		–	
25–34	0.28**	.08	-0.45***	.08	-0.02	.02	-0.22***	.02
35–44	0.25**	.08	-0.50***	.08	0.02	.03	-0.22***	.03
45–55	0.35***	.07	-0.51***	.07	0.07**	.02	-0.23***	.02
Relationship status:								
Not living with anyone (ref)	–		–		–		–	
Cohabiting or married	-0.06	.05	0.17***	.04	0.06**	.01	-0.04**	.02
Youngest child:								
No children <18 in household (ref)	–		–		–		–	
Child <3	0.29**	.09	-0.01	.07	0.11***	.03	0.24***	.03
Child 3–4	0.25**	.09	-0.02	.06	0.16***	.03	0.23***	.03
Child 5 or older	0.15**	.06	0.06	.04	0.12***	.02	0.13***	.02
ISCED:								
Low (ref)	–		–		–		–	
Medium	0.02	.06	0.03	.04	0.001	.02	-0.05*	.02
High	0.03	.07	-0.06	.05	0.01	.03	-0.06*	.02

(continued)

Table 11.3: Average marginal means of characteristics associated with long part-time hours and short part-time hours (reference full-time) for employed women in the Netherlands (ESS 2014) and Australia (HILDA 2014) (continued)

	Netherlands				Australia			
	Long part-time hours		<20 part-time hours		Long part-time hours		<20 part-time hours	
	Marginal mean	SE	Marginal mean	SE	Marginal mean	SE	Marginal mean	SE
Income (deciles):								
Lowest 20% (ref)	–		–		–		–	
	−0.12	.09	0.003	.07	−0.07*	.03	−0.08**	.03
	−0.19*	.08	0.001	.06	−0.08*	.03	−0.07*	.02
	−0.08	.08	−0.08	.06	−0.10**	.03	−0.09**	.03
Highest 20%	−0.20*	.08	−0.05	.07	−0.12***	.03	−0.08**	.03
ISCO-88:								
Managers (ref)	–		–		–		–	
Professionals	0.19	.10	0.06	.05	0.14***	.02	0.09***	.02
White collar	0.15	.10	0.15**	.05	0.20***	.02	0.14***	.02
Blue collar	0.05	.11	0.22**	.07	0.19***	.03	0.16***	.03
N	472				3,893			

Notes: [a] Discrete change from the base level holding all other measures constant at their means.
† p < .10; * p < .05; ** p < .01; *** p < .001.

hours were treated uniformly. Age is no longer uniformly significantly and negatively associated with part-time work. In the Netherlands, age is positively associated with long part-time work hours but negatively associated with short part-time work hours. This effect likely reflects the prevalence of short part-time work hours among young people in the Netherlands, suggesting that women over the age of 24 are more likely to work long part-time hours. In Australia, age remains significantly and negatively associated with working short part-time hours but is not significantly associated with long part-time work hours, except for women aged 45–55, who are more likely to work long part-time hours in comparison to full-time.

In further contrast to the simplified full-time/part-time model, living with a partner is positively and significantly associated with working long part-time hours in Australia, but negatively and significantly associated with working short part-time hours. In the Netherlands, relationship status only matters for short part-time work hours. Married and cohabitating Dutch women are significantly more likely to work short part-time hours in comparison to unmarried/ non-cohabitating women. Having children under 18 in the household remains associated with working part-time in Australia, both short hours and long hours. In the Netherlands, however, having children under 18 is only positively and significantly associated with working longer part-time hours. In contrast to the simplified model, women with higher levels of education are significantly less likely to work short part-time hours in Australia. Higher household income is significantly and negatively associated with both forms of part-time work in Australia. However, in the Netherlands, household income is only significantly and negatively associated with long part-time work hours for women in the third and fifth highest quintiles. Lastly, in Australia, occupation remains significantly and positively associated with part-time work. In comparison to women who are in managerial occupations, those in all other occupation groups are significantly more likely to work part-time. This association is stronger for long part-time hours than short part-time hours. In the Netherlands, however, occupation is only significantly associated with short part-time work hours. Women in white- and blue-collar occupations are significantly more likely than managers to work short part-time hours.[4]

Conclusion and discussion

The dualisation of labour markets creates a situation in which one group of workers enjoys significantly better protection, wages, security and/or labour market prospects than another group of workers (Palier and Thelen, 2010; Emmenegger et al, 2012a). In many countries, part-time work may be associated with a secondary labour market, with part-time workers having less protection, lower wages, more insecurity and fewer labour market prospects than full-time workers. Yet, this chapter started from the premise that in the Netherlands, where part-time work is highly regulated and protected, there might be less evidence of dualisation than in other countries where part-time work is less regulated and/or protected.

In our comparison with Australia, we see mixed results. Some of our findings indicate that the part-time work context of Australia may differ from that of the Netherlands. For example, in our comparison of men and women, full-time work seems to be more important for household income in Australia than in the Netherlands. This suggests that the wages and salaries of part-time workers in the Netherlands may be better than in Australia, or that part-time work is distributed more evenly throughout the household income distribution in the Netherlands. However, further research is needed to determine the validity of such assumptions, particularly given conflicting empirical evidence on the wage effects of part-time work for Australian mothers (Hosking, 2010; Preston and Yu, 2015). Education appears to be a more important driver of part-time work for women in Australia than in the Netherlands, particularly for short part-time work hours. This finding could reflect the normalisation of part-time work among women of all educational levels in the Netherlands, although previous research suggests that more highly educated women are likely to work more hours as their earnings capacity is higher (Portegijs and Keuzenkamp, 2008; Portegijs and Van den Brakel, 2016).

In contrast to the Netherlands, mothers of young children in Australia are more likely to be in short part-time work, which suggests that motherhood is less compatible with longer working hours than in the Netherlands. We also see opposite findings for the Netherlands and Australia in terms of relationship status. Married and cohabitating women are more likely to work short part-time jobs in the Netherlands, whereas the opposite is true for Australia. Thus, our comparative analysis implies there is stronger evidence for dualisation in Australia.

On the other hand, our findings suggest that even in the Netherlands, where part-time work is well protected, dualisation exists. We find significant gender and occupational differences in the predictors of full- and part-time work. In the Netherlands, having children increases women's chances of working part-time, but not men's. Gender norms around parenthood continue to be an important driver of differences between full-time and part-time work for men and women (Yerkes and Den Dulk, 2015). In Australia, occupation is also an important driver of dualisation between part-time and full-time work (partly mediated by education for Australian mothers), and this effect appears to be consistent across both forms of part-time work. These findings are in line with previous research from Bardasi and Gornick (2008), who show clear occupational segregation into part-time work, which is greater in the more liberal welfare regimes of the US and the UK.

Crucially, our findings for the Netherlands suggest that dualisation also exists *within* part-time work. We find that while mothers of (particularly young) children are likely to work long part-time hours in the Netherlands (eg 'equalised' part-time workers, see Chapter 1), short part-time work is primarily driven by occupation (mediated, in part, by education), relationship status and age.[5] These findings point to a possible dualisation between women in more precarious short part-time work, who are primarily young, in white- and blue-collar occupations, and/or married/cohabiting, versus women in long part-time positions, who are 25 or older, mothers of (young) children and/or professionals working longer part-time hours. In the best-case scenario, women in these short part-time jobs are semi-secured or equalised (see Chapter 1), protected by part-time work regulations in the Netherlands. Despite these regulations, short part-time work carries significantly greater risks of long-term economic and career disadvantage for women than long part-time work or full-time work, even if it is voluntary and performed under (relatively) good working conditions.

Some caution is needed when interpreting these findings. To make the data sets comparable, we have excluded contract type. Further research is needed to determine the extent to which these apparent dual labour markets are a reflection of gender and occupational differences versus differences in permanent, fixed-term or casual contracts. Additionally, the sample size for the Netherlands is quite small. While the ESS data allow for a comparison with Australian data, our focus on women and men of childbearing age led to the exclusion of a large number of respondents. We are also limited by the cross-sectional nature of our analysis. Future research is needed to look at the causality of the relationships examined here, for example, through longitudinal panel analysis. While the Australian HILDA data offer a high-quality longitudinal panel, Dutch panel data are problematic from a comparability standpoint, particularly in relation to variables on occupation, which is a key variable in the analysis of part-time work.

Despite these limitations, our analysis offers important insights for the debate on dualisation and part-time work and work–family scholarship. While the protection offered to part-time workers in the Netherlands is relatively unique, it does not appear to prevent dualised labour markets from developing. As argued by Bardasi and Gornick (2008), the presence of these comparative differences in part-time work highlight the need for a better understanding of the effect of work–family and employment policies in maintaining or countering such dualisation effects. For example, the greater importance of income in the Australian models suggests that part-time work legislation in the Netherlands is possibly more effective in protecting the wages of part-time workers. Yet, Dutch legislation does not appear to be able to prevent occupational or age segregation within part-time work. While not denying the importance of protective legislation for creating decent working conditions for part-time workers (Yerkes and Visser, 2006), it suggests that further vigilance is needed, even in a country where part-time work is well protected. This vigilance is also warranted in preventing possible new, intersectional forms of dualisation, particularly among young women, or migrant women, who are increasingly taking part in the labour market.

These findings have important theoretical implications as well. Work–family theory suggests that parents, and mothers in particular, rely on flexible working forms, such as part-time work, to reconcile the demands of paid employment and the care for (young) children (Den Dulk et al, 2005; Miani and Hoorens, 2014). The gendered nature of part-time work (Hegewisch and Gornick, 2011; Miani and Hoorens, 2014) leads to dualisation in work between men and women, as confirmed by our findings in both countries.

Additionally, our finding that dualisation appears to exist *within* part-time work in the Netherlands has consequences for how part-time work is viewed from a work–family perspective. This finding suggests that a reliance on part-time work to achieve flexibility in reconciling work and family demands is driven not only by gender, but also by age and class. Thus, while work–family scholarship demonstrates that part-time work may suit mothers' work–care preferences (eg Lewis et al, 2008) or meet their flexibility needs, and that mothers often view these arrangements as fair (McDonald, 2013; Yerkes et al, 2017), structural constraints remain. There is a continued need for concern regarding gender and class equality in part-time work strategies for reconciling work and care.

Notes

1 The gender equity of part-time work can also be questioned in relation to whether part-time work is supply- or demand-driven, and hence whether part-time work is meeting employees' or employers' needs (Kalleberg, 2000).

2 Ideally, we would include partner income rather than household income because while household income may predict part-time employment, part-time employment may also cause variation in household income. However, ESS data do not include information on partner income.

3 Occupational effects may be partly mediated by education. In further analysis (not included here), we examined whether education was significant without controlling for occupation. We found that education became significant for Australian women, where women with medium and high levels of education were significantly less likely to be working part-time, but the results did not change for Australian men, or for men and women in the Netherlands.

4 In further analysis excluding occupation, for Australian women, the effects of education become larger and more significant. For Dutch women, the results change: women with high levels of education are significantly less likely to be working short part-time hours. This suggests that occupation may also be partly mediated by education here as well. Results are available from the authors.

5 Our findings on age are in line with OECD data, which show that young adults are increasingly likely to work part-time. In 2001, more than one third (34.2%) and less than half (46.8%) of men aged 15–24 worked part-time in Australia and the Netherlands, respectively. This percentage grew to 42.5% in Australia and 64% in the Netherlands by 2016. Among young women, part-time work has also become the norm. In 2001, just under half (48.6%) of Australian women aged 15–24 worked part-time compared to 58.7% in the Netherlands. These figures are now 55.6% and an overwhelming 79.2%, respectively. The large increase in part-time work among young adults has gone hand-in-hand with an increase in temporary work forms and precarious employment for young people, which can have significant detrimental effects on their transition to adulthood (Fagan et al, 2012; Knijn, 2012). Recent evidence from the Netherlands suggests that for some young women, this precarious position is temporary (Merens and Bucx, 2018). As young women progress in their career, they are able to move out of 'underemployment' (see Chapter 1) into jobs with more hours. In both the Netherlands and Australia, underemployment among young women also appears to shift towards 'equalised' part-time jobs as they have children and then 'choose' to work fewer hours (Cassidy and Parsons, 2017; Merens and Bucx, 2018). These age-related part-time work

questions deserve further attention in dualisation research but are beyond the scope of this chapter.

References

Annink, A. (2017) 'From social support to capabilities for the work–life balance of independent professionals', *Journal of Management & Organization*, 23(2): 258–76.

Bardasi, E. and Gornick, J.C. (2008) 'Working for less? Women's part-time wage penalties across countries', *Feminist Economics*, 14(1): 37–72.

Bartoll, X., Cortès, I. and Artazcoz, L. (2014) 'Full- and part-time work: gender and welfare-type differences in European working conditions, job satisfaction, health status, and psychosocial issues', *Scandinavian Journal of Work, Environment & Health*, 40(4): 370–9. Available at: http://doi.org/10.5271/sjweh.3429

Baxter, J. and Hand, K. (2016) *Flexible child care: key findings from the AIFS evaluation of the child care flexibility trials*, Melbourne: Australian Institute of Family Studies.

Budig, M.J. and Hodges, M.J. (2010) 'Differences in disadvantage: variation in the motherhood penalty across white women's earnings distribution', *American Sociological Review*, 75(5): 705–28. Available at: http://doi.org/10.1177/0003122410381593

Cassidy, N. and Parsons, S. (2017) 'The rising share of part-time employment', *The Reserve Bank of Australia Bulletin*, September, pp 19–26.

Connelly, R., Gayle, V. and Lambert, P.S. (2016) 'Statistical modelling of key variables in social survey data analysis', *Methodological Innovations*, 9: 1–17. Available at: http://doi.org/10.1177/2059799116638002

Dekker, R. (2007) 'Non-standard employment and mobility in the Dutch, German and British labour market', Universiteit van Tilburg, Tilburg.

Den Dulk, L., Peper, A. and Van Doorne-Huiskes, A. (2005) 'Work and family life in Europe: employment patterns of working parents across welfare states', in A. Peper, A. van Doorne-Huiskes and L. den Dulk (eds) *Flexible working, organizational change and the integration of work and personal life*, Cheltenham: Edward Elgar, pp 13–38.

Dex, S., Ward, K. and Joshi, H. (2008) 'Changes in women's occupations and occupational mobility over 25 years', in J. Scott, S. Dex and H. Joshi (eds) *Women and employment: changing lives and new challenges*, Cheltenham: Edward Elgar, pp 54–80.

Dickens, W.T. and Lang, K. (1993) 'Labor market segmentation theory: reconsidering the evidence', in W. Darity Jr (ed) *Labor economics: problems in analyzing labour markets*, Boston, MA: Kluwer Academic Publishers, pp 141–80.

Emmenegger, P., Hausermann, S., Palier, B. and Seeleib-Kaiser, M. (2012a) 'How we grow unequal', in P. Emmenegger, S. Hausermann, B. Palier and M. Seeleib-Kaiser (eds) *The age of dualization: the changing face of inequality in deindustralizing societies*, Oxford: Oxford University Press, pp 3–26.

Emmenegger, P., Hausermann, S., Palier, B. and Seeleib-Kaiser, M. (eds) (2012b) *The age of dualization: the changing face of inequality in deindustrializing societies*, Oxford: Oxford University Press.

Fagan, C., Kanjuo-Mrčela, A. and Norman, H. (2012) 'Young adults navigating European labour markets: old and new social risks and employment policies', in T. Knijn (ed) *Work, family policies and transitions to adulthood in Europe*, Basingstoke: Palgrave Macmillan, pp 130–54.

Gallie, D., Gebel, M., Giesecke, J., Halldén, K., Van der Meer, P. and Wielers, R. (2016) 'Quality of work and job satisfaction: comparing female part-time work in four European countries', *International Review of Sociology*, 26(3): 457–81. Available at: http://doi.org/10.1 080/03906701.2016.1181839

Hegewisch, A. (2009) *Flexible working policies: a comparative review*, Manchester: Institute for Women's Policy Research and Equal Human Rights Commission.

Hegewisch, A. and Gornick, J.C. (2011) 'The impact of work–family policies on women's employment: a review of research from OECD countries', *Community, Work & Family*, 14(2): 119–38.

Hobson, B. (ed) (2014) *Worklife balance: The agency and capabilities gap*, Oxford: Oxford University Press.

Hobson, B. (2016) 'Gendered dimensions and capabilities: opportunities, dilemmas and challenges', *Critical Sociology*. Available at: http://doi.org/10.1177/0896920516683232

Hosking, A. (2010) *The influence of children on female wages: better or worse in Australia?*, Queensland: University of Queensland.

Javornik, J. and Kurowska, A. (2017) 'Parental leave as real opportunity structure for families and the source of gender and class inequalities', *Social Policy & Administration*, 51(4): 617–37.

Kalleberg, A.L. (2000) 'Nonstandard employment relations: part-time, temporary and contract work', *Annual Review of Sociology*, 26(1): 341–65. Available at: http://doi.org/10.1146/annurev.soc.26.1.341

Kangas, O. and Rostgaard, T. (2007) 'Preferences or institutions? Work family life opportunities in seven European countries', *Journal of European Social Policy*, 17(3): 240–56. Available at: http://doi.org/10.1177/0958928707078367

Knijn, T. (ed) (2012) *Work, family policies and transitions to adulthood in Europe*, Basingstoke: Palgrave Macmillan.

Korpi, W. (2010) 'Class and gender inequalities in different types of welfare states: the Social Citizenship Indicator Program (SCIP)', *International Journal of Social Welfare*, 19: S14–S24.

Lewis, J., Knijn, T., Martin, C. and Ostner, I. (2008) 'Patterns of development in work/family reconciliation policies for parents in France, Germany, the Netherlands, and the UK in the 2000s', *Social Politics: International Studies in Gender, State & Society*, 15(3): 261–86. Available at: http://doi.org/10.1093/sp/jxn016

Martin, B., Hewitt, B., Baird, M., Baxter, J., Heron, A., Whitehouse, G. et al (2011) *Paid parental leave evaluation: phase 1*, Canberra: Research Publications Unit, Research and Analysis Branch, Australian Government Department of Families, Housing, Community Services and Indigenous Affairs.

Martin, B., Baird, M., Brady, M., Broadway, B., Hewitt, B., Kalb, G. et al (2014) *PPL final report: paid parental leave evaluation*, Brisbane: Institute for Social Science Research, The University of Queensland.

McDonald, P. (2013) 'Societal foundations for explaining low fertility: gender equity', *Demographic Research*, 28(34): 981–94. Available at: http://doi.org/10.4054/DemRes.2013.28.34

Merens, A. and Bucx, F. (2018) *Werken aan de Start*, Den Haag: The Netherlands Institute for Social Science Research, The University of Queensland.

Miani, C. and Hoorens, S. (2014) *Parents at work: men and women participating in the labour force*, Brussels: Rand Europe.

Mood, C. (2010) 'Logistic regression: why we cannot do what we think we can do, and what we can do about it', *European Sociological Review*, 26(1): 67–82. Available at: http://doi.org/10.1093/esr/jcp006

OECD (Organisation for Economic Co-operation and Development) (2017) *Labour force statistics*, Paris: OECD.

O'Reilly, J. and Fagan, C. (1998) *Part-time prospects: an international comparison of part-time work in Europe, North America and the Pacific Rim*, London and New York, NY: Routledge.

Palier, B. and Thelen, K. (2010) 'Institutionalizing dualism: complementarities and change in France and Germany', *Politics & Society*, 38(1): 119–48. Available at: http://doi.org/10.1177/0032329209357888

Portegijs, W. and Keuzenkamp, S. (eds) (2008) *Nederland deeltijdland. Vrouwen en deeltijdwerk*, Den Haag: The Netherlands Institute for Social Research.

Portegijs, W. and Van den Brakel, M. (2016) *Emancipatiemonitor 2016*, Den Haag: The Netherlands Institute for Social Science Research, The University of Queensland.

Preston, A. and Yu, S. (2015) 'Is there a part-time/full-time pay differential in Australia?', *Journal of Industrial Relations*, 57(1): 24–47. Available at: http://doi.org/10.1177/0022185614545902

Prosser, T. (2016) 'Dualization or liberalization? Investigating precarious work in eight European countries', *Work, Employment and Society*, 30(6): 949–65. Available at: http://doi.org/10.1177/0950017015609036

Roeters, A. and Craig, L. (2014) 'Part-time work, women's work–life conflict, and job satisfaction: a cross-national comparison of Australia, the Netherlands, Germany, Sweden, and the United Kingdom', *International Journal of Comparative Sociology*. Available at: http://doi.org/10.1177/0020715214543541

Rose, J., Brady, M., Yerkes, M.A. and Coles, L. (2015) '"Sometimes they just want to cry for their mum": couples' negotiations and rationalisations of gendered divisions in infant care', *Journal of Family Studies*, 21(1): 38–56. Available at: http://doi.org/10.1080/132294 00.2015.1010264

Summerfield, M., Bevitt, A., Freidin, S., Hahn, M., La, N., Macalalad, N. et al (2016) *HILDA User Manual – Release 15*, Melbourne: Institute of Applied Economic and Social Research, University of Melbourne.

Treas, J., Van der Lippe, T. and Tai, T.-O.C. (2011) 'The happy homemaker? Married women's well-being in cross-national perspective', *Social Forces*, 90(1): 111–32. Available at: http://doi.org/10.1093/sf/90.1.111

Visser, J. (2002) 'The first part-time economy in the world: a model to be followed?', *Journal of European Social Policy*, 12(1): 23–42.

Watson, N. and Wooden, M. (2002) *The Household, Income and Labour Dynamics in Australia (HILDA) Survey: Wave 1 survey methodology* (HILDA project technical paper series, No. 1/02). Retrieved (2007) from Melbourne: www.melbourneinstitute.com/hilda/hdps-techn01.pdf

Whiteford, C.M. (2015) *Early child care in Australia: quality of care, experiences of care and developmental outcomes for Australian children*, Queensland: Queensland University of Technology.

Williams, J.C., Blair-Loy, M. and Berdahl, J.L. (2013) 'Cultural schemas, social class, and the flexibility stigma', *Journal of Social Issues*, 69(2): 209–34.

Yerkes, M.A. (2009) 'Part-time work in the Dutch welfare state: the ideal combination of work and care?', *Policy and Politics*, 37(4): 535–52.

Yerkes, M.A. (2014) 'Collective protection for new social risks: childcare and the Dutch welfare state', *Journal of Social Policy*, 43(4): 811–28. Available at: http://doi.org/10.1017/S0047279414000385

Yerkes, M.A. and Den Dulk, L. (2015) 'Arbeid-en-zorgbeleid in de participatiesamenleving', *Tijdschrift Voor Arbeidsvraagstukken*, 31: 510–28.

Yerkes, M.A. and Javornik, J. (2018) 'Creating capabilities: Childcare policies in comparative perspective', *Journal of European Social Policy*. Available at https://doi.org/10.1177/0958928718808421

Yerkes, M.A. and Visser, J. (2006) 'Women's preferences or delineated policies? The development of part-time work in the Netherlands, the UK and Germany', in J.Y. Boulin, M. Lallement, J. Messenger and F. Michon (eds) *Decent working time, new trends, new issues*, Geneva: ILO, pp 235–62.

Yerkes, M.A., Martin, B., Baxter, J. and Rose, J. (2017) 'An unsettled bargain? Mothers' perceptions of justice and fairness in paid work', *Journal of Sociology*, 53(2): 476–91. Available at: http://doi.org/10.1177/1440783317696361

12

Are female part-time workers dualised in South Korea? Institutional structures and employment conditions of South Korean female part-time jobs

Min Young Song and Sophia Seung-yoon Lee

Introduction

The dual structure of the labour market has become one of the most important social issues in South Korea (hereafter, Korea) following the increase in non-standard worker positions since the beginning of the millennium. Part-time employment is one such example of non-standard employment. Although less attention has been paid to part-time work than other types of non-standard employment, such as fixed-term employment and/or temporary employment, the number of part-time employment positions has been on the rise in the Korean female labour market in recent years. The Korean government actually paved the way for this rise in part-time employment positions for women through a series of policies intended to help families deal individually with the increasing risks of unstable employment and poverty (Lee and Baek, 2014), on the one hand, and to enhance work–life balance for married women, on the other.

Many Korean scholars have expressed concern over the negative implications of the expansion of part-time employment on the quality of the female labour market. They argue that the current part-time employment policy reinforces the gender gap in the Korean labour market because – compared to full-timers – part-timers tend to have less opportunities for wage increases, promotion and career development (Lee, 2012; Kim and Lee, 2014; Shin, 2015). In order to identify whether the Korean part-time employment policy is reducing or reproducing gender inequality in the labour market, we may need empirical evidence. Several studies have examined the overall characteristics of Korean female part-time employment (Ahn and Ban, 2007; Seong and Ahn, 2007; Jeong, 2010; Seong, 2014), but few have focused on working mothers in greater need of work–life balance because of their young children.

In this chapter, we will examine the characteristics of those who work part-time and have young children, including how much these workers are paid compared to full-time workers. Given that an individual's decisions regarding the type of job they take, as well as the outcomes of such decisions, are greatly affected by a complex configuration of related policies (Emmenegger et al, 2012), we will take a look at the institutional structure of the Korean female labour market as well. Accordingly, this chapter will be organised as follows. First, we provide an overview of recent trends in Korean female non-standard employment and part-time employment by referring to the Korea Labour and Society Institute (KLSI) report. Then, we will describe the development of labour market flexibility policies, female employment policies and childcare policies, which have constructed the current institutional structure of the Korean female labour market from the 1990s to the present. Lastly, we will compare the past employment history, uptake rate of work–life balance policies, socio-economic status and current employment conditions of Korean female part-time workers with young children to those of full-time workers by analysing data from the 2015 Korea National Survey on Fertility, Family Health and Welfare.

Part-time employment and women in the South Korean dual labour market

Since 2001, the Korean government has been surveying the detailed characteristics[1] of waged workers every August using an additional questionnaire attached to the National Survey of Economically Active Population.[2] The questionnaire asks whether or not an employee belongs to the following types: fixed-term employment, short-term employment, part-time employment, dispatched employment, employment through outside contractors, employment of special forms, daily employment or domestic employment. Statistics Korea (2016) defines employees as non-standard workers only if they fit into at least one of those seven categories. The KLSI criticises this classification scheme, asserting that it underestimates the size of non-standard workers as it excludes long-term temporary workers (eg permanent temporary workers, casual workers and seasonal workers) (Kim, 2016).

Given that aspects of temporary and daily work have long represented precarious workers according to the traditional criterion, we will describe the proportion and patterns of non-standard workers in Korea on the basis of the KLSI's definition. As seen in Figure 12.1 (panel a), non-standard workers comprised 44.5% of all wage-earners in 2016.[3] The share of total non-standard workers has been on a downward trend, whereas the share of part-time workers has grown from about 6% in 2001 to 12.7% in 2016. Figure 12.1 (panel b) additionally reports variations in the share of non-standard workers by sex. In 2016, the share of non-standard workers was higher among female wage-earners (54.5%) than among male wage-earners (36.7%). A more interesting characteristic is found in the association of marital status with employment status by gender. The share of non-standard workers was larger for the unmarried wage-earners (46.6%) than for the married wage-earners (32.7%) among men, whereas it was larger for the married wage-earners (59.5%) than for the unmarried wage-earners (43.0%) among women. We can see a similar tendency in the pattern of part-time employment, defined as working less than 36 hours per week. Under the general pattern indicating that part-timers were more frequently found among female wage-earners (20.6%) than among male wage-earners (6.5%) in 2016 in Korea, the share of part-timers was larger for the unmarried (10.5%) than for the married (4.8%) among men, whereas it was higher for the married (23.0%) than for the unmarried (15.0%) among women. This suggests that stable employment may be a resource used by men to get married or to maintain their marriage life, while marriage seems to act as a negative factor for women in maintaining their career.

Korean women's unstable employment is closely associated with discontinuity in their employment during their childbearing years (Lee and Baek, 2014). Figure 12.2 traces Korean women's age-specific employment rates back to the 1990s. A clear M-shape is found in the curve for 2016, as in the curve for 1991, indicating that a large number of Korean married women are still leaving their job after marriage or childbirth. The only change seen in the curves is a rightward movement of vertexes due to the increase in the age at first entry into the labour market (from 20–24 to 25–29)[4] and the age at first marriage and childbirth (from 25–29 to 30–39). The persistent M-shape curves correspond to the government's report that 48.2% of a total 9,053,000 Korean married women (including 1,812,000 unemployed women and 2,555,000 employed women) have experienced a career break due to marriage, childbirth or child-rearing (Statistics Korea, 2017: 11–12).

Figure 12.1: Proportion of non-standard and part-time workers among Korean wage-earners (%)

(a) % of NS and PT among all wage-earners (2001–16)

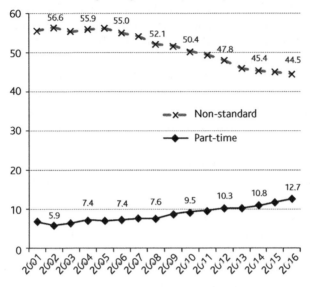

(b) % of NS and PT by gender and marital status (2016)

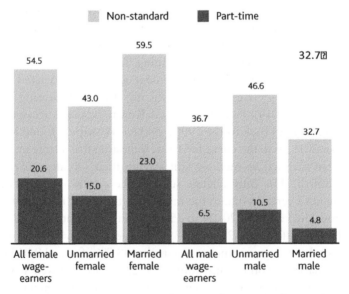

Source: Data from Statistics Korea, Survey of Economically Active Population and Kim (2016: 2, 4, 6, 10)

Figure 12.2: Korean women's employment-to-population ratio, by age, 1991–2016

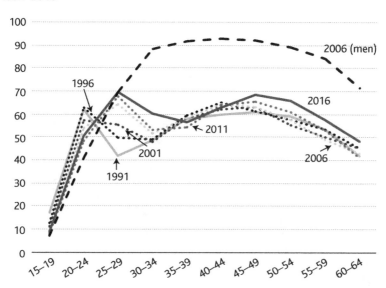

Source: ILOSTAT (no date)

As a result of this precarious status of employment and the ongoing tendency of career breaks, Korea has a much lower female employment rate compared to other post-industrial countries. The female employment-to-population ratio (15 and 64 years) was 56.2% for Korea in 2016, while it was 66.5% for Japan and an average of 59.5% for the Organisation for Economic Co-operation and Development (OECD, 2017). Furthermore, the gender gap in the employment rate has remained considerable in Korea. As seen in Figure 12.3, the employment rate of Korean women aged 15 and over has gradually increased from 41.3% in 1980 to 50.2% in 2016. Nevertheless, it is still about 20% lower than that of men, which has remained around 70% over the last 37 years.

Economic institutional structures of the South Korean female labour market

Korea is well known for its rapid and successful industrialisation, which commenced in the 1960s. Despite the noticeable increase in the employment-to-population ratio during the early period of industrialisation,[5] Korean female employment was very unstable and unorganised, concentrating on unmarried women in small-scale informal sectors. In the 1980s, the Korean government attempted

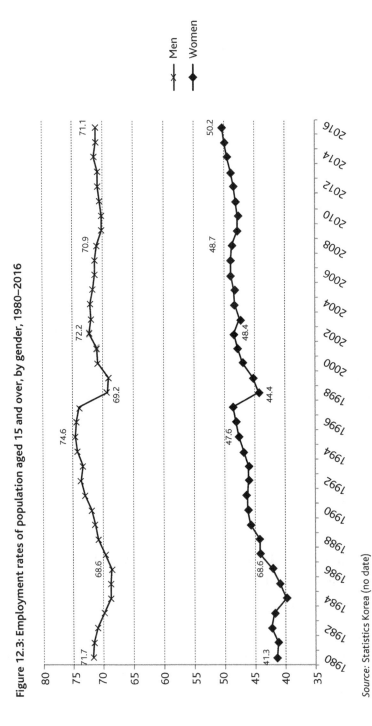

Figure 12.3: Employment rates of population aged 15 and over, by gender, 1980–2016

Source: Statistics Korea (no date)

to shift the core of the economy from light industries to heavy chemical industries. Accordingly, the labour market became more male-dominated and the gender division of work became stronger in Korea (Chang, 2011: 68–81).

Since the late 1990s, Korea has experienced three major social changes relating to female employment: a decline in the economic growth rate; an increasing awareness of gender equality; and a decrease in the fertility rate. The Korean government has tried to deal with these post-industrial social phenomena through such measures as labour market flexibility policy, female employment policy and childcare policy. Overall, it seems that the labour market flexibility policy has exerted a stronger influence on the employment status of Korean women over the last two decades than the other policies. The policy to protect female employment was often overwhelmed by neoliberal assertions that the government should increase flexibility in the labour market so as to overcome the economic crisis. Furthermore, it turned out that the childcare policy was not successful enough to lead to a fundamental change in the unequal division of labour between men and women in the family.

Labour market flexibility policy

The legislative process of introducing the labour market flexibility policy to Korea began in the late 1990s (see Table 12.1). The Labour Standards Act was amended in 1996 to allow 'dismissal for managerial reasons' (eg the closure of a business or financial difficulty) and to introduce a flexible working-hour system and part-time workers. However, a crucial moment in this advancement process was the financial crisis of 1997, which triggered a harsh bailout procedure. As the International Monetary Fund required the Korean government to enhance flexibility in the labour market, the Act on the Protection, etc. of Dispatched Workers was enacted in 1998 to justify massive layoffs and non-standard employment.

Since then, a series of measures, similar to those implemented by other post-industrial countries (Emmenegger et al, 2012), that are designed to handle growing employment instability and related social problems have been adopted in Korea. For example, throughout the 2000s, the government gradually extended the coverage of social insurance schemes, including employment insurance, the national pension, health insurance and industrial accident insurance, to non-standard workers. In 2007, the Act on the Protection, etc. of Fixed-term and Part-time Employees was enacted, imposing a two-year limitation on fixed-term employment. With this regulation, a guideline was announced in 2012 opening the way for fixed-term workers continuously employed for more than two years to become open-ended workers through a personnel appraisal. In addition, the issue of anti-discrimination against non-standard workers has been on the national agenda. Despite these efforts, however, the poor working conditions attached to non-standard work have improved very little. According to the Survey of the Economically Active Population, in 2016, the average wages per month and per hour for non-standard workers were only 49.2% and 55.4% of those for standard workers (Kim, 2016: 14, 16). Furthermore, the average rates of non-standard worker coverage by social insurance schemes have remained as low as 30–40% during the last 10 years; by contrast, nearly all standard workers were covered by the national pension (about 96%), health-care insurance (about 99%) and employment insurance (about 85%) (Kim, 2016: 25). More importantly, the two-year limitation on the fixed-term contract by the Act on the Protection, etc. of Fixed-term and Part-time Employees has been utilised against its original intent as giving employers an excuse to hire new temporary workers or outsource work instead of renewing contracts with existing fixed-term workers (Nam, 2007).

On the other hand, the government has continued to elaborate on the labour market flexibility policies, adding rules and regulations on working hours and dismissal procedures in 2008.

Table 12.1: Development of labour market flexibility policy

Year	Policy level	Key policy changes
1996	The Labour Standards Act	Introduced 'dismissal for managerial reasons' and a flexible working-hour system
1998	Establishment of the Korea Tripartite Commission	First introduction of a presidential advisory body comprising representatives of the labour, capital and the government to deal with important labour issues
	The Act on the Protection, etc. of Dispatched Workers	Provided regulations concerning massive layoffs and non-standard employment
2007	The Act on the Protection, etc. of Fixed-term and Part-time Employees	Imposed a two-year limitation on the duration of fixed-term employment
2012	Guidelines of the above Act	Introduced a new type called open-ended term employment
2015	Agreement of the Tripartite Commission	A labour market reform that allowed employers to extend the duration of fixed-term employment and the range of operating dispatched workers

In addition, a presidential advisory body called the Economic and Social Development Commission reached an agreement on labour market reforms in 2015, which allowed the duration of fixed-term employment and the range of operating dispatched workers to be extended. Although the agreement stipulated both strengthening the protection of non-standard workers and rationalising the regulations of employment, it was expected to be more beneficial to employers rather than non-standard employees. Before long, the government announced new guidelines in relation to this reform. The guidelines included many clauses weakening workers' positions in the workplace. For example, employers were then permitted to dismiss employees for no reason other than 'low performance' and to revise work rules against the labour union's will if justified on the basis of so-called 'collective rationality' (Lee et al, 2016).

Female employment policy

The low fertility trend since the 2000s has made the Korean government pay attention to enhancing the work–life balance of working mothers and protecting their employment (see Table 12.2). For example, the schemes for both maternity leave (introduced in 1953 by the Labour Standard Act) and parental leave (introduced in 1988 by the Gender Equal Employment Act) have greatly expanded as key policies of the Basic Plan to Address Low Fertility and Ageing Society enacted in 2006. The Amendment of the Act on Equal Employment and Support for Work–Family Reconciliation from 2007 is another important piece of legislation that contributes to the development of work–family balance policies. In particular, certain aspects of the parental leave scheme involving the payment, length and flexibility of the scheme were modified. However, these expanded modifications to the leave policies were applicable only to standard workers as the current parental leave scheme still imposes very strict restrictions on the eligibility of non-standard workers. It requires workers to be covered by employment insurance for at least 180 days before applying for both maternity leave and parental leave. Moreover, employers can refuse to grant parental leave to workers employed for less than one year at the current company. Although the government has introduced such measures as subsidies for employers who hold contracts with fixed-term or dispatched female workers in pregnancy or on maternity leave, such measures have not yet proven effective.

On the other hand, since 2010, the government started creating new part-time jobs for women under the guise of social investment

Table 12.2: Policy initiatives to increase female employment

Year	Policy level	Key policy changes
2001	The Labour Standard Act	Extension of the length of maternity leave up to 90 days
	The Gender Equal Employment Act	The parental leave scheme turned into paid leave
2006	The 1st Basic Plan to address Low Fertility and Ageing Society	A rise in the payment of both maternity leave (to 100% of ordinary earnings with a ceiling of 1,350,000 KRW) and parental leave (to 500,000 KRW per month)
2007	The Act on Equal Employment and Support for Work–Family Reconciliation	Expansion of the parental leave schemes including the payment (40% of ordinary earnings with a ceiling of 1,000,000 KRW and a minimum of 500,000 KRW), the length (one year for each parent) and the flexibility (possible to choose between full-time leave and the reduced working hour scheme; possible to use the leave for two separate periods until the child passes the age of eight years or the second grade in elementary school)
2010	The National Employment Strategy 2020	Proposed a plan for part-time employment in standard (ie permanent) position (eg a total of 930,000 new part-time jobs in 2013)

– highlighting the efficient use of human capital and the harmony between female employment policy and family policy (Lee and Baek, 2014). As a part of the National Employment Strategy 2020, the government proposed a plan to expand regular part-time employment contributing to work–family balance in 2010. It was followed in 2013 by a policy that aimed at providing married women with opportunities to get quality part-time jobs. In particular, the government proposed creating a total of 930,000 new high-quality part-time jobs. This tool was implemented in 2014 by introducing the time-selective employment category to the public sector and offering subsidies to employers who created part-time jobs in the private sector. Concerns have been raised, however, over the sustainability of the subsidy programme. Critics argued that the expiration of the subsidy programme would result in unstable and low-paying jobs, even adding non-standard employees to the Korean female labour market (Kim and Lee, 2014).

Childcare policy

Korea is one of the East Asian countries with strong familialism and patriarchal ideals (Chang and Song, 2010), which generated a care regime in which women in the family were the sole care providers. The continuous decline in fertility rates, however, has raised awareness of alternatives to the patriarchal familial care institution. In search of a new care regime, the Korean government developed a series of childcare service policies, which were first implemented in the 2000s, including the Mid- and Long-term Comprehensive Development Plan of Childcare Business, the Infant Care Act, the Childcare Support Policy Measures, the Basic Plan to Address Low Fertility and Ageing Society, and, finally, the Childcare Support Act (see Table 12.3). The Childcare Support Act introduced the 'universal childcare service' policy for all children aged 0–2 in 2012 and expanded it to include children aged 3–5 in 2013, with no income constraints (Baek, 2009; Committee for 50 Years of Korean Population Policy, 2016).

As a result, the enrolment rates of children under six in childcare facilities increased from 53.2% in 2006 to 67.0% in 2014. However, Korea's childcare policies had a critical limitation in establishing a new care regime: rather than directly providing an in-kind childcare service, which would have required significant amounts of time and money to construct, the government opted to offer vouchers for the use of private childcare facilities. According to the National Childcare Statistics, private childcare facilities comprised about 87% of total childcare facilities and took care of 76% of the total children who enrolled in any type of childcare in 2014. The problem with this system is that mothers are dissatisfied with the quality of private childcare services – which may be associated with the poor working conditions of childcare service workers and the lack of governmental supervision (Kim, 2015; Committee for 50 Years of Korean Population Policy, 2016).

Furthermore, there was an attempt to turn the direction of childcare policies from *defamilialisation* to *(re)familialisation* in the mid-2010s. If we define *defamilialisation* of childcare as a process that makes childcare available outside of the family unit, Korea's childcare policies during the early period of expansion followed such a definition. Given concerns over the increase in the childcare budget, however, the government launched a pilot project limiting the eligibility of full-time childcare services for children aged 0–2 to only working mothers in 2015. In 2016, the project, referred to as the 'tailored childcare service' policy, was finally applied to the whole country (Kim and Lee, 2016).

The policy reducing the coverage of childcare services was paralleled by the expansion of the home childcare allowance. When first introduced in 2009, the childcare allowance was offered only to second-tier poor households with children who were younger than

Table 12.3: Development of childcare policy

Year	Policy level	Key policy changes
2001	The Mid- and Long-term Comprehensive Development Plan of Childcare Business	Aimed to enhance the quality of public childcare services, to improve the expertise and working conditions of childcare workers, and to reform the childcare administrative system
2004–05	Amendment of the Infant Care Act	Modify standards for childcare facilities and strengthen public childcare systems
	Announcement of Childcare Support Policy Measures	Develop an integrated childcare system on a cross-ministry basis
2006	The 1st Basic Plan to Address Low Fertility and Ageing Society	Provided the basis of the collaboration among Ministry of Health and Welfare, Ministry of Education, and Ministry of Gender Equality and Family
2009	The Infant Care Act	Introduced the home childcare allowance to second-tier poor households with children aged under 24 months
2012	The Childcare Support Act	Abolished income constraints on providing childcare vouchers for all children under the age of six
2013	The Infant Care Act	Expanded the home childcare allowance to all households with children aged under six years
2014	The Childcare Support Act	'Tailored childcare service' limiting the use of full-time childcare services on the basis of the employment status of parents

24 months. The government expanded its coverage and benefit to all households with children who were younger than six years in 2013, regardless of household income level, if not using any childcare facilities. In addition, the part-time childcare voucher was introduced in 2014 as a corresponding policy to the part-time female employment policy (Committee for 50 Years of Korean Population Policy, 2016). From the perspective that these policies assume mothers in the family to be the main caregivers, the direction of the policies can be defined as *(re)familialisation*.

Employment conditions among female part-time workers in South Korea

As mentioned earlier, Korea's part-time employment policy was introduced as a way to enhance the work–life balance of married women and reduce the risk of career breaks due to childbirth and childrearing. In this section, we will examine the employment conditions of Korean female part-time workers with young children by analysing data collected through the South Korean National Survey on Fertility, Family Health, and Welfare in 2015. A total of 11,009 married women aged between 15 and 49 years[6] were surveyed about their marriage, childbirth, childrearing and career (including current and past employment).[7] Regarding current employment status, the respondents were asked whether or not they work, whether they work full-time (ie 36 hours or more per week) or part-time (ie less than 36 hours), whether they were wage-earners (ie regular workers, temporary workers, daily workers) or non-wage-earners (ie the self-employed, non-paid workers for the family business), and whether they were in permanent employment (ie the duration of employment is not specified) or in temporary employment (ie the duration of employment is specified).[8]

Female permanent or temporary employment

Figure 12.4 reports the employment pattern of married Korean women aged between 15 and 49. Overall, 56.5% of the respondents were employed at the time of survey, of which 21.1% were working on a part-time basis. The share of temporary employment among wage-earners was 41.7%.[9] It is worth noting that the share of permanent employment is a crucial difference between full-timers and part-timers. The share of permanent employment among the total part-time wage-earners was only 10.7% (= 0.9/[0.9 + 7.5]), while that among the total full-time wage-earners was 69.7% (= 24.4/[24.4 + 10.6]). In other words, most Korean female part-time wage-earners had a low level of employment protection in common, whereas full-time wage-earners were divided into a highly protected employment group, on the one hand, and a loosely protected employment group, on the other.

In addition, we examined the employment status of married women by age of the youngest child. In Korea, it is assumed that children under the age of nine typically need careful parental care and attention, for example, workers are allowed to take parental leave until their children turn nine years old (or become second graders in elementary school). As seen in Figure 12.4, the employment rate of those whose youngest child was under nine (45.5%) was about 10 percentage points lower than the total average. On the other hand, the proportion of part-timers among the employed with young children (25.7%) was more than 4 percentage points higher than the total average. The proportion of non-standard workers among the wage-earners grew with the increase in the age of the youngest child because middle-aged Korean married women who re-enter

Figure 12.4: Employment pattern of 15- to 49-year-old married Korean women, by motherhood status (%)

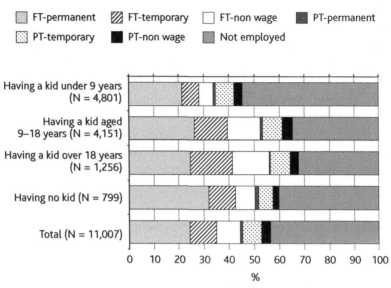

Notes: Employees with an open-ended contract are included in the category of permanent workers. Non-wage-earners include the self-employed and non-paid workers for the family business.

Source: Korea National Survey on Fertility, Family Health and Welfare 2015

the labour market are likely to be given non-standard positions (Lee et al, 2016).

Hereinafter, we will compare the employment condition of part-time workers with that of full-time workers having young children under the age of nine in order to verify whether part-timers are more marginalised than full-timers in the Korean female labour market. Among the various aspects of the employment condition, we will focus on 'wages'. In order to control differences attributed to the different working hours between part-timers and full-timers, we will look at 'hourly wage' instead of monthly or weekly wage. Prior to examining the employment condition, we will look at past employment history, the uptake rate of work–life balance policies and socio-economic status, which helps us identify who Korean female part-time workers are. Most importantly, we will make a distinction between full-time 'permanent' wage-earners (FT-Ps) ($n = 1,026$) and full-time 'temporary' wage-earners (FT-Ts) ($n = 326$) given that whether or not the duration of employment is specified greatly affects manifold employment conditions, including eligibility for employment insurance membership in Korea. The number of part-time 'permanent' wage-earners was so small that we included only part-time 'temporary' wage-earners (PT-Ts) ($n = 350$) in our analysis. None of the non-wage-earners were included because the labour market policies discussed in the previous section only apply to wage-earners.

Employment history in relation to the use of work–family policy measures

Although we categorised our respondents based on their current employment status at the time of the survey, they were also asked several questions about their employment history regardless of their current employment status. For example, the survey included questions about the number of years of employment not only at the current workplace, but also at all workplaces in which they had been employed until the time of survey. In addition, the respondents were asked whether they had been continuously employed without a career break during one year around such life events as marriage and childbirth (ie from six months before each lifetime event to six months after the event).

As seen in Figure 12.5, the duration of Korean female wage-earner work experience varied according to the type of employment contract rather than working-time arrangement. PT-Ts and FT-Ts had similar years of both total employment and current employment (9.0 years and 2.2 years for PT-Ts; 8.8 years and 2.3 years for FT-Ts), which is much shorter than for FT-Ps (11.3 years and 7.5 years). A similar pattern was found in the proportion of those who had experienced continuous employment from six months before their first marriage to six months after marriage. This indicator shows us how many women worked without a career break around such a life event since we excluded those who had never been employed or had left their job during that year from our respondents who had experienced the life event. The share of those who had experienced continuous employment around their first marriage was only 48.4% among PT-Ts and 42.1% among FT-Ts, whereas it was as high as 82.7% among FT-Ps. The rate of continuous employment around the time of childbirth dropped much more rapidly among temporary workers on both a part-time and a full-time basis than permanent workers. The share of those who had been continuously employed from six months before their first childbirth to six months after the life event was below 20% among both PT-Ts and FT-Ts. On the contrary, the proportion among FT-Ps hovered around 70% without a rapid decrease.

In brief, Figure 12.5 informs us that a large number of Korean female temporary workers in both full-time and part-time arrangements left

Figure 12.5: Employment history of Korean female workers with at least one child under nine

(a) Duration of employment

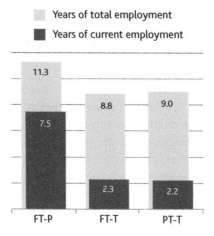

(b) % of continuous employment during one year between six months before and six months after marriage and childbirth

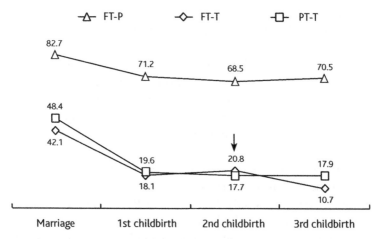

Source: Korea National Survey on Fertility, Family Health and Welfare 2015

a previous job after marriage or childbirth. This trend raises some questions: why did they leave their jobs? Did the Korean government's expansion of work–family reconciliation policies, which were first implemented in the 2000s, not alleviate these problems? Figure 12.6 clearly shows that these temporary workers have been excluded from the female employment protection system. As presented in Figure 12.6, the take-up rate of maternity leave was less than 20% for both PT-Ts and FT-Ts, while for FT-Ps, it was over 70%. These proportions are nearly identical to the proportions of female workers who were continuously employed after childbirth, suggesting that maternity leave is a critical employment protection system for workers who have given birth. This further indicates how closely the dual structure of the labour market is associated with the mechanism reproducing the precarious status of female non-standard workers in Korea. In other words, it shows us that Korea's female employment protection system benefits only labour market insiders (ie permanent workers), offering hardly any assistance to outsiders (ie temporary workers).

As to the take-up rate of parental leave, the overall average is much lower than that of maternity leave. Nevertheless, the trend for uptake rates is similar to the trend for maternity leave as the rates were much lower for temporary workers (less than 10% for both PT-Ts and FT-Ts) than permanent workers (about 48% for FT-Ps). Meanwhile, the take-up rates of reduced working hours and flexible working hours were very low even among FT-Ps (6.0% and 4.5%). This reminds us how long working hours actually are in Korea. According to the OECD (2018), in 2016, the average number of annual hours worked per worker was 2,069 hours in Korea – 306 hours higher than the OECD total average.

Figure 12.6: Uptake rates of work–life balance policies by Korean female workers with at least one child under nine (%)

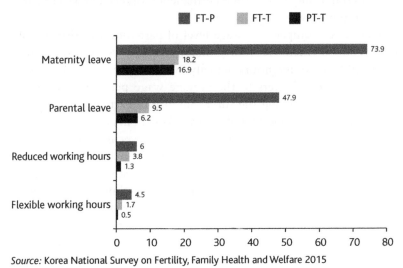

Source: Korea National Survey on Fertility, Family Health and Welfare 2015

The socio-economic status and wage level of part-timers

According to the previous section, the employment history of Korean female workers, including career breaks related to family change, is associated with the type of employment contract (ie permanent or temporary employment) rather than the working-time arrangement. In other words, there was no critical difference in employment history between part-timers and full-timers if they were in temporary positions.

However, we found that socio-economic status had some significant association with working-time arrangement even among those in temporary positions. Figure 12.7 illustrates how much a respondent's husband earned on average over the three months preceding the survey and how many respondents had attained a college degree. The average monthly spousal income revealed a significant difference between part-timers and full-timers in temporary positions: husbands of PT-Ts earned 3,258,000 KRW a month on average, while husbands of FT-Ts tended to earn a much smaller amount of money (2,912,000 KRW) during the same period of time. This suggests that lower spousal earnings likely increase the working hours of Korean female temporary workers.[10] In addition, Korean female full-time temporary workers had a lower socio-economic status than part-time temporary workers in terms of educational level. The proportion of those with a college degree was significantly lower among FT-Ts (48.8%) than among PT-Ts (59.8%). In other words, it is probable that Korean female full-time temporary workers are a more disadvantaged population compared not only to full-time permanent workers, but also to part-time temporary workers in Korea.

Now let us compare the wage level of part-timers to that of full-timers. We defined the hourly income as follows: hourly income = monthly income/(hours actually worked per week*4), where 'monthly income' refers to the average wage per month over the three months preceding the survey and 'hours actually worked per week' refers to the typical number of working hours with no particular reference week. As seen in Figure 12.8, the average hourly income of part-timers (11,000 KRW) was lower than that of full-timers (13,000 KRW). Given that the wage level is greatly affected by years of employment at most Korean workplaces, part-timers' lower income might be significantly associated with their shorter duration of current employment (3.1 years) compared to that of full-timers (5.9 years).

For temporary workers, however, we saw somewhat different features. First, the average years of current employment of PT-Ts

Figure 12.7: Socio-economic status of Korean female workers with at least one child under nine

(a) Average monthly wage of spouse (10,000 KRW)

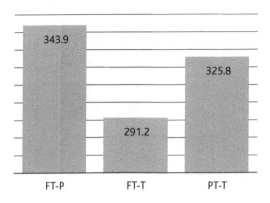

(b) Share of population with tertiary education (%)

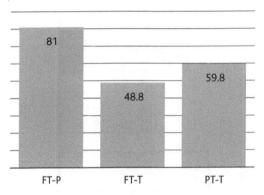

Source: Korea National Survey on Fertility, Family Health and Welfare 2015

(2.2 years) and FT-Ts (2.3 years) were similar. Second, and perhaps more importantly, it was not PT-Ts (12,000 KRW), but FT-Ts (9,000 KRW), who had lower wages per hour. Previously, we found that the spouses of Korean female FT-Ts tended to earn less money than those of Korean female PT-Ts. Furthermore, these FT-Ts had lower levels of educational attainment than PT-Ts. To put all these findings together, Korean female full-time temporary workers without a college education might be compelled to take very low-paying jobs and extend their working hours because of their low household income.

In addition, we saw a sign of dualisation within part-time workers in Figure 12.8. Part-timers with a college education earned as much

Figure 12.8: Average hourly income of Korean female workers with at least one child under nine

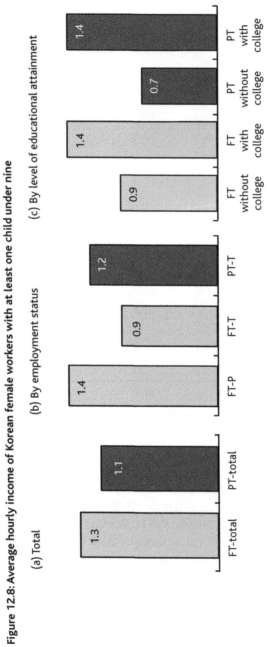

continued

	Monthly income (10,000 KRW)	Hours actually worked per week	Hourly income (10,000 KRW)	Years of current employment
Full-time				
Standard (N = 1026)	242.2	42.3	1.4	7.5
Non-standard (N = 326)	149.2	42.7	0.9	2.3
Non-wage earners (N = 271)	180.9	44.4	1.1	4.1
High school or below (N = 456)	153.4	44.1	0.9	4.2
College or above (N = 1167)	236.6	42.2	1.4	6.5
Total (N = 1623)	213.3	42.7	1.3	5.9
Part-time				
Standard (N = 42)	137.6	27.2	1.3	3.5
Non-standard (N = 350)	94.2	23.5	1.2	2.2
Non-wage earners (N = 168)	87.9	24.4	1.1	4.9
High school or below (N = 197)	73.4	26.5	0.7	2.4
College or above (N = 363)	107.6	22.7	1.4	3.5
Total (N = 560)	95.6	24.0	1.1	3.1
Total (N = 2183)	183.1	37.9	1.2	5.2

Note: Hourly income = monthly income/(hours actually worked per week*4)

Source: Korea National Survey on Fertility, Family Health and Welfare, 2015

income per hour as full-timers with a college education (14,000 KRW on average), while the average hourly income of part-timers without a college education (7,000 KRW) was much lower than that of full-timers without a college education (9,000 KRW). As a result, the wage gap by education level was bigger among part-timers (7,000 KRW) than among full-timers (5,000 KRW). This implies a potential dualisation of Korean part-time employment, which seems to be highly associated with such factors as educational achievement and skills required for the job. Figure 12.9 further suggests the heterogeneity of Korean female part-timers by plotting the distribution of hourly income by occupation of all wage-earners with a childbirth experience (regardless of the age of their youngest child) in our data set. As seen in the graphs, the range of income distribution was much wider for part-time temporary workers than full-time permanent workers. In contrast, only a small variation was found among full-time temporary workers as most full-time temporary employees are concentrated in low-paying jobs.

Conclusion

The Korean government has encouraged married women to take up part-time jobs since the 2010s in order to increase female employment rates. Under the strong influence of the labour market flexibility policy, however, most part-time jobs have been created on the basis of temporary contracts. Furthermore, the Korean childcare regime has not sufficiently defamilialised or degenderised to allow these women to actually choose between work and child-rearing. Consequently, it seems that Korea's part-time employment policy has achieved neither of its goals as families have been unable to independently manage their poverty risks and married women with young children have not achieved a work–life balance. The social security system in Korea is not sufficiently developed for married women from a family at risk of poverty to reduce their working hours and still make a living. On the other hand, a part-time job is not an attractive option for those from a middle- or high-income family because its employment condition does not match their expectations. If they have already experienced a career break and if they are not so poor that they 'can' choose between working again and staying at home, they tend to choose the latter. This is because it is so difficult for them to find a decent job or enter into male-dominant jobs (regardless of working-time arrangement) while balancing responsibilities for childcare and housework.

Figure 12.9: Distribution of hourly income of Korean female workers with a childbirth experience, by occupation

(a) Within FT-Ps (N = 2,438)

(b) Within FT-Ts (N = 1,014)

(c) Within PT-Ts (N = 749)

Note: Classification of occupations: (1) managers, professionals, armed forces; (2) clerical support workers; (3) service and sales workers; (4) craft workers, machine operators and assemblers; and (5) forestry and fishery workers, elementary occupations (STATA version 12.0 was employed to generate the box plots).

Source: Korea National Survey on Fertility, Family Health and Welfare 2015

We found that, on the whole, the hourly income of female part-timers with young children was lower than that of full-timers in Korea in 2015. This was because most part-time jobs were coupled with temporary employment in which the wage level was much lower than permanent employment. On the other hand, a sign of dualisation was found within the Korean female part-timers. The gap in the average hourly income between those with a college degree and those without was wider among part-timers than among full-timers. Furthermore, the distribution range of hourly income was much wider for part-time temporary workers than for full-time temporary workers. More research will be required to investigate how these factors are involved in the dualisation process of part-time employment. In addition, we should improve the quality of part-time jobs – in terms of, for example, the level of employment protection and wages – so that married women (and men) can actually consider a part-time job as a real option to maintain both the quality of life and the balance between work and family.

While most feminists have been highlighting issues of gendered segregation in the labour market, part-time work-related policies have always been a matter targeting females. However, recently, the Korean government and policymakers seem to have taken the problem of female concentration in temporary and part-time work more seriously, due to the continuous low fertility rate and high speed of demographic change. The fast demographic transition facilitated discussion on fathers' parental leave (with a higher level of parental leave benefits when fathers take it up from 2019). Also, the historical rapid increase in the minimum wage in 2018 sparked a discussion on shared working hours, offering the possibility of developing policy to create part-time jobs for male permanent workers. However, the gendered division of labour is still rigid and the unionisation rate of female workers (who are concentrated in temporary full-time and part-time jobs) is also very low, which suggests that to mitigate the concentration of mothers in part-time work in Korea may require a more configurational approach in reforming the existing policy arrangements.

Acknowledgement

This work was supported by the Ministry of Education of the Republic of Korea (ROK) and the National Research Foundation of Korea (NRF – 2015S1A3A2046566).

Notes

[1]   For example, type of employment contract, expected duration of current employment and whether or not the worker will be covered by social insurance schemes.

[2]   This national survey has been conducted every month since 1963 in order to examine the employment status and conditions of the South Korean people in general. Its sample included every person aged 15 or over belonging to 33,000 households selected from all regions of the country through a stratified three-stage cluster sampling method in 2016.

[3]   This KLSI calculation is 11.7% higher than Statistics Korea's calculation (Kim, 2016; Statistics Korea, 2016). There are no available data for an international comparison of the proportion of non-standard workers. However, it is reported that Korea has a much higher proportion of temporary workers (21.9%) compared to other countries, such as Japan (7.2%), the UK (6.0%) and Germany (13.1%) as of 2016 (OECD, 2017).

[4]   This is attributed to the significant increase in the share of the female population with tertiary education: from 11.9% (55–64 years), 30.9% (45–54 years) and 57.9% (35–44 years), to 74.8% (25–34 years) (OECD. stat, 2018).

[5]   The employment rate of the female population aged 15 and older has increased from 34.3% in 1963 to 41.3% in 1980 and 46.2% in 1990 (Statistics Korea, no date).

[6]   This survey, which first began in the 1970s, has a long history. At that time, Korean mothers' age at childbirth was much younger than nowadays, which was why the survey defined the childbearing age as between 15 and 49.

[7]   The respondents were all married women who were between 15 and 49 years old and residing at the time of the survey in 12,000 households selected from all regions of the country through a stratified three-stage cluster sampling method.

[8]   The survey included 221 open-ended contract workers. Since all of them were regular workers and their duration of employment was not specified, we classified them as permanent workers rather than temporary workers.

[9]   This is already high enough, and it increases if we include married women aged 50 years or older, as we saw earlier.

[10] This corresponds to the findings of previous research (eg Yang and Park, 2016).

References

Ahn, M.B. and Bahn, J.H. (2007) 'Part-time work of women: choice and motivations', *Monthly Labour Review: Korea Labor Institute*, November: 27–47 (in Korean).

Baek, S.H. (2009) 'Evaluation on childcare policy during 10 years of Kim, Dae-Jung and Roh, Moo-Hyun's administrations: focus on national plans', *Journal of Critical Social Policy*, 28: 95–141 (in Korean).

Chang, K.-S. (2011) *South Korea under compressed modernity: familial political economy in transition*, New York, NY: Routledge.

Chang, K.-S. and Song, M.-Y. (2010) 'The stranded individualizer under compressed modernity: South Korean women in individualization without individualism', *The British Journal of Sociology*, 61(3): 539–64.

Committee for 50 Years of Korean Population Policy (2016) *From antinatalist to pronatalist*, Sejong: Korea Ministry of Health and Welfare and Korea Institute of Health and Social Affairs (in Korean).

Emmenegger, P., Häusermann, S., Palier, B. and Seeleib-Kaiser, M. (2012) *The age of dualisation: the changing face of inequality in Europe*, Oxford: Oxford University Press.

International Labour Organization (ILO), ILOSTAT (no date) 'Key indicators of the labour market'. Available at: www.ilo.org/ilostat (accessed 8 January 2018).

Jeong, S.-M, (2010) 'Present conditions and characteristics of Korean female part-time workers', *Labour Review: Korea Labor Institute*, December: 73–86 (in Korean).

Kim, E.-J. and Lee, H.-S. (2016) *Evaluation of the impact of Child Care Subsidy Program*, Sejong: Korea Institute for Health and Social Affairs (in Korean).

Kim, S.-J. (2015) 'The trilemma of childcare service: Korean strategy and its consequences', *Economy and Society*, 105: 64–93 (in Korean).

Kim, Y. and Lee, S.-Y. (2014) 'Analysis of the time selective job policy: a comparative study on South Korea, Netherlands and Germany', *Korea Social Policy Review*, 21(3): 93–128 (in Korean).

Kim, Y.-S. (2016) 'The size and pattern of non-standard employment: the results of survey on economically active population (additional module, August 2016)', KLSI Issue Paper Vol. 9, Korea Labour and Society Institute (in Korean).

Lee, J.H. (2012) 'Policy alternatives for improving labor rights of women: a holistic response to Wollstonecraft dilemma', *Journal of Korean Women's Studies*, 28(3): 35–62 (in Korean).

Lee, S.S.Y. and Baek, S.H. (2014) 'Why the social investment approach is not enough – the female labour market and family policy in the Republic of Korea', *Social Policy & Administration*, 48(6): 686–703.

Lee, S.Y., Ahn, J.Y. and Kim, Y. (2016) 'Why women are left as outsiders in the labour market: a comparative study on the labour market between South Korea and Japan', *Korea Social Policy Review*, 23(2): 201–37 (in Korean).

Nam, W.K. (2007) 'The Act on Protection of Non-Standard Employment: between dismissal and discrimination', *Non-Standard Employment*, 59: 12–26 (in Korean).

OECD (Organisation for Economic Co-operation and Development) (2017) 'Employment rate (indicator)'. Available at: https://data.oecd.org/emp/employment-rate.htm (accessed 29 August 2017).

OECD (2018) 'Hours worked (indicator)'. Available at: https://data.oecd.org/emp/hours-worked.htm (accessed 6 April 2018).

OECD.Stat (2018) 'Educational attainment and labour-force status'. Available at: http://stats.oecd.org (accessed 6 February 2018).

Seong, J.M. (2014) 'The expansion of female part-time jobs and its implications in Korea', *Labour Review: Korea Labor Institute*, July: 20–33 (in Korean).

Seong, J.M. and Ahn, J.Y. (2007) 'Voluntariness and job satisfaction of part-time employment', *Labour Economy Studies*, 30(1): 109–37 (in Korean).

Shin, K.-A. (2015) 'The marginalization of permanent part-time women workers in organizations', *Journal of Korean Women's Studies*, 31(2): 131–79 (in Korean).

Statistics Korea (no date) 'Survey of Economically Active Population'. Available at: http://kostat.go.kr/portal/eng/index.action (accessed 8 January 2018).

Statistics Korea (2016) 'The results of Survey on Economically Active Population', additional module, August, press release, 3 November (in Korean).

Statistics Korea (2017) 'Indicators of work–life balance in 2016', press release 15 December (in Korean).

Yang, H.S. and Park, J.W. (2016) 'Choice of women with young children between full-time and part-time work', *Korea Social Policy*, 25(2): 151–81 (in Korean).

13

Conclusion and prospects

Hanne Cecilie Kavli and Heidi Nicolaisen

Introduction

Understanding the consequences of part-time work and how it might shape the position of workers as 'insiders' or 'outsiders' is an important, but also a challenging, task. While part-time work has some characteristics common to most countries, it evades a clear classification: is part-time work good or bad? Contrasting perspectives have developed within different policy domains based on which problems part-time work is intended to solve. Part-time work is affected by the interconnectedness of employment policy, family policy and gender-equality policy. These domains are linked, but their intentions, logics and effects are not necessarily harmonised. One example is that labour market policy often aims at mobilising women into the labour market, especially during periods of labour shortages. In many countries, however, this aim is not supported by a dual-earner family policy. If parental leave is short with low compensation rates, and publicly provided childcare is not easily available or affordable, few mothers will take up paid work. Moreover, while part-time work can be regarded as a path towards greater gender equality by increasing women's presence in the labour market and perhaps also men's presence at home, it can be argued that integrating women into the labour market through bad part-time work puts them in a marginalised position, with unfortunate effects for gender equality. Moreover, even for equalised part-time workers who voluntarily take up part-time positions with good working conditions and social benefits, part-time work may have long-term consequences in terms of, for example, lower pension benefits, fewer career opportunities and lower wages.

In this concluding chapter, we will not repeat in detail the evidence presented in the introduction and in the contributing chapters. Instead, we will return to one of the key questions of this book: do policies that regulate social protection and labour relations increase or decrease the divide between labour market insiders and outsiders? In the words of Emmenegger and colleagues (2012: 11–12), while the concepts of polarisation, segmentation and marginalisation emphasise the outcomes among individuals, dualisation stresses the role of policy. This volume has engaged with issues around both politics and outcomes for individuals. Whether political change results in the widening, deepening or creation of new inequalities is an empirical question. The book's point of departure was to investigate whether dualisation, or at least greater diversity, occurs not only between full-time and part-time workers, but also within the overall category of part-time workers. In contrast to much of the existing literature on the regulations of part-time work, we have emphasised that while policy may be passed at the supranational and national levels, its implementation involves a range of actors with different priorities, power and strategies. To study the role of policy therefore includes the study of policy implementation, the role of organisations and the dynamics within families.

The remainder of this chapter gives a brief overview of the book's main findings, before we discuss the future prospects for part-time work and part-time workers.

Main findings

While some intriguing changes have occurred over time, the general picture is that part-time work is a stable labour market phenomenon. Across countries and regimes, it is still predominantly women who work part-time, and part-time workers have a higher risk of precarious or marginal employment than full-time workers. That said, and as many of the chapters in this volume demonstrate, there are also important differences in the quality of part-time work and in the conditions of part-time workers both across and within countries. Among the conditions that have been discussed are involuntary part-time (in almost all chapters), temporary employment (Chapters 3, 6 and 11), pay penalties (Chapters 8 and 10), access to other flexible working-time arrangements (Chapters 5 and 8), work scheduling (Chapters 4 and 8) and social protection (Chapters 2, 3, 10 and 12). Part-time workers face harsher conditions than comparable full-time workers with regard to the majority of these conditions. Access to flexible working-time arrangements is the only example where part-timers enjoy better or similar working conditions as full-timers (Chapter 5).

The descriptions of part-time work quality across countries clearly show that part-time is neither 'always bad' nor 'either good or bad'.

The quality of part-time work and the conditions among part-time workers form a more complex phenomenon and should be studied as such. For this purpose, we have developed a typology of part-time work (presented in Chapter 1). In order to determine where a part-time job is located along a 'good–mixed–bad' dimension, we need to examine if working less than full-time is voluntary or not, as well as the quality of working conditions and social protections attached to the job. The structures surrounding a part-time job will vary between policy regimes and labour markets. Moreover, the workers' mobility and future prospects are important. Mobility between categories of working time has been explored in this book within the Nordic countries, illustrating, for example, that migrants have a significantly higher mobility from part-time to full-time compared to natives, but also a higher risk of labour market exit (see Chapters 7 and 9).

Part-time work exists within a broad framework of regulatory institutions and policies, creating a complex structure of opportunities and constraints for working men and women. Policies are exercised at different levels, and their regulatory strength and effectiveness varies. Regulations regarding part-time work exist at the supranational (the International Labour Organisation, the European Union [EU]) and the national levels (national laws and collective agreements). The contributions in this book show that the answer to why part-time work in different countries continues to be more or less widespread, gendered and marginalised, is mainly to be found at the national level. EU policy and regulations seem to have a limited influence on the country-specific profile of part-time work (see Chapter 2). Labour market structures are more influenced by national labour laws, collective agreements, welfare state arrangements, traditions and norms.

With regard to policies to increase employment, and the employment of women and mothers in particular, the effects of policies vary by context and comparative studies are key to understand this. Employment policies and work–life balance policies that look rather similar on paper can have very different effects on women's labour market participation in dissimilar countries. The unique country characteristics of labour market structures, welfare arrangements and gender cultures influence how well policy works in practice. There are cases of both 'colliding policy logics' and 'implementation deficits'. In the first case, policy aiming to improve the quality of part-time work is contradicted by other – and more powerful – policy measures intended to increase the flexibility enjoyed by employers (see, eg, Chapters 10 and 12). In the second case, policy measures to improve the quality of part-time jobs may be diverted by employers' strategies to keep control over staffing procedures (see Chapter 4).

Workers with low education end up with the most precarious or marginalised forms of part-time employment. This aspect of part-time jobs cuts across all country differences. Low-educated workers are more exposed to short and involuntary part-time work and have poorer working conditions and less access to social protection. We have seen that while policies and regulations are important, they only have a limited capacity to provide good part-time jobs to those at 'the bottom' of the labour market. Even in countries known for egalitarian norms and high-quality working conditions for most workers, there is inequality between part-time workers. Yet, the overall conclusion is that regulations and politics matter, and that they can modify the influence of both demand and supply factors. Vulnerable workers have many of the same characteristics across countries, but the numbers of precarious or marginalised workers, as well as the true extent of their challenges, vary. With a slight rewording of the formulation of the political scientist Stein Rokkan, we might conclude that regulations count, but resources decide.

The pattern of men's part-time work that was identified more than 20 years ago (Delsen, 1998) still seems quite accurate. Men work part-time less often than women. Furthermore, when they do work part-time, it is primarily upon labour market entry and exit, for shorter periods, or during economic downturns. Yet, it is worth noting that there are also signs of diversity among male part-time workers, as illustrated in Chapters 5, 6 and 12. Over the last decade, part-time work has increased among men in almost all countries. Moreover, men are more likely to work part-time on an involuntary basis than women. So far, it is a reasonable assumption that while the presence of work–life balance policies in some countries has had an impact on women's labour market participation, it is still less important for men. In their discussion of the future prospects of part-time work, O'Reilly and Fagan (1998) suggested a demarginalisation and a degendering of part-time work as a way forward. In an account of how societies perceive women's part-time work over time, Ellingsæter and Jensen (2019) suggest an alternative pathway. Based on an analysis of the last 20 years of discourse on part-time work in Norway, they suggest that a degendering of *full-time* work fits better. Rather than envisaging men's entry into part-time positions, we might think more in terms of women's entry into full-time work.

Dualisation of part-time work

This book illustrates that the characteristics of part-time workers vary, both in their motivations to work part-time, in their working conditions, in their access to social protection and in their prospects of transitioning from a position as a labour market outsider to a position as a labour market insider (for elaboration, see the presentation of the typology of part-time work in Chapter 1). The contributions in this volume give little reason to expect that this will change. In this final section, we briefly discuss the capacity of politics and regulations to increase or decrease the dualisation of part-time work. We argue that part-time work is undergoing a process of dualisation where the divide between insiders and outsiders endures and diversifies – and that it is notoriously difficult to protect the most vulnerable workers.

Active labour market policy is an important trend in Europe and North America and may influence the development and the position of labour market outsiders. The activating state expects an engaged role for citizens, including marginalised citizens (Jensen, 2005; Taylor-Gooby, 2005; Dean, 2007). Activation is often divided into two types: the work-first type and the human capital/social investment type. The former gives priority to labour market participation on the premise that any job is better than none, while the latter emphasises the development of skills that will enable people to find not only 'any job', but a good job (Dean, 2003; Hagelund and Kavli, 2009; Morel et al, 2011). In the activating state, income support is tied to active participation in training programmes, and conditions for citizens often include obligations to take any available job offers, regardless of their quality in terms of working conditions or social rights. As pointed out by Rubery et al (2018), this may normalise non-standard forms of employment as a route out of unemployment. By pushing the unemployed, or the underemployed, to take precarious or marginalised work, activation policy may, in effect, supply employers with cheap and flexible labour at the cost of the workers. As a central aspect of activation policy is its conditionality, the consequence can be a reduction in the power of workers to reject precarious or marginalised work (Rubery et al, 2018). By withholding income support from workers who already have limited power resources, activation of the 'work-first' type will shift the power relations even more in favour of the employers. Some categories of workers are particularly exposed to this development, including young people, migrants and workers with limited formal education. These are also workers with comparative low levels of unionisation that might otherwise have provided them with a stronger bargaining position. That said, the unions are not necessarily protective of workers who are either outside or at the margins of the labour market. With a priority to protect the 'insiders' in the labour market, unions have often failed to include and advance, or have not prioritised, the interests of more precarious workers (see, eg, Chapter 3). Of course, there are also exceptions in this regard. In the Nordic countries, collectively agreed wage levels were extended to immigrant workers outside the trade unions to avoid a dualised wage structure between 'old' and 'new' workers in the same industries (Arnholtz et al, 2018).

The contributions to this volume also illustrate a well-known paradox with regard to the capacity of regulations to decrease the divide between labour market insiders and outsiders: regulations work best for those who need them least (Crouch, 1982). In the primary labour market, workers are protected through their education and the skills they offer to employers, but they are also better protected through higher-quality regulations and better-organised industrial relations. In the secondary labour market, it is the other way around. Low-skilled workers are more dependent on regulations and trade unions to secure decent working conditions. Several chapters in this volume show that workers with high education are more likely to achieve a match between actual and preferred working time. Education will probably continue to be the single most influential factor in the determination of good and bad part-time contracts. It may also very well grow in importance as increased demand for formal qualifications is spreading. The composition of work tasks and occupational groups in the labour market has changed rapidly since the 1990s in Europe as well as in the US. A particular growth has taken place in the number of jobs that require either quite high or quite low education (Autor and Dorn, 2013; Goos et al, 2014). While politics matters, the differences that stem from education and skills are hard to remove completely.

The current and future composition of industries, with the service sector growing, indicates growth both in part-time work and in the divide between insiders and outsiders. Currently, there is also an important debate on how automation and digitalisation will influence future jobs (Autor and Dorn, 2013; Goos et al, 2014; Autor, 2015; Arntz et al, 2016; Nedelkosta and Quintini, 2018). It is not yet clear how technological developments may change the number or the type of jobs available or how they will affect the need for competence and higher education among workers. While some have argued that a large number of jobs will disappear (Brynjolfsson and McAfee, 2014), others maintain that this process will be more gradual and less dramatic. While automation may be technically possible, it may not always be cost-efficient (Autor, 2015). Increased productivity through automation may also increase the demand for services and labour in other parts of the economy, thus creating new job opportunities. There are, however, indications that these processes will lead to skill-biased demand shifts (Autor and Salomons, 2017).

Today, the service sector employs a large proportion of low-skilled workers, and automation and digitalisation can affect the future of this sector. Compared to the post-war manufacturing trade unions, the service sector unions have less ability to influence the quality of working conditions for low- or semi-skilled workers. Service sector trade union influence has always been weak compared to union influence in many other industries because of a number of reasons, for example, low unionisation rates, poorly organised employers and poor cooperation between the parties. The contributions to this book illustrate that several actors at different levels influence the quantity and quality of part-time work. The most important are governments and organised labour and capital. To understand how regulations work, we also need to examine mechanisms for enforcement and articulation between the different regulatory bodies and levels.

Work–family reconciliation policies will continue to influence the quality and consequences of part-time work. The contributions to this volume illustrate that the country context is decisive for the effect of such policies on female labour market participation, the quality of work for female part-timers and gender equality. Although work–life balance policies are implemented, female workers in many countries end up with precarious or marginalised part-time jobs (see, eg, Chapter 12) unless the country provides wider institutional support to the 'dual-earner/dual-carer' model (Ellingsæter and Leira, 2006) through affordable and available childcare and sufficient parental leave schemes.

Policy domains that have traditionally had little relevance to part-time work may also influence the current and future prospects of part-time work. One example is retirement policy. Part-time work at the end of the career is increasingly normal and more than half of the EU's member states have implemented national or sector-level partial retirement schemes to improve the sustainability of their pension systems (Dubois et al, 2016). There is still limited knowledge about the effects of such schemes, but concerns are raised with regard to unequal effects for different groups of workers, both in terms of access to such schemes and the conditions attached. Hence, inequality between labour market insiders and outsiders may become manifest in unequal access to part-time work at the end of the career. The winners can gradually and voluntarily step down towards retirement, while this is less of an option for lower socio-economic groups. What part-time work will look like in the years to come depends on numerous factors. As illustrated throughout this volume, some are well within the reach of political action, while others are far more challenging to address. The gender difference in part-time work has drawn much attention; the difference between women and the dualisation of part-time work less so. A good way forward would be to apply a more nuanced perspective of what part-time work entails for different categories of workers within different contexts. We will then be in a better position to understand this complex phenomenon and to address the effects that it has on individuals and societies alike.

References

Arnholtz, J., Meardi, G. and Oldervoll, J. (2018) 'Collective wage bargaining under strain in Northern European construction: resisting institutional drift?', *European Journal of Industrial Relations*, 24(4): 341–56.

Arntz, M., Gregory, T. and Zierahn, U. (2016) 'The risk of automation for jobs in OECD countries: a comparative analysis', OECD Social, Employment and Migration Working Papers, No. 189.

Autor, D.H. (2015) 'Why are there still so many jobs? The history and future of workplace automation', *Journal of Economic Perspectives*, 29: 3–30.

Autor, D. and Dorn, D. (2013) 'The growth of low-skill service jobs and the polarization of the US labor market', *The American Economic Review*, 103: 5.

Autor, D. and Salomons, A. (2017) 'Does productivity growth threaten employment?', ECB Forum on Central Banking, 2017, Sintra, Portugal.

Brynjolfsson, E. and McAfee, A. (2014) *The second machine age: Work, progress, and prosperity in a time of brilliant technologies*, London: W.W. Norton & Company.

Crouch, C. (1982) *Trade unions: the logic of collective action*, Fontana New Sociology.

Dean, H. (2003) 'The Third Way and social welfare: the myth of post-emotionalism', *Social Policy & Administration*, 37: 695–708.

Dean, H. (2007) 'The ethics of welfare-to-work', *Policy & Politics*, 35: 573–89.

Delsen, L. (1998) 'When do men work part-time?', in J. O'Reilly and C. Fagan (eds) *Part-time prospects: an international comparison of part-time work in Europe, North America and the Pacific Rim*, London and New York: Routledge.

Dubois, H., Runceanu, G. and Anderson, R. (2016) European Foundation for the Improvement of Living and Working Conditions (Eurofound), doi: 10.2806/004233, ISBN 978-92-897-1541-6. EU-Publications: Publications Office of the European Union.

Ellingsæter, A.L. and Jensen, R.S. (2019) 'Politicising women's part-time work in Norway: a longitudinal study of ideas', *Work, Employment and Society*. Available at https://doi.org/10.1177/0950017018821277

Ellingsæter, A.L. and Leira, A. (2006) *Politicising parenthood in Scandinavia: gender relations in welfare states*, Bristol: The Policy Press.

Emmenegger, P., Häusermann, S., Palier, B. and Seeleib-Kaiser, M. (2012) 'How we grow unequal', in P. Emmenegger, S. Häusermann, B. Palier and M. Seeleib-Kaiser (eds) *The age of dualization: the changing face of inequality in deindustrializing societies*, New York: Oxford University Press.

Goos, M., Manning, A. and Salomons, A. (2014) 'Explaining job polarization: routine-biased technological change and offshoring', *The American Economic Review*, 104(8): 2509–26.

Hagelund, A. and Kavli, H. (2009) 'If work is out of sight. Activation and citizenship for new refugees', *Journal of European Social Policy*, 19: 259–70.

Jensen, P.H. and Pfau-Effinger, B. (2005) 'Active citizenship: the new face of welfare', in P.H. Jensen, J.G. Anderson, A.-M. Guillemard and B. Pfau-Effinger (eds) *The changing face of welfare: Consequences and outcomes from a citizenship perspective*, Bristol: The Policy Press.

Morel, N., Palier, B. and Palme, J. (2011) 'Beyond the welfare state as we knew it', in N. Morel, B. Palier and J. Palme (eds) *Towards a social investment welfare state*, Bristol: Policy Press, pp 1–30.

Nedelkoska, L. and Quintini, G. (2018) *Automation, skills use and training*, OECD Social, Employment and Migration Working Papers No. 202, Paris: OECD Publishing. Available at: https://doi.org/10.1787/2e2f4eea-en

O'Reilly, J. and Fagan, C. (1998) *Part-time prospects: an international comparison of part-time work in Europe, North America and the Pacific Rim*, London: Routledge.

Rubery, J., Grimshaw, D., Keizer, A. and Johnson, M. (2018) 'Challenges and contradictions in the "normalising" of precarious work', *Work, Employment and Society*, 32: 509–27.

Taylor-Gooby, P. (2005) 'Ideas and policy change', in P. Taylor-Gooby (ed) *Ideas and welfare state reform in Europe*, Hampshire: Palgrave Macmillan.

Index

Printed and bound by CPI Group (UK) Ltd, Croydon, CR0 4YY

23/04/2025

14661025-0005